SETTING THE STANDARD FOR

# PROJECT BASED
# LEARNING

A PROVEN
APPROACH TO
RIGOROUS
CLASSROOM
INSTRUCTION

W9-CDY-639

# SETTING THE STANDARD FOR
# PROJECT BASED
# LEARNING

## A PROVEN APPROACH TO RIGOROUS CLASSROOM INSTRUCTION

JOHN LARMER || JOHN MERGENDOLLER || SUZIE BOSS

**ASCD** Alexandria, VA USA

BIE
BUCK INSTITUTE
FOR EDUCATION

1703 N. Beauregard St.
Alexandria, VA 22311-1714 USA
Phone: 800-933-2723 or 703-578-9600
Fax: 703-575-5400
Website: www.ascd.org
E-mail: member@ascd.org
Author guidelines: www.ascd.org/write

Buck Institute for Education
18 Commercial Blvd.
Novato, CA 94949 USA
Phone: (415) 883-0122
Fax: (415) 883-0260
Website: www.bie.org

Judy Seltz, *Executive Director*; Stefani Roth, *Publisher*; Genny Ostertag, *Director, Content Acquisitions*; Julie Houtz, *Director, Book Editing & Production*; Deborah Siegel, *Editor*; Louise Bova, *Senior Graphic Designer*; Mike Kalyan, *Manager, Production Services*; Valerie Younkin, *Production Designer*; Kelly Marshall, *Production Specialist*

Copyright © 2015 ASCD. All rights reserved. It is illegal to reproduce copies of this work in print or electronic format (including reproductions displayed on a secure intranet or stored in a retrieval system or other electronic storage device from which copies can be made or displayed) without the prior written permission of the publisher. By purchasing only authorized electronic or print editions and not participating in or encouraging piracy of copyrighted materials, you support the rights of authors and publishers. Readers who wish to reproduce or republish excerpts of this work in print or electronic format may do so for a small fee by contacting the Copyright Clearance Center (CCC), 222 Rosewood Dr., Danvers, MA 01923, USA (phone: 978-750-8400; fax: 978-646-8600; web: www.copyright.com). To inquire about site licensing options or any other reuse, contact ASCD Permissions at www.ascd.org/permissions, or permissions@ascd.org, or 703-575-5749. For a list of vendors authorized to license ASCD e-books to institutions, see www.ascd.org/epubs. Send translation inquiries to translations@ascd.org.

All referenced trademarks are the property of their respective owners.

All web links in this book are correct as of the publication date below but may have become inactive or otherwise modified since that time. If you notice a deactivated or changed link, please e-mail books@ascd.org with the words "Link Update" in the subject line. In your message, please specify the web link, the book title, and the page number on which the link appears.

PAPERBACK ISBN: 978-1-4166-2033-4    ASCD product #114017   n5/15

PDF E-BOOK ISBN: [978-1-4166- 1954-3]; see Books in Print for other formats.

Quantity discounts: 10–49, 10%; 50+, 15%; 1,000+, special discounts (e-mail programteam@ascd.org or call 800-933-2723, ext. 5773, or 703-575-5773). For desk copies, go to www.ascd.org/deskcopy.

**Errata:** For corrections to the first printing of this book, see the Errata link at www.ascd.org/publications/books/114017.aspx.

**Library of Congress Cataloging-in-Publication Data**
Larmer, John.
    Setting the standard for project based learning : a proven approach to rigorous classroom instruction / John Larmer, John Mergendoller, Suzie Boss.
        pages cm
    Includes bibliographical references and index.
    ISBN 978-1-4166-2033-4 (pbk. : alk. paper) 1. Project method in teaching. I. Mergendoller, John R. II. Boss, Suzie. III. Title.
    LB1027.43.L37 2015
    371.3'6—dc23
                                                                                    2015005753

23 22 21 20 19 18 17 16          3 4 5 6 7 8 9 10 11 12

# SETTING THE STANDARD FOR PROJECT BASED LEARNING

# Acknowledgments

Many people contributed to this book, and we would like to acknowledge them. Most important, we want to thank the many teachers and instructional coaches who shared their strategies and passion for project based teaching and learning, including Myla Lee, Todd Wigginton, Leah Obach, Heidi Hutchison, Jim Bentley, Nathan Mulhearn, Rosine Borello, Jennifer Lee, Jody Passanisi, Shara Peters, Shawn Swanson, Jason Irwin, Valerie Hoover, Don Doehla, Luann Lee, Mark Gomez, and Danette McMillian.

PBL teachers are most successful when they have school leaders and organizations that understand and support project based learning. Principal Aaron Brengard helped us imagine how PBL can transform summer learning experiences, and then a whole school. Superintendents Eric Williams and Steve Matthews taught us about effective PBL leadership and school change. Public Health Management Corporation of Philadelphia showed us how PBL could animate out-of-school-time settings.

BIE staff were also significant contributors, most especially in leaving first author John Larmer alone as he hunkered down in the writing bunker. While he was there, Gina Olabuenaga capably shouldered many duties, and she and Alfred Solis were always on hand to offer feedback and ideas, and most important, to make us smile. Jennifer Cruz, Cris Waldfogel, and Rody Boonchouy contributed their experience and wisdom to the chapter for school leaders, and David Ross provided useful critique throughout the writing process.

BIE's stellar National Faculty—too many to name—shared their PBL expertise and lessons gained providing PBL professional development to thousands of teachers and school leaders. Todd Felton contributed significantly to the chapter on PBL in Informal Education; we value his storytelling and good thinking.

We convened a group of representatives from many organizations we consider experts, friends, and fellow travelers to critique our model for Gold Standard PBL, and we are grateful to them all: Aaron Brengard, Shannon Buerk, Milton Chen, Marc Chun, Ben Daley, Kristin DeVivo, Ryan Steuer, Patrick Howlett, Bob Lenz, Ron Marx, Rosanna Mucetti, Glen O'Grady, Bob Pearlman, Elizabeth Phillips, Tim Presiado, Andy Rothstein, Helen Soulé, Jennifer Sparrow, Bernie Trilling, Eric Williams, and Tsuey-ling "Doris" Wu.

Ken Kay and the other members of the BIE board of directors put us on this path to find gold and refresh our thinking about project based learning. It was a perceptive and timely move, and we are grateful for their vision.

Finally, we appreciate the counsel and critique of our editors at ASCD, especially Genny Ostertag for her initial interest in a PBL book and her patience in our delivery.

# Preface

Project based learning (PBL) is not a new instructional approach, but it now has a new respectability and an ever-growing number of proponents. The Buck Institute for Education (BIE) has played a central role in PBL's growth, and for the past 20 years, it has worked to identify and shape PBL best practices. Initially this effort seemed pointless in an era of "covering standards" and test-based accountability. Rigor was defined by recitation and excellence by compliance. But times have changed. Current concerns with college and career readiness, and the performance-based emphases of Common Core State Standards, have caused educators to take another look at project based learning and recognize its ability to not only help students develop deep content understanding, but also to help students learn and practice the skills they will need for college, career, and life success.

A Google search for "project based learning" yields over 3,000,000 results. Newspapers feature back-to-school stories about PBL. Parents and school boards are encouraging their schools to adopt PBL, and many charter schools are making it a centerpiece of their program. An ever-growing number of PBL teachers are connecting online to share ideas and to blog about their experiences. You can find 30,000 of them in the BIE PBL Community on Edmodo (see https://www.edmodo.com/publisher/biepbl). More and more publishers and curriculum providers are producing materials to meet the demand. Organizations such as New Tech Network, Asia Society International Studies

Schools, Expeditionary Learning Schools, Envision Schools, and the National Academy Foundation's career-oriented academies, which place PBL at their instructional core, have grown dramatically. Virtually every national and state education conference has sessions about PBL. The methodology of AP classes and the nature of the SAT are adapting to meet the movement toward PBL. Momentum is building.

Popularity, though, has an unavoidable result: variation in quality. Project based learning, like any worthwhile instructional method, requires time, thought, and careful planning to achieve quality. If PBL is not done well, its reputation will suffer. Poorly designed and poorly executed projects can result in wasted time, misdirected student energy, and failure to achieve learning goals. Some projects might be "too loose," with students taking part in a variety of activities that do not add up to much beyond "fun" and a low-quality product or two. On the flip side, some teachers might simply add a group report and presentation to a traditionally structured unit and call that a project— which will fail to yield the promised benefits of PBL. Another threat to the reputation of PBL comes from what we call "dessert projects" (more on that in Chapter 4), which are hands-on activities that are easily completed with little planning, thought, or research. Do we really need to see another classroom stocked with sugar-cube pyramids or Styrofoam solar systems? To ensure that PBL doesn't become another one of yesterday's innovations (remember open classrooms?), we need to make sure that the best PBL practices rise to the top.

In 2010, BIE wrote an article for ASCD's *Educational Leadership* magazine entitled "7 Essentials for Project Based Learning" to describe what differentiated rigorous PBL from simply "doing projects" that bordered on busywork. Our publications and professional development workshops for teachers were infused by these "Essential Elements"—later increased to 8 with the addition of "Significant Content" as a reminder that PBL was meant to teach content, not just build "soft skills" as some stereotypes had it. Those 8 Essential Elements have served us well in promoting effective classroom practices, but now it's time to step it up a notch with a more comprehensive, research-based model for PBL.

We've written this book to help teachers and school leaders understand and implement the highest-quality project based learning—what we refer to as *Gold Standard PBL*. As you will see, a number of educational thinkers and researchers have contributed to the development of Gold Standard Project Based Learning, which brings together proven instructional practices and learning strategies. Gold Standard PBL is systematically planned and carefully facilitated, and the work students do is assessed, both formatively and summatively, by teachers, students, and often an external audience.

Gold Standard PBL involves more than students working to complete products; it explicitly includes teachers and the judicious use of traditional instructional practices—what we call *project based teaching*. PBL requires much more of the teacher than finding or creating a project and then turning it over to the students. Teachers' modeling, explanation, scaffolding, and coaching, among other traditional instructional methods, continue to be important. Teachers also need to help students adjust to the new learning demands of PBL, a process that requires time for students to develop new skills and self-expectations (Schmidt, Boshuizen, & de Vries, 1992).

To develop this new model for Gold Standard PBL, we have ourselves used best PBL practices. We collaborated with our board of directors and as a staff. We engaged in an iterative process of critique and revision, by sharing our work-in-progress at the PBL World gathering in June 2014, in several blog posts, in numerous conference presentations, in meetings of our 60-strong National Faculty, and with a group of representatives of several PBL-savvy organizations. We reflected on what we heard—resulting in 42 draft versions of the Gold Standard language—and are now ready to make our work public.

We believe PBL is vital for preparing young people for the modern world, and we want to help ensure that PBL becomes a regular practice in more and more classrooms. Making this vision a reality will require the combined efforts of teachers and school leaders—and, of course, students—with the support of parents and communities. We've written this book with all these stakeholders in mind.

This book is intended to be practical as well as visionary and inspirational. Our first three chapters make the case for PBL, describe what Gold Standard PBL looks like, and provide an overview of what research says about PBL. The middle chapters explain how teachers can successfully design and manage projects, including notes and examples for teachers in the primary grades through high school. Following this is a chapter for school and district leaders, because their supportive policies, structures, and culture are what will make PBL a systemwide practice. Finally, we discuss the possibilities for PBL in informal education spaces such as after-school clubs, community programs, and summer learning. Appendix A contains sample projects of a variety of types, in a wide range of grade levels and subject areas.

Project based learning is gaining traction around the world. A growing number of educators on every continent recognize the need for new approaches to teaching and learning in the 21st century. Three of the project snapshots you'll read about and that are described in Appendix A attest to PBL's global appeal; they are from Mumbai, India, Manitoba, Canada, and Crestmead, Australia. In recent years we've also gotten to know educators interested in PBL from Canada, Mexico, Korea, England, China, South Africa, Singapore, Costa Rica, Pakistan, Japan, Brazil, Jordan, Taiwan, the Dominican Republic, and many more places. Although we use terminology and descriptions of schooling drawn mainly from the United States' system of education, we think the project design principles and management practices we recommend can be applied anywhere.

We hope this book will bolster the few who are already doing Gold Standard PBL, guide the many who want to improve their practice of PBL, and lead many more to begin using PBL with their students—all of whom need and deserve it.

John Larmer
John Mergendoller
Suzie Boss
February 2015
Novato, California

# 1 Why Project Based Learning?

In the hundreds of "PBL 101" workshops conducted each year by the Buck Institute for Education across the United States and in other nations, we ask teachers and administrators to describe an "ideal graduate" from the K–12 system. Our school and district partners sometimes do the same exercise in their communities with parents, people from local businesses and civic organizations, and other stakeholders. Every time, everywhere, the lists generated are remarkably similar, with items such as these:

- Problem solver
- Responsible
- Works well with others
- Can work independently
- Critical thinker
- Confident
- Manages time and work effectively
- Communicates well with a variety of people

When asked *how* students learn these qualities of an ideal graduate, teachers and administrators say that it sometimes happens in traditionally taught classrooms, but they acknowledge that it's inconsistent at best. Our workshop participants then go on to learn how project based learning (PBL) provides opportunities for students to build these qualities, as well as more deeply learn traditional academic content and understand how it applies to the real world.

We do have to be wary of excessive hype in today's education landscape. Some advocates for PBL make it sound like a cure-all for what ails schools: PBL will inspire and motivate passive students, restore the joy of teaching, rebuild communities, help solve world problems, and... dramatically raise test scores! Although PBL is not a panacea, there is some truth behind (most of) these claims. We can confidently state that project based learning is a powerful teaching method that does the following:

- Motivates students.
- Prepares students for college, careers, and citizenship.
- Helps students meet standards and do well on tests that ask students to demonstrate in-depth knowledge and thinking skills.
- Allows teachers to teach in a more satisfying way.
- Provides schools and districts with new ways to communicate and to connect with parents, communities, and the wider world.

Let's take a closer look at how PBL benefits students, teachers, and schools.

## Motivating Students

Elementary school children are typically motivated to learn and do good work in school because they arrive with a natural desire to learn about the world and they want to be able to read, write, and use numbers. They also tend to like and want to please their teachers, and the teaching methods—especially in the primary grades—often still have an element of fun and play. But even young students may grow tired of worksheets, drills, or other traditional instructional methods if such approaches are used too much.

Once they reach middle school and especially high school, many students report that they are not engaged at school for much of the time. Some might still be motivated by the desire to earn good grades and please their teachers and parents, but far too many simply go through the motions of listening to their teachers, completing assignments, doing homework, and studying for tests. Even many "model" students with high GPAs who take challenging courses admit that, although they know how to play the game of school, they don't find their work intrinsically interesting or meaningful. Generally speaking, students are driven to learn by external factors, not the real "need to know" that is one of the keys to PBL's motivational effect.

The High School Survey of Student Engagement (Yazzie-Mintz, 2010) surveyed 275,925 students in the United States from 2006 to 2009. It found that 49 percent of students in grades 9 through 12 reported being bored in at least one class every day; another 17 percent were bored in every class, every day. In response to a question about why they were bored, the students gave various reasons, with these as their top three:

- "Material wasn't interesting" (81 percent)
- "Material wasn't relevant to me" (42 percent)
- "No interaction with teacher" (35 percent)

The students were also asked about what instructional methods engage them most. Here are their top four responses:

- Discussion and debate (61 percent)
- Group projects (60 percent)
- Projects and lessons involving technology (55 percent)
- Student presentations (46 percent)

Grant Wiggins, author and cofounder of Understanding by Design, found similar results when he recently surveyed students at a "typical American high school" in a Midwestern suburban community. Most students reported being bored much of the time and suggested that teachers should "make learning active and fun," do more "hands-on activities," and provide opportunities to "discuss my ideas with others" (Wiggins, 2014).

## More Motivated, Better Behaved

Experienced teachers know that when students are deeply engaged by a topic or a task, a lot of classroom management issues fade away. Students who used to disrupt class behave differently when they're doing active work on a project that engages them (Lambros, 2002). Students who previously did not do their assignments, or turned in shoddy work, become more responsible and step up their work quality when they care about a project.

The results of these surveys clearly point to the need for instruction that's more engaging, and project based learning is just that. Interesting and relevant topics, issues, and challenges are central to every well-designed project. Interaction with the teacher is likewise baked into the whole process, as we describe in detail in the following chapters. Discussions and debates occur frequently in projects, whether as a whole class or in small groups. Most projects today involve technology to some extent, and student presentations are also a key element.

A survey of gifted high school students showed they, too, were often bored and disengaged from classroom learning (Kanevsky & Keighley, 2003). The researchers listed five features that distinguished "boring from learning experiences": control, choice, challenge, complexity, and caring teachers. Once again, project based learning fits the bill.

## Motivating Students to Stay in School

Students drop out of school for many reasons, and one of them is being bored and disengaged. According to a 2006 report on high school dropouts (Bridgeland, Dilulio, & Morison), the response "classes were not interesting" was the top vote-getter in surveys, a reason given by 47 percent of students. When asked in the survey about what might help them stay in school, 81 percent of the students said there should be more real-world learning. The report's authors recommended that schools "improve teaching and curricula to make school more relevant and engaging and enhance the connection between school and work" (p. iv). This is exactly what well-designed project based learning does.

**Motivating Students to Stay in School—(*continued*)**

In another study of the dropout problem (Balfanz, 2007), the author noted an additional benefit that projects give to students who are at risk:

It is also paramount that avenues for short-term success through projects, performances, and experiential learning be built in. If you enter high school significantly below grade level it will require hard work and considerable time to produce quality high school work. In the meantime, students need to be experiencing success. (pp. 19–20)

## Preparing Students for College, Careers, Citizenship, and Life

Much of the talk about getting students "ready for college and career" focuses on making sure they take the right courses and learn enough in math, science, English/language arts, history, and other subjects. But being ready for the next step beyond the K–12 school system has another aspect, which has more to do with attitudes, habits, and skills that fall outside the boundaries of traditional academic disciplines.

A major study (Conley, 2005) of what it takes to succeed in entry-level college courses found the following general "habits of mind" to be key, along with subject-specific knowledge and skills:

- Critical-thinking skills
- Analytical-thinking skills
- Problem-solving skills
- Open to and utilizes critical feedback
- Open to possible failures at times
- Clear and convincing written and oral expression
- Can weigh sources for importance and credibility
- Can draw inferences and reach conclusions independently
- Time management skills

When employers are asked what it takes to succeed in the workplace, in addition to job-specific knowledge and skills, they generate a similar list. Take a look at one example:

- Critical-thinking and analytical-reasoning skills
- The ability to analyze and solve complex problems
- The ability to effectively communicate orally
- The ability to effectively communicate in writing
- The ability to apply knowledge and skills to real-world settings
- The ability to locate, organize, and evaluate information from multiple sources
- The ability to innovate and be creative
- Teamwork skills and the ability to collaborate with others in diverse group settings (Hart Research Associates, 2013, p. 8)

The consensus is clear: students need more than basic subject-area knowledge. The competencies and personal qualities included in these various lists have been given many names: 21st century skills, cross-curricular skills, soft skills, interdisciplinary skills, habits of mind and work, deeper learning, and college- and career-readiness skills. We call them "success skills." Some are as old as Socrates; some are products of the modern age. But can traditional schooling meet the need to teach them?

As we mentioned at the beginning of this chapter, many of the things educators, parents, colleges, and employers want to see in a graduate tend to fall between the cracks of traditional subject areas and teaching methods. Some teachers might teach, say, critical-thinking skills as they pertain to a specific discipline, but others may not at all. And even if such opportunities are provided, they may only be implicit or assumed to be embedded in an assignment or activity.

But a good project brings it all together like nothing else can. In PBL done well, students not only find themselves needing to use college- and career-readiness skills; they are explicitly taught them, assessed on them, and asked to reflect on their growth in them. Students who graduate from school systems in which they have completed multiple projects over the years will have had many more opportunities to gain these skills, and systematic support in doing so, than students who have had only scattered or unfocused opportunities.

By the way, we are *not* saying that students should learn college- and career-readiness skills at the expense of learning how to read, write, do math, and know something about history, literature, and other traditional subjects. Even though information on any topic is readily available in our digital age, people still need some background knowledge to be able to make sense of the information and to be well-rounded, culturally literate members of society. Learning key knowledge and understanding should always be one of the twin goals of a project, along with gaining key success skills. After all, students need something to think critically or communicate *about* in a project, and they can't solve a problem simply by applying a process devoid of content knowledge.

## College Challenges

When some educators and parents hear about PBL, they might say, "But that's not how students are taught in college, so wouldn't we be doing them a disservice? Shouldn't they learn to listen to lectures, take notes, and take tests that measure how much information they've memorized?"

We offer two responses to this concern. First, it's true that listening and note taking are important skills that students should practice in high school, but such opportunities can be included within a project. Contrary to some stereotypes, there's still room for lectures in PBL. During a project, the best way for students to learn something—once they see a genuine need to know it—might, in fact, be a lecture by the teacher. Or they might be called upon to interview an expert and take notes. Likewise, a test on content knowledge might be an effective and necessary assessment tool in a project.

Second, as students advance through college they will encounter more and more courses that are not lecture based. Even at fairly traditional colleges and universities, undergraduates will be asked to work in teams, to use knowledge in real-world applications, to analyze problems, and to communicate findings to an audience. A growing number of postsecondary institutions are using an explicitly project-based approach, particularly in the fields of engineering, architecture, and business. Olin College of Engineering, for example, emphasizes collaborative projects throughout its curriculum. Harvard University's undergraduate Applied Physics 50 course is entirely project based (Perry, 2013). Stanford University's popular Design for

Extreme Affordability and MIT's D-Lab are multidisciplinary project based courses in which students develop products and services for the world's poor.

Additionally, students who develop a sense of being independent learners through PBL are well prepared for the self-advocacy and initiative it takes to thrive in a college environment. Although the findings are preliminary, because most of its graduates have not yet completed college, students from the PBL-infused New Tech Network high schools have been found to have high rates of persistence into their second year of college (New Tech Network, 2014). Envision education schools show similar results (www.envisionschools.org/impact/). A 2014 study found high rates of college success among students from high schools that feature "student-centered instruction," which researchers defined as including project based teaching, collaborative learning, relevant curriculum, and performance-based assessments (Friedlaender, Burns, Lewis-Charp, Cook-Harvey, & Darling-Hammond, 2014). For example, 97 percent of the graduates from City Arts and Technology High School in San Francisco who enrolled in four-year colleges were still enrolled in their fourth year, as were 69 percent of the graduates from Life Learning Academy in Oakland. Both schools far exceeded national averages for their high-minority populations, which included many students who were the first in their families to attend college.

## The Modern Economy

School systems designed more than a century ago to send workers into that era's industrial economy emphasized only the basics: the 3 Rs and a little knowledge of history and civics. Factory jobs did not require much else and mainly called for the ability to follow routines. Although jobs like that still exist, they're fewer in number, and even those require more complex skills than they used to.

In today's "knowledge economy," success at most jobs demands the kinds of skills seen on the lists presented earlier in this chapter. The report *Dancing with Robots: Human Skills for Computerized Work* (Levy & Murnane, 2013) makes the case that because of technology, "the future of middle-class work will necessarily have to rely on uniquely human brain strengths" such as flexibility, solving nonstandard problems, and working with new information and communicating it to others (p. 4).

On the job, and even in college, people also benefit from having leadership skills. It pays to be able to organize a team, get others to do their best work, and manage a complex, extended set of tasks that must be accomplished by a deadline. Projects provide students—sometimes especially those who are not the typical leaders in a classroom—with multiple and varied occasions to build these kinds of skills. Equally valuable are self-management skills, such as being able to organize one's time and tasks, work independently, handle stress, and take the initiative. Rigorous projects require all of the above.

Finally, it's a fact in today's economy that most people will change jobs several times, requiring them to stay flexible and to know how to learn new skills. Students get practice in this by taking on new and varied roles in projects. In a shifting economy, personal qualities such as persistence and resilience—also known as grit—will come in handy. A project-based environment in school helps build these capabilities, as students investigate questions and issues that do not lead them down a straightforward path. It's almost a given that any project will involve unexpected twists and turns, setbacks, reconsideration of ideas, and recognition that something more must be learned.

## Citizenship and Life

Becoming an informed, active citizen in a community, state, or nation requires many of the same skills asked for by colleges and employers. Whether it's discussing issues with fellow members of a community, asking a government or a corporation to address a need, negotiating a bureaucracy to get something done, or simply voting in an election, it pays to be able to think critically, evaluate information, communicate well, and make defensible decisions. And just as in the workplace, citizens in a diverse society must be able to work well together to identify and solve problems.

Finally, we should also note that PBL helps prepare young people for life in general, where adults tackle many "projects," from planning a wedding to building a toolshed to taking a road trip. Everyone can benefit from learning how to set goals, plan a complex undertaking, gather resources, and successfully complete a "performance-based assessment."

## Helping Students Meet Standards and Do Well on Rigorous Tests

Most states in the United States, whether they have updated their own standards or adopted the Common Core State Standards (CCSS) for English/Language Arts and Mathematics, are asking students to reach new kinds of learning goals, for which PBL is especially well suited. A growing sense is developing in the United States and around the world that knowing a lot of facts (which older standards documents often listed at length) is not enough for today's students. Information in the modern world is easily accessible; what's needed is the ability to ask the right questions, find the best information, and apply it to the real world. So rather than "cover content," these standards ask teachers to help students gain deeper conceptual understanding and learn how to apply their knowledge.

Recent standards also emphasize the interdisciplinary, 21st century competencies described earlier. Here are some examples from states that have not adopted CCSS:

• *Texas Essential Knowledge and Skills for English Language Arts and Reading:* "Students work productively with others in teams."

• *Indiana Academic Standards, English Language Arts:* "Create engaging presentations that include multimedia components."

• *Virginia Standards of Learning, English:* "Analyze, evaluate, synthesize, and organize information from a variety of sources to produce a research product."

### Common Core State Standards and PBL

"Aligned with CCSS" is a claim made all too readily these days by school district curriculum committees, publishers of instructional materials, and purveyors of educational tools and programs. But to say project based learning "aligns" with the Common Core State Standards is an understatement. Although we can't claim that PBL is the *only* way to achieve the goals of the Common Core, it is one of the *best* ways. As we said in the preface, PBL's recent popularity is evidence that educators are recognizing this.

It's widely acknowledged that instructional methods have to change in order to meet new standards. We believe PBL should be one of the key methodologies in every teacher's toolbox, for two reasons. First, PBL reflects the broad implications and underlying principles of the standards:

• *Fewer standards, more depth (ELA and mathematics)* —Well-designed projects have always emphasized deep conceptual understanding and critical thinking when solving problems, developing and answering a driving question, and creating high-quality products.

• *More emphasis on reading informational text in a variety of content areas (ELA)*—Many projects are interdisciplinary and create a purposeful context for reading a wide variety of texts to find information, from reference books to new media, from expert interviews to web pages.

• *More emphasis on inquiry and evidence-based reasoning (ELA)*— Close reading of a text in search of meaning is a form of inquiry—an important skill that is often built into a project. The standards also call for students to ask questions, do research, evaluate sources, and develop well-supported answers—processes that are fundamental to PBL.

• *Real-world applications (mathematics)*—The Common Core's Standards for Mathematical Practice highlight the ability to apply math to solve "problems arising in everyday life, society, and the workplace"—exactly what happens in a good project.

Second, a project enables a teacher to teach several specific standards in one context rather than as isolated lessons. For example, students could learn, through various assignments and activities scattered throughout a year of traditional instruction, how to make multimedia presentations, have collegial conversations with peers, and conduct research to investigate a self-generated question (all of which appear in new standards for ELA). But imagine how much more frequent and focused the opportunities to build these skills would be if students were engaged regularly in projects that require them every time.

Most ELA standards for reading and language, as well as standards for mathematics, could be taught in the context of projects. But some specific standards for ELA are especially well suited for PBL, as shown in Figure 1.1.

## New and Revised Assessments

For states that are members of either the Smarter Balanced Assessment Consortium (SBAC) or the Partnership for Assessment of Readiness for College and Careers (PARCC), PBL is an excellent "test prep" methodology—although most PBL practitioners would shun that term. One part of the tests these organizations are developing will be a performance task, in which students will have to *do* something rather than simply select the best multiple-choice answer.

For example, to measure research skills, the SBAC test asks students to read and compare various points of view on an issue, then write an evidence-based argument for a real-world situation (Smarter Balanced, 2014). Students who are used to the demands of a project will be comfortable with these kinds of tasks when they sit down to take the test. PARCC is developing similar research simulation tasks. Both groups are creating performance tasks for mathematics that call for modeling and application in a real-world context or scenario—familiar territory for students who have been taught with PBL.

## Next Generation Science Standards

The Next Generation Science Standards (NGSS) are also a good fit with PBL. The standards were developed by a group of 26 states, with a writing team coordinated by Achieve, Inc. (see http://bit.ly/1iGN9c2). Like Common Core, NGSS marks a shift to a "focus on understanding and application as opposed to memorization of facts devoid of context" (Next Generation Science Standards, 2013).

**Figure 1.1**    How PBL Applies to Common Core State Standards for English/Language Arts

| CCSS for ELA | Application to PBL |
|---|---|
| *Writing 6.* Use technology, including the Internet, to produce and publish writing and to interact and collaborate with others. | Many projects feature a written product created with word-processing tools and self-publishing websites. Student project teams can use online tools for sharing documents, conducting meetings, and keeping track of tasks and deadlines. |
| *Writing 7.* Conduct short as well as more sustained research projects based on focused questions, demonstrating understanding of the subject under investigation. | Most projects include research of some sort, whether it's reading a variety of sources to develop and support an answer to a driving question, conducting a scientific study, or interviewing experts, community members, or end users to inform the creation of a product. Student-generated questions that guide investigations are a hallmark of PBL. |
| *Speaking and Listening 1.* Prepare for and participate effectively in a range of conversations and collaborations with diverse partners, building on others' ideas and expressing their own clearly and persuasively. | In a project, when students work in teams, they have regular and multiple opportunities to discuss plans, ideas, and products. They may also talk with outside experts, mentors, and family and community members. |
| *Speaking and Listening 4.* Present information, findings, and supporting evidence such that listeners can follow the line of reasoning and the organization, development, and style are appropriate to task, purpose, and audience. | Projects culminate when students present their work to a particular public audience, depending on the nature of the project. In addition to showing their final product or explaining their answer to a driving question, students defend their reasoning and describe their process. |
| *Speaking and Listening 5.* Make strategic use of digital media and visual displays of data to express information and enhance understanding of presentations. | When students present project work to a public audience, they must be clear and persuasive, choosing the most appropriate digital media and creating effective visual displays. |
| *Speaking and Listening 6.* Adapt speech to a variety of contexts and communicative tasks, demonstrating command of formal English when indicated or appropriate. | Many projects require students to interact with other adults, not just teachers, and make presentations to audiences beyond their classmates and teacher, creating a variety of opportunities to practice formal speech. |

Compared to earlier state standards for science, NGSS also has a much greater focus on engineering—a natural link to projects in which students design and build models, devices, structures, and other such products. The following NGSS "Science and Engineering Practices" align with practices common in PBL:

• Asking questions (for science) and defining problems (for engineering)
• Developing and using models
• Planning and carrying out investigations
• Analyzing and interpreting data
• Using mathematics and computational thinking
• Constructing explanations (for science) and designing solutions (for engineering)
• Engaging in argument from evidence
• Obtaining, evaluating, and communicating information

Some of the science standards, like many in Common Core, even point directly to potential projects:

• *Grade 3–5 Physical Science:* Plan and conduct an investigation to provide evidence of the effects of balanced and unbalanced forces on the motion of an object. (3-PS2-1)
• *Middle School Physical Science:* Undertake a design project to construct, test, and modify a device that either releases or absorbs thermal energy by chemical processes. (MS-PS1-6)
• *High School Life Science:* Design, evaluate, and refine a solution for reducing the impacts of human activities on the environment and biodiversity. (HS-LS2-7)

## SAT, Advanced Placement, and Other Tests

In 2014, College Board President David Coleman, who helped write the Common Core State Standards, announced changes to the SAT test for 2016. Many of the changes reflect the PBL-friendly trend seen in CCSS and other recent state standards, such as a greater emphasis on thinking skills in ELA, coverage of fewer topics in math, and "problems grounded in real-world contexts" (see https://www.collegeboard.org/delivering-opportunity/sat/redesign).

According to the College Board,

• The Evidence-Based Reading and Writing section will feature "continued emphasis on reasoning alongside a clearer, stronger focus on the knowledge, skills, and understandings most important for college and career readiness and success." (See https://www.collegeboard.org/delivering-opportunity/sat/redesign/compare-tests.)

• The Math section will feature "multistep applications to solve problems in science, social science, career scenarios, and other real-life contexts. Students will be presented with a scenario and then asked several questions about it. This allows students to dig into a situation and think about it, then model it mathematically." (See https://www.collegeboard.org/delivering-opportunity/sat/redesign.)

Advanced Placement courses and tests are also changing in ways that support greater use of PBL. According to the College Board, AP is shifting toward a "greater emphasis on... inquiry, reasoning, and communication skills" and "a balance between breadth of content coverage and depth of understanding" (see http://advancesinap.collegeboard.org/overview). The new exam and curriculum for AP Physics, AP Biology, and AP U.S. History are the first to reflect this shift.

In addition, AP has created a Capstone diploma program designed to "equip students with the independent research, collaborative teamwork, and communication skills that are increasingly valued by colleges" (see http://advancesinap.collegeboard.org/ap-capstone). This program, for which students accustomed to a PBL environment would be well prepared, requires them to do the following:

• Consider and evaluate multiple points of view to develop their own perspective on complex issues and topics.
• Hone critical- and creative-thinking skills.
• Ask questions and conduct inquiry and investigation.
• Work in teams.
• Make a public presentation, performance, or exhibition.

Another well-known test is considering changes that move in the direction of PBL. In *Leading Assessment into the Future*, a report for the National Assessment of Educational Progress (NAEP), a panel recommends using new technologies to "assess new constructs, such as critical thinking, problem solving, and collaboration" (NCES, 2012, p. 9).

An international test that already reflects the goals of PBL is the Programme for International Student Assessment (PISA). The test is given every three years to 15-year-old students in over 65 countries in schools that join the Global Learning Network, run by the Organisation for Economic Co-operation and Development (OECD). The network's goal is to "help more students succeed at globally competitive levels" (America Achieves, n.d.). PISA assesses how well students can apply their knowledge of reading, mathematics, and science in real-world contexts. It has recently begun offering a test of "creative problem solving" that measures students' ability to respond to a "non-routine situation"—which is exactly what every good project is (OECD, 2014).

## Allowing Teachers to Teach in a More Satisfying Way

> What we need are schools organized in ways that put the joy back into teaching and that do not confuse rigor with rigor mortis.
> —Phil Schlechty

In today's era of standards, testing, and accountability, many teachers feel constrained in their choices about curriculum and instruction, or are actually told they must teach in a certain way. In schools where raising test scores is the be-all and end-all, a "test-prep" approach dominates, which might entail following a prescribed script for a lesson and using only approved instructional materials. All teachers must be on the same page on the same day, following a pacing guide. In our PBL workshops we've noted that many teachers who have entered the classroom in recent years, especially in the elementary grades, have not even had the opportunity to plan a unit. It's always been done for them.

Schools dominated by the need to raise test scores claim to have no time for "frills" (the arts and other untested subjects), connecting with the community, using technology in new ways, or teaching students how to work in teams and make presentations. They say it's impossible to spend the time it takes to create high-quality products students can be proud of. Pedagogies such as PBL are discouraged or even outright forbidden because they're seen as too unstructured and inefficient in terms of "covering" the standards.

Many teachers faced with this situation still find ways to inject their personality into the classroom and make their teaching as creative and lively as they can. Others go along with the program, but grow weary of the constraints and hate seeing their students lose interest in learning when it's textbooks, worksheets, and drills every day. Some teachers might even leave the profession or move to a charter or private school where they can teach in a more satisfying way.

Most teachers like to plan their own lessons and units, not simply "deliver instruction" based on off-the-shelf materials or a long march through a textbook. They like to teach about topics and issues they and their students find interesting. They want to see their students get actively engaged in learning, and they like learning new things themselves. They enjoy engaging closely alongside young people, rather than always directing a whole group from the front of the classroom. All of these things happen in a PBL environment.

We get feedback along these lines in our PBL professional development workshops, where teachers often say, "This is how I've always wanted to teach!" Some veteran teachers might put it differently: "This is how I used to teach!"—although they might have to admit that their projects back in the day were not as rigorous as they should have been. In either case, they now feel liberated once they see that PBL can work in a standards-based world. The appeal of PBL to teachers was confirmed by a 2010 study of a project-based high school economics curriculum, in which teachers who used the PBL approach felt more satisfied with their teaching methods than those who did not (Finkelstein, Hanson, Huang, Hirschman, & Huang, 2010).

**Is PBL for Everybody?**

Some teachers might *not* prefer to use PBL. Some are concerned about controlling the classroom and planning every minute, so conducting a project with student voice and choice just seems too "messy" and fraught with uncertainty. Other teachers, particularly in high schools, prefer traditional teaching methods over PBL because they're more focused on their academic discipline than on working as closely with young people as PBL requires. They like being the "sage on the stage" and would find the role of "guide on the side" unfamiliar and uncomfortable. We offer two thoughts for teachers who don't feel PBL is for them:

- *You can still have structure and use traditional instructional tools in a project-based approach.* Especially in their first few projects, we advise teachers to design the key pieces of the project in advance and map out a project calendar in detail, allowing for more limited student input than you might have assumed PBL requires. As teachers gain experience with PBL, they begin to see how much they are able to let go and trust the process. And rest assured, traditional tools such as lectures and structured lessons have a place in PBL—when and as needed.

- *Try it—you might like it! And your expertise still has a place.* Some high school teachers tell us, after they've done their first project or two, that although they found it challenging to work with teenagers in new ways, it was more fulfilling and, well, fun. And they could still give that wonderful lecture about Civil War battles or the DNA evidence for evolution, but now students paid more attention because they saw its purpose in the context of an engaging project.

## Providing Schools and Districts with New Ways to Connect with Parents, Communities, and the Wider World

We've talked about what PBL can do for students and teachers—but how about what it can do for a school as a whole or a school district? Let's start with a couple of stories.

## Communicating with Stakeholders

Katherine Smith Elementary School is a public K–6 school in San Jose, California, part of the Evergreen School District. It has a high number of English language learners, and most of its students come from low-income families. Faced with the need to dramatically improve student achievement and reenergize its culture of disengaged students and parents, the school reinvented itself in 2012.

With an eye on the demands of the Common Core, teachers and newly hired principal Aaron Brengard made a commitment to "deep learning" and teaching students how to think critically, collaborate, communicate, create, and innovate. They adopted a "college bound, no excuses" attitude, brought in technology, and beautified the campus. And they adopted project based learning as a primary teaching method in all grades, for all students, providing teachers with extensive professional development and coaching. The parent community, when they were informed about the school's new direction, rallied in support. The school's turnaround efforts have been paying off, and it's now a very different place.

In the spring of 2013 and again in 2014, Katherine Smith School hosted an Exhibition Night at which students shared their project work with the public. Students made interactive presentations and walked visitors through displays of project products, explaining the process they had followed and reflecting on what they had learned. Many of the students had first delivered their project presentations earlier in the year to other public audiences, such as realtors' associations and the city council. (You can see a video about the 2013 Exhibition Night at https://www.youtube.com/watch?v=PQ_xnExy4LI.)

The other story involves two school districts: Metropolitan Nashville Public Schools in Tennessee and York County School Division, southeast of Richmond, Virginia. Both partnered with the Buck Institute for Education in a multiyear effort to implement project based learning in all their schools by providing teachers with extensive professional development and creating systemic support. In 2014, both districts took a bold step and asked students, teachers, and administrators to conduct a public exhibition of the students' project work.

York asked each of its 19 schools to conduct its own event in April or May, so the format of the exhibitions varied. Some were held during the day and others were evening events. Some showcased particular projects, subject areas, or grade levels, whereas other exhibitions were more like fairs, with tabletop displays of a variety of projects, hosted by students. Teachers, other students, parents, community members, and representatives of local businesses attended.

Metro Nashville decided to hold one big exhibition in April from 8:00 a.m. to 8:00 p.m. at a local community college's exhibit hall. More than 300 projects were on display, hosted by student teams. Over 900 people attended, including middle school and high school students, parents, teachers, administrators, and partners from the business community.

## Highlighting More Than Test Scores

In both of these stories, the schools and districts met a need to communicate with stakeholders in new ways. Traditionally, community members learn about a school or district through stories in the local media and word-of-mouth. Parents might also hear from their children and teachers, attend events on campus, read newsletters, or visit websites. A key piece of information these people use to judge the quality of a school or district is its test scores.

But as any teacher would tell you, a test score is only a snapshot of what happens in a classroom; students learn more than what's measured on standardized tests. Parents see evidence of that when their children bring work home from school, at a parent-teacher conference, or when they visit a classroom on Open House night. A public exhibition of students' project work takes this a big step further, by helping schools and districts tell more of the story.

What Katherine Smith, Metro Nashville, and York are doing, then, is more than a celebration of students' accomplishments and a way to build a shared vision for a new form of instruction. It's more than an opportunity for students to present their work to an audience, which is one of the essential elements of PBL that we discuss in the next chapter. A public exhibition is a powerful way to tell stakeholders, "We're more than our test scores."

Some schools and districts that do not have high test scores have adopted PBL as an instructional strategy because they believe it can improve student achievement on traditional measures, but meanwhile helps them meet other goals. In these places, a public exhibition of project work sends the message that, despite the current scores, "Great things are happening here." Students are not only learning important content knowledge; they're also gaining skills such as critical thinking, problem solving, collaboration, and self management. And they're fully engaged in their education.

According to instructional coach Sonya Mansfield of Metro Nashville, many people in the city have a negative view of the public schools and the students in them. But at the PBL exhibition, "When people from the business community and parents came in, it gave them a different perspective on the students and what they're learning."

For schools and districts whose test scores are generally high enough to satisfy their stakeholders, a public exhibition of students' project work can meet a related but slightly different need. Teachers and school leaders may want to tell parents and the community, "We're not satisfied with high test scores alone. We want our students to learn in more depth, build 21st century success skills, and gain real-world experience. We want them to care about what they do at school, not just their grades. PBL is how we're doing it, and this is what it looks like."

As Eric Williams, past superintendent of York County Schools, said about the PBL exhibition, "It shows we don't just have a test-prep mentality. Parents of high-achieving students concerned about test scores saw the depth of learning."

## Connecting Schools to Communities and the World

Many schools today want to be more closely involved with parents, local businesses, community organizations, and people in the outside world rather than remain islands in their communities. Projects can present many opportunities for a school to connect with its community. Teachers can contact local businesses or other organizations to get ideas for projects, to find resources for students, or to ask them to act as clients, mentors, and audiences.

For example, in the *Farmer Appreciation Project* described in the Appendix, 1st graders planned and hosted an event that brought dozens of local farmers to the school. To launch the *Home Sweet Home* project (see Appendix), teachers contacted an education expert at the Detroit Zoo about writing a letter to 4th graders asking them to design new animal habitats. A parent who had worked at a zoo gave students feedback on their plans during the project, and the Detroit Zoo's education director attended their final presentations. In Telannia Norfar's high school math class in Oklahoma City, students act as consultant teams who work with local businesses to help improve their services or marketing.

Some schools want to take it a step further, and they involve their students in addressing real-world issues and solving problems that have a significant impact on others. Project based learning allows them to accomplish these goals. For example, at Maplewood High School in Nashville, teacher Danette McMillian organized an economics/personal finance project that included working with real estate agents and local bankers and focused on increasing home ownership in the community (see *The Home Ownership Project* in Appendix). Pamela Newman, another Nashville teacher, led her 5th graders at Dupont Haley Middle School in a project that grew out of her students' interest in one of their classmates who was a cancer survivor. The class decided to raise funds for the local children's hospital by conducting an event that included dinner and exhibits based on student research on cancer and its treatments (see *The Cancer Project* in Appendix A). A project with international reach was conducted by Leah Penniman of Tech Valley High School in Rensselaer, New York. Her 9th graders met the need of a nonprofit organization that works in Haiti to design a simple, low-cost solar oven.

## From the Why to the What and How

We're convinced that project based learning is an instructional strategy that can enable you and your students to go beyond content coverage and develop the deep understandings and success skills needed to thrive in today's complex world. As we explained in the preface, we've written this book to present a new vision of PBL—what we call Gold Standard Project Based Learning—and to give you concrete suggestions for infusing your own teaching with this vision. We describe Gold Standard PBL in the next chapter, with a review of the history and theory from which it derives, and then describe the research that supports it. Later chapters explain how to make PBL a reality your classroom, school, and district. Rather than going on to Chapter 2, readers who want to see what PBL looks like in practice might want to go directly to the Appendix. The stories from real teachers about real kids provide compelling testimony about the power of PBL.

# 2 | What Is Gold Standard PBL?

We'll begin our in-depth exploration of project based learning by looking back at its development. The path to Gold Standard Project Based Learning is not a direct one but is rather the story of several teaching innovations that share instructional methodologies and common assumptions about learning. Gold Standard PBL blends them into a pedagogy that combines the best practices of each as reflected in current research, theory, and the experience of the many expert teachers we work with and learn from each year.

## Precursors to Gold Standard Project Based Learning

Although the beginning of PBL is often associated with progressive education and John Dewey's belief that learning is a social process, it turns out that the essence of project based learning was being practiced several centuries before the birth of either Dewey or progressive education.

### The Beginning: *Progetti*

In 16th century Italy, architects, painters, and sculptors were considered to be skilled artisans. This designation did not sit well with them. They believed their occupations were different from other skilled trades, such as stone masonry or carpentry. They felt their work was built on the union of scientific and artistic knowledge. They wished to be recognized as professionals whose work was based on special training and theoretical knowledge rather than on oral tradition and practice. Schools were necessary to develop, systematize, and disseminate this knowledge, and in 1577, under the patronage of Pope Gregory XIII, an art school called the Accademia di San Luca was founded in Rome (Knoll, 1997).

Like other educational institutions of the time, this new school used the lecture as its primary instructional method. For nascent architects and sculptors, however, a lecture-based course of preparation was obviously inadequate: they needed the opportunity to apply and test what they were learning about form and function. As students became more advanced, they were required to complete scale models of churches, monuments, or palaces—what we might today call "design challenges." These assignments were called *progetti* (projects), to indicate that they were works of imagination and creativity, as opposed to constructions that would actually be built in the real world. This was the first time that the word *project* was used to signify a methodology for teaching and learning (Marconi, Cipriani, & Valeriani, 1974). About 20 years later, the Accademia began holding competitions in which students' models were judged against specific criteria.

These 16th century competitions established many of the characteristics that define Gold Standard PBL today. First, *progetti* were organized around the solution of a *challenging problem*. The importance of this concept—organizing learning around active problem solving and knowledge application, as opposed to listening, understanding, internalizing, and recalling—cannot be overstated. Rather than requiring students to simply listen and remember, *progetti* gave them the opportunity to think, solve problems, and apply what they had been learning.

Second, *progetti* were intended to reflect the experience and professional expectations of the working architect and to include the sorts of tasks architects confront daily, such as producing design specifications while meeting deadlines, or convincing others of the worth of the design. Today, we would say the *progetti* were *authentic*.

Third, in addressing the realistic problems posed by the teacher, students had considerable *voice and choice* in deciding how they would solve these problems and create their models. Multiple correct answers were possible.

Fourth, the goal of *progetti* was to create a *public product* that could be viewed and examined by others. The word *product* comes from the Latin verb *producer*, meaning "to bring forth." A product is the tangible result of the creative process. It's a way of making learning visible. Once visible, as John Hattie and others have pointed out, it can be discussed, reflected upon, critiqued by the learner and others, and improved (Hattie, 2012; Ritchhart & Perkins, 2008). It's through a process of rigorous *assessment, critique, and revision* that learners encounter the strengths and deficiencies of their initial ideas and efforts, add missing details and elaborate their products, recognize misunderstandings, and, finally, deepen their learning.

It's striking that 16th century *progetti* brought together five of the essential project design elements that define what we call Gold Standard Project Based Learning: a challenging problem or question, authenticity, student voice and choice, critique and revision, and a public product. These elements established a model for vocational training that has continued to be an essential part of vocational preparation to this day, in both Europe and the United States (Knoll, 1997). These ideas, however, were to cross over from vocational preparation to K–12 schooling with the help of two educational philosophers at Columbia University's Teachers College.

## William Heard Kilpatrick and John Dewey

In the fall of 1918, William Heard Kilpatrick published an influential essay titled "The Project Method." Kilpatrick had been one of John Dewey's students, and his thinking was influenced by Dewey's philosophy as well as contemporary psychological thought. Kilpatrick's description of the Project Method caught the attention of educators in the United States for more than a decade and focused attention on the importance of student engagement (what we might today refer to as "flow") and the "purposeful act" in which students are engaged (Csikszentmihalyi & Csikszentmihalyi, 1991). In Kilpatrick's thinking, the goal of projects was to foster student motivation by encouraging students to freely decide the "purposes" they wanted to pursue. He believed that unless students were given unfettered voice and choice, schoolwork would only be drudgery, and this would alienate students and be counterproductive to the ultimate educational goal of producing productive citizens.

Although this rather romantic vision of education has resonated among writers from Rousseau to A. S. Neill, it did not resonate with John Dewey. Dewey believed Kilpatrick's focus on unrestricted student choice was misguided (as do we). Student choice was important, but not absolute. Dewey also questioned Kilpatrick's emphasis on spontaneous and total student engagement, and he criticized Kilpatrick's emphasis on "purposeful activity." Rather than focusing on the significance of activity, Dewey called attention to the "act of thinking," an iterative process whereby students encounter a conceptual or practical obstacle, plan a solution, try it out, and *reflect* upon their results (Knoll, 1997). It was the teacher's job, Dewey believed, to place just such obstacles in front of students. Effective projects were carried out through a "common enterprise" in which "the teacher becomes a partner in the learning process, guiding students to independently discover meaning within the subject area" (Dewey, 1938; Dewey & Small, 1897). Projects with no attention to teacher judgment, guidance, and interaction were likely to fail or, at a minimum, fail to challenge students (Dewey & Small, 1897). Dewey asserted that students still had important things to learn from the teacher, including high standards and a sense of excellence:

> The danger that children undertaking too complex projects will
> simply muddle and mess, and produce not mere crude results
> (which is a minor matter) but acquire crude standards (which is an
> important matter) is great. (Dewey, 1916, p. 205)

Those who mistakenly associate Dewey with the "muddle and mess" of laissez-faire education will be surprised to learn that he was very concerned that students develop high standards for their work through rigorous critique and guidance. Although Kilpatrick gained fame as the popularizer of the Project Method, his ideas eventually fell into disfavor, and he even began to question them himself (Knoll, 1997). For the development of Gold Standard Project Based Learning, it is Dewey's criticisms of Kilpatrick, and his own attention to "the cognitive act," that are foundational. Dewey felt that it was important to engage students in purposeful project activities and to grant some degree of student voice and choice, but student engagement and decision making were neither absolute nor sufficient for learning. Teachers were indispensible, for they created the context in which student learning took place. Teachers conceived situations where students engaged in thinking, *sustained inquiry*, and *reflection*. Using today's language, the teacher's job was to design and plan projects, making sure they lead students to grapple with things worth knowing (generally defined by accepted standards), scaffold learning and materials so that students succeed, assess student progress, engage and coach students toward learning goals, and, finally, manage the project process, turning over as much responsibility to students as is productive, given the goals of the project and students' readiness to assume responsibility for their own learning. We summarize these practices as *project based teaching*.

Beyond drawing on Dewey's ideas to inform Gold Standard PBL, we would argue that Dewey's concern with the "act of thinking" also moves project based learning beyond a purely vocational focus to encompass philosophical (unanswerable) questions—questions such as *What is beauty? What is ethical? What is the purpose of education?* Although Dewey would consider the more concrete problems of architectural design as worthwhile problems to be solved through experimentation, thought, and reflection, as a philosopher he would also advocate that students wrestle with more abstract questions of life and ethics.

Although the paternity of project based learning doesn't trace directly back to Dewey, his thinking has had considerable influence on all those who teach using PBL and has strongly influenced our own conceptualization of Gold Standard Project Based Learning. He drew our attention to the importance of the teacher as an indispensable mentor and senior partner in PBL design, planning, management, coaching, assessment, and reflection. He demonstrated that abstract questions, in addition to design challenges, could be approached through an iterative method of thought and reflection. Finally, he emphasized that engagement alone was an insufficient justification for PBL, and learning in general.

## Medical Education and Problem Based Learning

During the 1960s, medical educators at Canada's McMaster University were concerned that their students were not learning the clinical and diagnostic skills they would need to practice as effective physicians. They were also troubled by the traditional medical school curriculum, an approach emphasizing the memorization of fragmented biomedical knowledge rather than the integration of the knowledge, skills, and dispositions typical of successful doctors. They wanted to try a new teaching approach.

The approach they developed—*problem based learning*—was immediately adopted by several institutions, including Maastricht University in the Netherlands and Michigan State University in the United States. Other institutions watched and over the next 50 years increasingly adopted the new approach to professional education. Today problem based learning is an accepted pedagogy in nearly every medical school in the world, including Yale, Harvard, and the University of California (Camp, 1996). Professional training programs in other fields, including architecture, business, education, social work, law, and engineering, have also embraced some form of problem based learning (Mergendoller, Markham, Ravitz, & Larmer, 2006).

Although schools vary in how they implement problem based learning, the differences are outweighed by the commonalities. First, as with the original *progetti*, materials are created that describe a *challenging problem*. These problems are ill structured, ill defined, or "messy." They do not have an obvious answer and sometimes no obvious solution path to be followed. They reflect the type of problems people face in the real world, where there may be missing or conflicting information, multiple stakeholders and value positions, and no incontestable correct answer. Such problems call out for discussion, analysis, and logic—and they present very powerful questions to build a project around. The problems are made as realistic as possible. In medical schools, for example, problems are presented to students via documents describing patient symptoms, interviews, and lab reports, and they may even include a live actor playing the role of the patient. Business schools might present students with cases containing divisional revenue and expense reports, market surveys, and business plans.

Second, teams of students are formed and expected to collaborate on the problem solution. Students on each team identify and master "learning issues"—the information and concepts they need to learn and understand to solve the problem. For medical students, learning issues often include disease characteristics and trajectories. For architects, they might include materials or building codes. Different team members are assigned to research different issues and then pool their knowledge in jigsaw fashion (Aronson, 1978). This *sustained inquiry* process requires students to set individual goals, *manage themselves and their learning*, and then contribute their individual work toward a common goal. The *success skills* of "learning to learn" and to collaborate productively as a team are as important a goal as mastering the knowledge and understandings needed to solve the problem. Team members discuss what they've learned that is relevant to the problem and agree on what they believe to be the best solution. Individual teams often report to the entire class the conclusions they've reached and explain the logic used in reaching these conclusions.

Finally, students reflect on the entire learning experience and often share their thoughts with other students and the teacher. The process of *reflection*—what others might call metacognition—not only gives students the opportunity to examine how they solved the problem and consider ways to improve their performance, but also helps them to internalize the problem-solving process and recognize the problem type they have just addressed when it arises in the future (Bransford, Brown, & Cocking, 2000; Hung, Jonassen, & Liu, 2007).

In closing this discussion of problem based learning, we should note that often the distinction between *problem based* and *project based learning* is academic and possibly arbitrary. We've found that many teachers describe the classic problem based learning sequence when asked to describe the projects they're doing with their class. Consider, for example, the California history *22nd Mission Project* found at PBLU.org (see http://pblu.org/projects/the-22nd-california-mission) or the high school Project Based Economics curricula developed by BIE (available from Social Studies School Service at http://bit.ly/1ph7Rcx). Both of these projects are simulations of real-world problems. Both are messy and allow for multiple correct answers (as well as multiple incorrect answers). Both require research and discussion, and are resolved on the basis of logical argument. And, finally, both employ essential Gold Standard Project Based Learning design elements.

## From Problem Based Tutor to Project Based Teaching

In medical school, problem based learning takes place under the guidance and scrutiny of a more experienced facilitator who has encountered the problems the students are addressing. Such facilitators are traditionally called "tutors"—although they work with small groups, not individual students—and are typically physicians from the school or surrounding community. Tutors monitor and mentor student groups and help guide the conversation as students share their learn ing and questions (Savery, 2006). The goal is to promote discussion and reflection and to provide resources and scaffolding while avoiding direct instruction and answers. Instead, students are questioned in order to extend their own thinking and reasoning, and encouraged to develop their skills as independent, self-directed learners.

Howard Barrows is a leading practitioner, author, and theoretician of problem based learning, and he has written a classic essay about the role of the tutor and the importance of "metacognitive modeling" in scaffolding student thinking and problem solving:

> The oral statements and challenges he [the facilitator] makes
> should be those he would make to himself when deliberating over
> such a problem or situation as the one his students are working
> with. His questions will give them an awareness of what questions
> they should be asking themselves as they tackle the problem and
> an appreciation of what they will need to learn. In this way he does
> not give them information or indicate whether they are right or
> wrong in their thinking. (Barrows, 1992, pp. 4–5)

[The teacher] can ask, "Why?" "What do you mean?" "What is the evidence?" "Are their other explanations?" "Have you thought of everything that needs to be considered?" "What's the meaning of that?" to crank up tension and interest. To decrease the challenge, he can ask questions such as "Should we just tackle a piece of this problem (or task)?" "Let's revise our objectives and tackle those that are most important in this task." "Maybe we ought to stop here and read some resources or go talk to an expert?" "Would it be better to get the big picture now and fill in the details later?" etc. (Barrows, 1992, p. 11)

Other experts in problem based learning also emphasize the importance of monitoring student progress in solving the problem in order to guide students toward more sophisticated thinking and problem solutions. Linda Torp and Sara Sage (2002) recommend that problem based teachers keep five activities in mind: (1) diagnosing students' learning needs, (2) mentoring by helping students build intellectual bridges from their current understanding to more complete and complex understanding, (3) encouraging student progress, (4) questioning student thinking, and (5) modeling the inquiry process.

Problem based learning thus draws attention to the importance of student thinking, discussion, and collaboration, as well as to the importance of tactful, and respectful, teacher guidance (shades of Dewey!). Students are assumed to be novices needing the prodding, modeling, and praise of a more knowledgeable and experienced problem solver.

Although we also believe in the importance and power of the facilitative, metacognitive-focused instructional approach described above, we believe that as a description of what an excellent (Gold Standard) teacher does, it is insufficient. Project based teaching requires considerably more than facilitating student thinking in small groups. The role—and experience—of a problem based tutor in medical or professional schools, where self-selected, bright, and motivated students pay money to attend, is not analogous to that of a K–12 teacher (Maxwell, Bellisimo, & Mergendoller, 2001). In addition to differences in student characteristics, there are differences in the numbers of students for whom teachers are responsible, and differences in the multitude of tasks they must accomplish to make project based learning successful. The project based teachers we know spend considerable time creating or adapting the projects they do with their students. They still have to make sure that students learn the skills and concepts they will be tested upon each year, and they have to assess students and communicate to students and their parents about academic progress and problems. Although they may instruct their students in ways similar to that of a problem based tutor, they are responsible for so much more.

The concept of project based teaching is meant to incorporate the instructional and managerial skills and behaviors necessary for Gold Standard Project Based Learning. We will outline those skills and behaviors at the end of this chapter.

## Gold Standard Project Based Learning

Beginning with 16th century architectural training, adding ingredients from William Kirkpatrick and John Dewey, and concluding with the importation of major aspects of problem based learning, we arrive at our conception of Gold Standard Project Based Learning described via the graphic in Figure 2.1. Although this (or any) description of Gold Standard Project Based Learning can be subjected to critique, debate, and reformulation (which we've done more than 40 times in the preparation of this book!), we've tried to accomplish several goals. First, we wanted to draw on our predecessors' thinking about effective project based learning, as well as that of today's expert PBL educators, from whom we've learned immeasurably and to whom we owe a great deal. Second, we wanted to be simple and terse, believing that a straightforward diagram and concise description would be more easily remembered and make the translation to teacher practice more easily than complex and lengthy distinctions. Third, we wanted to base our thinking on recent educational research and theory, especially that conducted under the general umbrella of the "learning sciences" (Bransford, Brown, & Cocking, 2000).

We should also note that we are aware that there are differences between the Gold Standard ideal and the reality of typical PBL classroom practice. Gold Standard PBL is meant to be an aspirational goal, a composite of the best research-based and classroom-proven project design elements and instructional practices. The overall goal for both teachers and students is to become more competent—teachers moving toward Gold Standard PBL while students learn deeply and develop the skills they will need for success in college, career, and life. Our formulation of Gold Standard PBL is not meant to be formidable or discourage newbies from trying PBL. It is, rather, a description of what PBL looks like when it is done really well—a North Star to shoot for and approach through problem solving, practice, and reflection.

**Figure 2.1**   Gold Standard Project Based Learning

Copyright © 2015 Buck Institute for Education. Used with permission.

## Student Learning Goals

At the center of this diagram are the student learning goals at the heart of Gold Standard Project Based Learning. The purpose of the Gold Standard conceptualization—and the rationale for all we do as educators—is to enable students to develop the knowledge, understanding, and success skills that prepare them for successful school and life experiences

**Key Knowledge and Understanding**. PBL is an instructional approach that encourages both students and teachers to dig deeply into a subject, going beyond rote learning and grappling with the concepts and understandings fundamental to the subject and the discipline. Gold Standard Project Based Learning focuses on information and concepts that go beyond the superficialities of a Google search, that have nuance, and that require thought and analysis.

Such depth of thinking has not always been associated with PBL. In the 1970s many teachers attempted project based learning but didn't understand that PBL is a disciplined way to learn, not just an enjoyable way to engage students. Even today, some teachers think of PBL as a way to motivate rather than a way to teach. William Kirkpatrick made the same mistake by focusing on "wholehearted purposive activity" as opposed to learning.

Gold Standard Project Based Learning, although a motivating experience for students, emphasizes the purpose of this experience, which is learning with understanding. Enjoyment and motivation are a thankful corollary, but the goal is to learn deeply, mastering knowledge and concepts. Although it is impossible to separate the doing from the learning, as they interact and inform each other, the emphasis must ultimately be placed on what students will learn. Project activities are the means; knowledge and understanding is the goal (Blumenfeld, Solloway, Marx, Krajcik, Guzdial, & Palincsar, 1991).

**Key Success Skills**. Gold Standard PBL aims to develop not only students' understanding but also their ability to use and apply that understanding in the future. Students need to be able to mobilize their learning to think about and analyze current issues, solve new problems, and contribute to the civic dialogue. Cognitive psychologists describe this as "transfer": students are able to transfer what they've learned to new situations and problems. The Hewlett Foundation uses the term "deeper learning" to communicate a very similar idea (Hewlett Foundation, n.d.; see http://www.hewlett.org/ programs/education/deeper-learning).

But even if students can use and apply what they have learned, there are additional skills necessary for college, career, and life success. We call these—not surprisingly—*success skills.* Gold Standard PBL identifies three specific success skills that are necessary for success in the modern workplace, are highly valued by the American public, and also contribute to effective project based learning. (For views of U.S. business leaders, see AMA, 2012, and Casner-Lotto & Barrington, 2006; for a view of U.S. public opinion, see Partnership for 21st Century Skills, 2007.) These three success skills are *critical thinking/problem solving, collaboration,* and *self-management.* Although arguments could be made for adding other success skills, we believe that Gold Standard PBL will be more effective and attainable if priorities are set. Communication, which frequently appears on lists of 21st century skills, is certainly important but is contained within content standards for reading, writing, and speaking and listening. Creativity, often linked with innovation, appears on many lists of competencies valuable in today's economy and is an obvious candidate for addition. From our perspective, critical thinking/problem solving is foundational for innovation and addresses many, if not most, of the competencies generally that make up creativity and innovation. And although some projects may encourage students to express their creativity or be innovative, *all* projects should provide students with opportunities to think deeply, solve problems, work with others, and manage their own learning, time, and tasks.

An interesting thing about these success skills is that at the same time they represent learning goals for a project, they also represent the processes necessary to achieve project goals. If you want students to become problem solvers, then you have to give them problems to practice solving! The same is true for critical thinking, collaboration, communication, and self-management. Students need structured opportunities to learn these competencies, as they do for learning anything else, and Gold Standard PBL provides these opportunities. (For more on using project based learning to develop students' success skills, see Buck Institute for Education, *PBL for 21st Century Success: Teaching Critical Thinking, Collaboration, Communication, and Creativity*. http://bie.org/shop/product_detail/6777.)

## Essential Project Design Elements

With student learning goals in mind, teachers create or modify projects that embody the essential project design elements shown in Figure 2.1: (1) a challenging problem or question, (2) sustained inquiry, (3) authenticity, (4) student voice and choice, (5) reflection, (6) critique and revision, and (7) a public product. These design elements, and the degree of their representation within the project, determine how closely a project attains the goals of Gold Standard Project Based Learning. Let's examine each of them in more detail.

**Challenging Problem or Question**. Problems and questions provide the organizing structure for Gold Standard Project Based Learning and make learning meaningful because they give learning a purpose—students are not just gaining knowledge in order to remember it; they're gaining knowledge in order to use it. By focusing on a problem or question, students not only master new knowledge but also learn when and how this new knowledge can be used. This makes it more likely that they'll be able to use and apply this knowledge in the future (Brown, Bransford, Ferrara, & Campione, 1983; Brown, Collins, & Duguid, 1989). Many research studies—not to mention daily experience—demonstrate that knowledge perceived as meaningful and purposeful is more easily recalled than random knowledge (Bransford et al., 2000; Ebbinghaus, 1913). Questions focus students' attention on what is important to be learned and help students distinguish between relevant and irrelevant information. They also can prompt students to activate their prior knowledge, which is a key part of the process of organizing new information and connecting it to what is already known (Dean, 2012). As students work to solve the problem, they generate knowledge and understandings that remain with them and that they can use again in the future.

Educational research has shown that challenge is an important factor in producing learning outcomes (Hattie, 2012). But determining the optimal level of challenge in a diverse classroom is difficult and requires careful consideration of the scaffolding and support that some learners will need (which is part of project based teaching). Too much challenge and too little challenge turn students off; so Gold Standard PBL seeks a "Goldilocks" level of challenge—not too difficult, not too easy, but just right. Determining what's appropriate for a particular group of students within a specific project with certain learning outcomes rests with the professional judgment of the teacher. Harder (more complex, longer, more difficult) projects will not necessarily be more successful projects.

Several different elements contribute to the "challenge level" of a problem or question. First is the difficulty of understanding and applying the underlying information and concepts students will need to learn. As experienced teachers know, some ideas, concepts, and procedures are more difficult to understand and more difficult to use. Projects can be used to address such difficult concepts, but teachers should make sure they continually check for students' understanding and provide clarification (from other students and/or the teacher) as needed. Second is the degree of structure found within the problem. When problems are ill structured and require students to develop their own solution methods, they are more challenging than problems that have students follow a familiar solution path. Although ill-structured problems provide opportunities for students to learn how to structure and carry out investigations—what activities to undertake, what tools to use, what questions to ask, what order to follow—they can be very challenging for students and may require considerable scaffolding for successful completion. The third element that contributes to challenge is the complexity of procedures and the number of steps students will have to complete in order to solve the problem (Blumenfeld, Mergendoller, & Swarthout, 1987).

**Sustained Inquiry**. John Dewey's thought animates much of Gold Standard Project Based Learning, but it is his insistence on the importance of inquiry that wields the strongest influence. Challenging problems or questions are used to launch an inquiry designed to solve the problem or answer the question. The Latin root of *inquiry* means "to ask," and the classic PBL project begins by students asking, "What do we know?" and "What do we need to know?" to solve the problem or answer the driving question. These questions lead students (generally with teacher guidance and assistance) to identify investigations and research to be conducted and tasks to be completed, and plan the public product they will create. It's important to note that inquiry does not just mean research in its simplest sense of "finding information" from a book or website. To answer their questions, students might interview an expert, do field work, or conduct an experiment. They might inquire into the needs of the users of a product or service, or of the audience with whom students will share their work. As students find answers to their initial questions, new questions emerge, and they seek more answers; their inquiry becomes a cycle, or a spiral, as students dig deeper and deeper.

Within the world of education, the word *inquiry* evokes diametrically opposed reactions. Educational conservatives (e.g., Kirschner, Sweller, & Clark, 2006) decry inquiry, maintaining that such learning is inefficient, overloads student cognitive capacity, and generally wastes teachers' and students' time. On the other hand, progressive educators and those aligned with the "learning sciences" view inquiry as the heart of all meaningful learning (Bransford et al., 2000; Bruner, 1966; Hmelo-Silver, Duncan, & Chinn, 2007) and argue that the learning conservatives don't really understand the practice of inquiry (or project based) learning. Count us unapologetically part of the learning sciences crowd. We believe that inquiry—done well—is not the same as turning students loose to discover things to be learned. In project based learning, it is the project itself, carefully planned by the teacher, that structures student inquiry and guides learning activities toward project goals. In a project, challenging problems or questions establish a purpose for learning. We believe that students—actually, anyone—learn more efficiently, more quickly, and more deeply if they understand why they are learning and perceive their learning as purposeful. It is this intentional and purposeful pursuit of a solution or answer that is at the heart of inquiry.

It is important that the inquiry be sustained. One of the goals of Gold Standard PBL is to build the success skills of critical thinking/problem solving, collaboration, and self-management. If this is to occur, then students need to confront problems and questions that are not resolved in a few class meetings. Difficult questions take more time to think through and solve. Collaborative teams go through developmental phases as well as emotional ups and downs. Developing the interactive skills necessary to contribute to an ongoing team takes time. Finally, if students are to develop self-management skills that will be useful in college, career, and life, then they must be able to manage themselves over the course of weeks, rather than days. (Additionally, we should note, building these skills requires students to experience several projects a year, not just a few over the course of their education.)

**Authenticity**. PBL educators generally agree that authenticity is a not-so-secret sauce that both frames and enhances students' engagement in projects. Research has shown that authenticity not only increases motivation but can also increase achievement (Blumenfeld, Kempler, & Krajcik, 2006; Brophy, 2013; Hickey, Moore, & Pellegrino, 2001).

Authenticity is a complex concept, but it's generally synonymous with making a learning experience as "real" as possible. Teachers (and students) can make projects authentic in multiple ways and in varying degrees. Authenticity should not be considered an all-or-nothing proposition, but rather a PBL best practice that can be addressed in four different ways, possibly at the same time. (The following discussion draws on the concepts advanced by Strobel, Wang, Weber, & Dyehouse in their 2013 article on engineering education. For other perspectives on authenticity, see blogs by Sam Siedel [http://bie.org/blog/authenticity_to_self_engaging_students_identities_in_project_based_learning] and John Larmer [http://bie.org/blog/what_does_it_take_for_a_project_to_be_authentic].)

First, the *context* of a project can be authentic, as when elementary students design and create restaurant menus, or high school students, acting as advisors to the president, advocate for specific economic or social policies. Although such projects may require some suspension of disbelief—students are not creating actual menus that customers will use or making their living as policy wonks—the context matches what happens in the actual world.

Second, the *tasks* students complete, and the tools they use, can make a project authentic if those tasks and tools match what people do in the "real world." Many career-focused projects emphasize real-world tasks and real-world performance standards. Other projects that use real-world tasks focus on the problems, dilemmas, and ways of thinking that people face each day, when they design websites, schools, or living spaces; arrange exhibitions; analyze competing alternatives; prepare budgets; conduct telephone surveys; or write letters to the editor.

Third, projects can have an authentic *impact* on the world, as when students make a presentation to the school board proposing the redesign of a school playground, write books and create a tutoring program for younger readers, design and sell note cards to raise money for a wildlife sanctuary, or conduct research projects and submit data that will be used to better understand climate change. Research suggests that such authentic-impact projects are especially motivating, and students often choose to work on them before and after school and at recess (Barron et al., 1998; Cognition and Technology Group at Vanderbilt, 1998, McCombs, 1996; Pintrich & Schunk, 1996).

Finally, projects can have a *personal* authenticity because they speak to students' personal concerns, interests, or issues in their lives, or because they engage the needs, values, language, and cultural practices of students' communities. Community health fairs, oral and community history projects, and projects that bring the neighboring community into the school have the added benefit of helping newly arrived students connect to the rituals and expectations of schooling (Moll, Amanti, Neff, & Gonzalez, 1992). Authenticity is one of the Gold Standard design elements where more is better than less. Experienced PBL teachers tell us that projects that include multiple forms of authenticity—tasks, real-world standards, social and personal impact—are more powerful and productive than projects with less authenticity (Laur, 2013).

**Student Voice and Choice**. Faced with a challenging problem or question, students must be able to exercise judgment and make decisions about how to resolve it. Otherwise the project becomes an exercise, a set of directions to follow. Gold Standard PBL calls for students to voice their ideas and make choices over the course of the project. This requirement has consequences for both learning and motivation. Dewey's description of "the cognitive act" suggests that student voice and choice are a prerequisite to critical thinking and problem solving. Students need some freedom to act and to reflect on their actions if they are to learn from the situation. In terms of motivation, giving students an opportunity to express their own ideas and opinions and make choices during project work validates the basic drives of autonomy and competence, and contributes to intrinsic motivation (Brophy, 2013).

This does not mean, however, that student self-determination is unlimited. Teachers have the responsibility of determining how much choice students should exercise and what kinds of choices are most beneficial to their learning and to getting the project done. If students are expected to choose the methodology they'll use in a science project but don't have the background knowledge about method needed to make such a choice, the project won't be a success (see, e.g., Marx, Blumenfeld, Krajcik, & Soloway, 1997). Degree of voice and choice must be made with an eye to what students are ready to handle, and what scaffolds and coaching will be available. We don't generally advocate, for example, that students be given the unfettered choice of who becomes a member of their project team. That said, Gold Standard PBL suggests that the more voice and choice students can be given, the better. Our goal is to encourage self-motivated students who can make logical, intelligent choices in their lives. The smaller-scale choices and opinions students express in PBL are a training ground for the more weighty choices they'll confront later in their lives.

**Reflection**. Nearly a century ago, anticipating today's interest in "metacognition," Dewey wrote, "We do not learn from experience. We learn from reflecting on experience" (1938). His concern with "the cognitive act" makes reflection a key part of project activities. Students—and the teacher—need to reflect throughout the project on the effectiveness of their inquiry and project activities, the quality of student work, the obstacles confronted, and how they can be overcome. Such reflections keep the project on track and help minimize PBL's "muddle and mess."

Gold standard PBL aims to prepare students who, when confronted with a problem, size it up and reflect on whether they've seen this type of problem before and whether they've already developed knowledge and strategies that they can use to solve it. If they have not, then their thinking moves on to how to solve the problem.

When reflection is applied to one's own thinking process—thinking about one's thinking—psychologists refer to it as metacognition, which ranks 14th in John Hattie's list of achievement influences, higher than prior achievement (Hattie, 2012). Reflection is thus two-pronged. Cast outward, it enables students to progress thoughtfully through project tasks and modify their behavior as needed. Cast inward, it provides awareness of the learning and problem-solving strategies they are using, and enables students to better understand and modify these strategies.

Careful reflection enables students to determine whether the problem solving strategies they are using are appropriate to the problem being solved. Problem solving and metacognitive strategies are frequently embedded in specific academic disciplines and do not transfer across subject areas (e.g., textual analysis strategies do not generally help students solve physics problems). Consequently, Gold Standard projects need to be designed to prompt subject-appropriate thought (Bransford et al., 2000).

**Critique and Revision.** For over a decade, John Hattie has been analyzing the impact of different factors on education in a groundbreaking effort to better understand what makes a difference in student learning. His analysis indicates that "providing formative evaluation" is the fourth most powerful influence in his list of 150 possible influences, more powerful than teacher-student relationships, prior achievement, or cooperative learning (Hattie, 2012). Hattie concludes that although formative evaluation is an essential teacher function, it is an equally essential student activity:

> [Students'] role is not simply to do tasks decided by teachers, but to actively manage and understand their learning gains. This includes evaluating their own progress, being more responsible for their learning, and being involved with peers in learning together about gains in learning. (Hattie, 2012, p. 88)

Other researchers have come to similar conclusions and have argued that formative assessment is a powerful but underused tool in most classrooms (Black & Wiliam, 1998; Schroeder, Scott, Tolson, Huang, & Lee, 2007). This situation may be the case in most classrooms, but formative assessment—what we call critique and revision—is a baked-in practice in Gold Standard PBL.

Gold Standard PBL emphasizes the importance of improving student work through critique and revision. By building in checkpoints, where students receive feedback on their work from their teacher, perhaps other adults such as experts or mentors, and their peers, students examine the quality of their work and have opportunities to revise and improve it. Students are taught how to examine each other's work and how to provide suggestions for improvement. Such critique and revision is a normal part of product creation and is generally carried out through protocols or other structured processes to ensure that the feedback is "specific, helpful, and kind" (Berger, 2003). Attention is also given to the overall progress each student team is making, which allows students to surface and reflect on both practical and interpersonal issues that may be impeding project progress, and to initiate midcourse corrections.

**Public Product**. Most schoolwork typically winds up on the teacher's desk, in an online folder, or squashed into student notebooks. In contrast, Gold Standard PBL provides the opportunity for students to create a product and share it with an audience beyond the classroom. This has several positive consequences. First, the products that result from a project are perceived as more real (i.e., authentic) and consequential than schoolwork that is only graded by the teacher and returned to the notebook. It also encourages students to do their best—nobody wants to look ill prepared or show a shoddy product in front of a public audience. Making student work public ups the ante for both students and teachers.

A public product can also increase student engagement. Research into job satisfaction and motivation has shown that workers become more committed and engaged when working on tasks that make a difference (i.e., are authentic), require a variety of skills, and for which they have some control from initiation to completion (Hackman &

Oldham, 1980). This sounds almost like a definition of project based learning! But let us focus here on the first finding, the motivation that arises from working on tasks that make a difference. Public products encourage students to perceive their work is worthwhile and taken seriously by others (not just the teacher). This happens during the project when student work is critiqued by peers, the teacher, and outside experts or product users. At the end of the project, students can publicly display and describe their products in an exhibition, at a community meeting, or online. This process continues to encourage students to feel pride in their products and accomplishments.

Public products, as we noted in our "Why PBL?" discussion in Chapter 1, also make an important contribution to school morale and community perceptions. By demonstrating to other students, parents, and the larger community what students know and can do, public exhibitions of student work build support for their school and instructional program. Public exhibitions of student work not only explain what project based learning is all about; they also engender goodwill and promote PBL as a powerful approach to teaching and learning.

## Project Based Teaching

The role of the teacher in project based learning has been described in various ways: a facilitator, a coach, a conductor; the guide on the side, not the sage on the stage. These metaphors all have some truth to them and can be useful in differentiating the role of the teacher in PBL from traditional teaching, but such depictions may prompt some to ask, "Don't teachers *teach* anymore in PBL?" They most certainly do, in our view. The teacher is still a content expert, a mentor, a motivator, and an assessor of learning. Teachers make instructional decisions based on their pedagogical content knowledge about how to best help students understand new ideas. They engage students in scaffolding conversations and monitor how the project is going. They devise new resources and provide coaching. They build a classroom culture that supports PBL. They act as instructional designers and project managers. Put together, you have the ensemble of practices we call *project based teaching* (see Figure 2.2).

**Figure 2.2**    Project Based Teaching

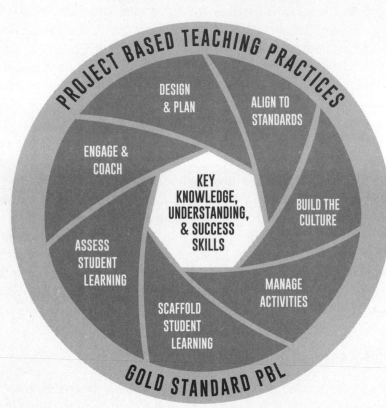

Copyright © 2015 Buck Institute for Education. Used with permission.

A common stereotype suggests that the teacher in PBL simply launches the project and then steps back to let students work, providing only as much guidance as needed. It's true that older students who are experienced with PBL should be given the maximum level of autonomy possible. But this is an ideal, and in reality most students will need some support from a teacher. So the rule of thumb should be, provide the *appropriate* level of autonomy.

There are also differences between what a PBL rookie teacher might be able to do versus a PBL veteran. A teacher who is experienced with PBL might be able to give students a great deal of voice and choice in some projects, treating them as co-designers, co-managers, and co-assessors. Generally speaking, we advise teachers who are less experienced with PBL, or whose students are new to it, to take the leading role in planning and guiding projects. But even a PBL veteran may decide that less student voice and choice is appropriate for some projects or at different points within a project, depending on the students, the topic, the products, and many other factors.

In the remainder of this chapter, we outline seven key practices essential to project based teaching. Although Gold Standard PBL emphasizes how and what students learn, it is the teacher who is paramount in ensuring such learning occurs. Students can help teachers carry out these practices—what matters is the nature of the practice, not who carries it out—but the adult teacher has ultimate responsibility to ensure that each function is done well. We will discuss each of these seven practices below.

## Project Design and Planning

A project starts with a gleam in a teacher's eye—or sometimes in students' eyes, if a teacher is attuned their interests and concerns. That's the first step in the project planning process: come up with an idea or, sometimes, adapt someone else's idea. Either way, teachers then flesh out the idea by designing a framework for the project, to make it work in their context, for their students. This task may be challenging—and enjoyable—for some teachers if they've mainly used "off the shelf" curriculum materials in the past.

As we explain in more detail in Chapter 4, a project framework includes the project's central focus and goals, the major products and how they'll be made public, and a driving question that makes the challenging problem or question engaging and doable.

## Aligning the Project to Standards

This step is part of the project planning process, but it is worth calling out as a separate teaching practice because it's so important. For some PBL teachers, content standards are an afterthought; they tend to plan a project first and then backfill the standards they think it will address. This approach is not optimal. We suggest teachers look at their content standards *at the same time* as they are developing an idea for a project. Indeed, the standards themselves may suggest a direction for a project, in terms of the topic and/or the skills on which to focus. Aligning a project with standards early on helps ensure that it's targeting content and understandings worth knowing, and that student time will be well spent.

What does it mean to "align" a project to standards? It means making sure the products students create will require the knowledge and skills laid out in the standards. The same goes for the challenging problem or question that frames the project; to solve or answer it, will students need to learn what's in the targeted standards? When it comes to critique and revision, how will these processes focus on what's described in the standards? How will the project's assessment practices, scaffolding, and coaching be directed at meeting the standards?

## Culture Building

A PBL classroom culture promotes independence, inquiry, and attention to quality. In practice, the teacher in Gold Standard PBL builds this kind of culture in ways both explicit (e.g., slogans on the wall or structured processes for inquiry) and subtle (e.g., how the teacher responds to student questions or how students are taught to speak to each other). In a healthy PBL classroom, student questions to guide the inquiry process are elicited and honored. Students know that it's OK to explore different pathways, to propose ideas or create product prototypes that need to be revised or even tossed out entirely, aka "failing forward." The teacher allows students to voice their opinions and offer ideas about the project, and makes sure students understand that the project truly is open-ended—that there is more than one way to investigate a topic, create a product, show what they know, and answer a driving question.

Another important aspect of a PBL classroom culture is encouraging a "growth mindset," or the shared belief that students' abilities are not limited by genes or background, and can be developed through dedication and hard work (Dweck, 2006). When students come to believe this, they learn more and apply themselves more consistently to new challenges. PBL teaching encourages a growth mindset through cycles of critique and revision where students have the opportunity to improve their products and, in so doing, increase and deepen their learning. Rather than focusing solely on the final product, teachers should focus their praise and recognition on students' effort, persistence, their strategies for overcoming difficulties, and the overall process of improvement. Every student should be "stretched" and given challenges requiring thought and effort.

## Managing Project Activities

In the business world, a project manager makes sure the work gets accomplished by organizing tasks; setting schedules, checkpoints, and deadlines; keeping people focused and productive; controlling quality; and handling a hundred other details. The job is pretty much the same in project based teaching—except with the added twist that it's done with children and teenagers, and you want to give them reasonable control and autonomy over the process. Indeed, with students who are project veterans, many PBL teachers actually think of themselves as facilitators instead of managers, since students do much of the "project management" on their own, with the teacher only providing support as needed.

For newcomers, managing a project is often one of the more challenging aspects of project based teaching because it's so different from what is called for in traditional teaching. Teachers are used to providing lessons, resources, and other scaffolding; they know how to assess student learning, at least for content knowledge; they've employed the practices of a coach when helping students do their work, even if they might not have used the term. But keeping a multi-week project on track, guiding student teams in the creation of products, coordinating the involvement of other adults in the process, dealing with the logistics of public exhibitions... that's unfamiliar territory for most classroom teachers. As we explain in detail in Chapter 5, managing a project includes preparing students for PBL, arranging resources, and creating a project calendar before the project starts, then steering the project from the launch to the big finish.

## Scaffolding Student Learning

As teachers work to scaffold student learning, traditional teaching practices mesh with project based learning. Scaffolding may include everything from structured lessons and lectures, to student handouts and readings, to tools and processes that support students in achieving project goals. Although it's used with other forms of instruction, the term *scaffolding* is particularly apt for PBL because of its emphasis on student independence. Here's how the online Glossary of Education Reform (edglossary.org) defines it:

> Scaffolding refers to a variety of instructional techniques used to move students progressively toward stronger understanding and, ultimately, greater independence in the learning process.... Like physical scaffolding, the supportive strategies are incrementally removed when they are no longer needed, and the teacher gradually shifts more responsibility over the learning process to the student.

A big part of scaffolding is *differentiation* for diverse learners, another term known well by today's teachers. PBL is very compatible with differentiated instruction, as we explain in Chapter 6. Teachers also play an important role in structuring, supporting, and monitoring group discussion. It's not enough to put students in a group and ask them to think deeply and collaborate. Students need explicit tasks and conversational expectations to turn random student talk into increased comprehension and critical thinking (Murphy, Wilkinson, Soter, Hennessey, & Alexander, 2009).

## Assessing Student Learning

Assessment in a PBL context includes many of the practices found in traditional instruction, but it requires teachers to go beyond the assignments, quizzes, tests, and other tools with which they might be most familiar. Conceptions of "balanced assessment" (Burke, 2010; Stiggins, 2005) emphasize the need for both *formative assessment*—used to inform the learner and teacher about progress toward a learning goal—and *summative assessment*—used to make a judgment about what has been learned. Both are important in a project.

Summative assessment in PBL, like formative, is a combination of traditional and, for many teachers, new practices. In a traditional curriculum unit, for example, a teacher might give a test or ask students to write an essay to determine whether they have learned what the teacher intended. In a project, those tools might still have a place—especially to assess content knowledge and conceptual understanding—but so does a final evaluation of a team-created product and of students' ability to employ critical thinking/problem solving, collaboration, and self-management skills. For that, teachers and students need to use criterion-referenced rubrics (for more on the use of rubrics, see Chapter 5).

In addition to formative and summative assessment, other kinds of "balance" apply in Gold Standard PBL. A project should include some degree of self-assessment, in which the student uses evidence and reflection to evaluate his or her own progress and achievements. For students who are old enough, peer assessment plays a role in evaluating the quality of a piece of work or one's participation as a member of a team. In addition to assessing individual work, teachers in a project-based classroom might need to assess the work done as a group. Because a project requires students not only to gain knowledge but to apply it, traditional measures of knowledge gained must be balanced with performance assessment. Finally, in addition to assessing knowledge, teachers need to assess conceptual understanding and success skills such as critical thinking/problem solving, collaboration, and self-management.

## Engaging and Coaching Student Performance

Many educators have observed the way PBL engages students. They know that meaningful projects, framed by a challenging problem or question, entice students to work hard and learn. Projects alone, however, are not uniquely responsible for student engagement. Teachers also play an important role. As the project unfolds, PBL teachers learn about students as individuals and can show their respect for student individuality and recognize student preferences. Teachers have opportunities to share students' accomplishments and frustrations. This emotional involvement and knowledge of students enable a teacher to act as ex officio team members, an informed "guide on the side," whose own engagement with students encourages, in turn, their engagement with learning. Teachers engage with students to encourage their own thinking, working, and learning.

Teachers' engagement with students is a precondition for an effective coaching relationship. The metaphors of "student as worker"/"teacher as coach" was coined by Ted Sizer, founder of the Coalition of Essential Schools (Sizer, 1984).

The terminology is a useful way to think about students engaged in a project, where the classroom should feel more like a modern workplace than an old-fashioned classroom with students sitting quietly at desks arranged in rows. In project based teaching, the teacher acts as a coach in several ways, much like the coach of a sports team, who (1) is an expert in the sport, (2) develops players' skills, (3) inspires and motivates, and (4) builds teams (Tomlinson, 2011).

As an expert in the subject matter and in how young people learn, the teacher in a project knows how to play the game: he or she understands the subject being addressed by the project and skills needed for successful project completion. The teacher knows what the goal is and holds up standards for high-quality performance. A teacher-as-coach develops skills systematically, first by believing that all students can become better at what they're doing, then by breaking it down into steps, providing practice, and giving lots of feedback. To motivate students, the teacher inspires them by talking about the worthiness of the project and the wonder and mystery of the topic. He or she reminds them of the goal of the project and how activities and tasks connect to it. If the team needs a pep talk midway through a project or an individual student needs some counseling, the teacher recognizes the need and delivers. Finally, a coach knows the importance of team spirit and works to build and sustain it over the long haul of a project—and leads the team in reflecting on and celebrating the work when it's done.

## Doing Gold Standard PBL in Your Classroom

This chapter has described the precursors and the components of a vision of PBL we call Gold Standard Project Based Learning. The approach is designed to be inclusive and inviting to PBL practitioners who associate themselves with differently named PBL traditions (problem based learning, challenge based learning, anchored instruction, place based learning, passion based learning, case studies, cognitive apprenticeship, deeper learning, and so on), all of which, in our opinion, are working to help students retain knowledge better, learn deeply with understanding, and develop the success skills they will need in college, career, and life.

The next chapter reviews the past 25 years of PBL research to reach some big conclusions about what we know about PBL. We hope these conclusions will convince you to give PBL a try, with the Gold Standard providing a North Star to guide your planning and teaching. You—and your students—are in for a challenging, fun, and rewarding journey.

# 3 | What Does the Research Say About Project Based Learning?

In preparing this book, we examined the last 25 years of research on *project* based and *problem* based learning. We've examined studies of both *project* based and *problem* based learning because we believe both PBLs have something to teach us. Like other educators, we wanted to know more about the evidence supporting PBL and the factors that contribute to its effectiveness. We know that PBL can be challenging to implement, and we wanted to make sure that there was evidence that meeting this challenge was worthwhile for both students and teachers.

Although our review of PBL literature was inclusive, the following summary is selective and identifies studies based on accepted, high-quality research designs. (By "high-quality," we generally mean research studies that have been published in peer-reviewed academic journals and, in the case of student-outcome studies, those based on either a *randomized controlled trial*—that is, one in which the participants are chosen randomly to be in a control group or an experimental group; or a *quasi-experimental design*—that is, lacking a random assignment of participants to one or both groups.) We begin with an overall review of PBL effectiveness organized according to subject area.

# Comparing the Impact of PBL and Traditional Instruction in K–12 Classrooms

FINDING: *Multiple K–12 research studies document that students engaged in PBL score higher on both traditional and performance-based assessments compared to similar students learning the same material using traditional instructional methods. This is a robust finding from dozens of studies involving thousands of students in varying grade levels and subjects. There is also evidence that students engaged in PBL score the same as students using traditional methods. We could find no published evidence in K–12 studies that PBL students score lower on assessments than traditionally taught students.*

## Science

Science education research is a fertile area for PBL research, mainly because science education generally emphasizes the importance of student inquiry and of working with other students to collect data or conduct experiments. This emphasis matches what students do during project based learning as they work to resolve a challenging problem or question. Studies comparing the effect of traditional, more didactic teaching with inquiry-oriented, PBL-like teaching in science have been conducted with 4th graders (Drake & Long, 2009); English language learners in the early elementary grades (Lee, Buxton, Lewis, & LeRoy, 2006); urban middle school students in the United States (Gordon, Rogers, Comfort, Gavula, & McGee, 2001; Kolodner et al., 2003; Lynch, Kuipers, Pyke, & Szesze, 2005; Rivet & Krajcik, 2004) and Turkey (Arazm & Sungur, 2007); and high school students (Schneider, Krajcik, Marx, & Soloway, 2002). Two additional middle school studies blend PBL and computer technology (Chang, 2001; Liu, Hsieh, Cho, & Schallert, 2006). All of these studies demonstrate that students in inquiry-oriented, PBL classrooms learned more *science content* than students in more traditional, didactic classrooms.

Research conducted in 18 public middle schools in Detroit is a good example of the effect of project based science instruction. Approximately 5,000 students—most of whom were African American and receiving a free or reduced price lunch—and 37 teachers participated in this two-year study. Students in the PBL classrooms worked on projects targeting physical science (*Why do I need to wear a helmet when I ride my bike?*), biological science (*What is the water like in my river?*), and earth science (*What is the quality of air in my community?*). At the end of the year, all students took the Michigan Assessment of Educational Progress (MEAP) administered by the state. Over the two-year course of the study, students in the project based classes scored significantly higher on the MEAP than students who had covered the same material using traditional methods. The PBL students also scored higher on the MEAP assessment of science process skills (Geier et al., 2008).

## Mathematics

Most mathematics educators and the Common Core Standards for Mathematical Practice emphasize the importance of reasoning, problem solving, reflecting, and communicating one's own mathematical understanding (Common Core State Standards Initiative, n.d.; Fennema & Romberg, 1999). Although these are key practices of project based learning, researchers have not conducted many studies that compare project based and traditional mathematics approaches.

One well-known study that did compare PBL with traditional mathematics instruction focused on the curriculum development project known as *The Adventures of Jasper Woodbury* (http://jasper.vueinnovations.com). This research demonstrated that the middle school students using the PBL approach not only developed greater skills in solving math word problems than did the comparison students, but also demonstrated more positive attitudes toward math (Cognition and Technology Group at Vanderbilt, 1998). The most thorough study of the effect PBL can have on mathematics learning was conducted by Jo Boaler (1998) in two British comprehensive schools in working-class communities. One school, "Amber Hill," used a traditional (textbook- and exercise-centric) approach to mathematics. A second school, "Phoenix Park," engaged students by having them work on open-ended mathematics projects and in heterogeneous groups. At the conclusion of the three-year study, all students completed the British General Certificate of Secondary Education (GCSE) exam. As a whole, Phoenix Park students scored higher than Amber Hill students. Boaler offers this explanation:

> The relative underachievement of the Amber Hill students in formal test situations may be considered surprising, both because the students worked hard in mathematics lessons and because the school's mathematical approach was extremely examination oriented.... [However, the] Amber Hill students had developed an *inert*... knowledge that they found difficult to use in anything other than textbook questions. In the examination, the students encountered difficulties because they found that the questions did not require merely a simplistic rehearsal of a rule or a procedure; the questions required students to understand what the question was asking and which procedure was appropriate. The questions further required the students to apply to new and different situations the methods they had learned. (p. 56)

Boaler's research is compelling and gets at the heart of what PBL can achieve—the ability to use and apply what has been learned to new and different situations. As Boaler puts it:

> The students at Phoenix Park did not know *more* mathematics than the students at Amber Hill. Rather, the students were able to use mathematics [they did know]. (p. 59)

## Social Studies

The achievement gap between richer and poorer students is well known and remains one of the most vexing problems we face as educators. An interesting study of 2nd grade students in four classrooms explored whether PBL could be used to increase the learning of low-SES students so that their tested achievement in social studies, reading, and writing would be equal to that of the higher-SES students in nearby schools. The experiment was successful, and the authors commented that the "study confirms the promise of project-based approaches... with a disadvantaged population" (Halvorsen et al., 2014, p. 30).

Another study focused on a six-week unit in 8th grade local history. One group of students made and presented video minidocumentaries showcasing their own interpretations of events in local history, while a second group studied local history as traditionally taught.

The research showed that the documentarians ("PBL students") not only learned more about 19th century local history than the students who were traditionally taught, but also demonstrated greater historical-thinking skills (Hernandez-Ramos & De La Paz, 2009). Similar results have been shown with gifted high school students in an American studies class (Gallagher & Stepien, 1996).

The *Knowledge in Action* research project at the University of Washington developed a PBL instructional approach and materials for Advanced Placement Government classes and compared their efficacy to traditional, textbook-based AP courses. This research continues under the auspices of Lucas Education Research. Reported results to date are promising. A higher percentage of students in the PBL courses scored 4 or 5 on the AP exam, compared to students in the traditional AP Government course. Results on an assessment of deep understanding, requiring the application of principles of U.S. government, were inconsistent: PBL students in a higher-achieving school showed deeper understanding than their peers in traditional AP classes, but there was no difference in ability to apply and use knowledge among PBL and non-PBL students from moderate-achieving high schools (Parker et al., 2013). The authors attribute this inconsistency to difficulties in assessing knowledge application.

Although all 50 states and the District of Columbia include economics in their education standards and 22 states require high school students to enroll in an economics course, for most students the subject remains true to its description as a "dismal science," filled with unfamiliar terms and concepts that are difficult to understand. The Buck Institute for Education created Project Based Economics (PBE) to address this problem, and this semester-long course was evaluated by WestEd as part of its work for the U.S. Department of Education (Finkelstein et al., 2010). Approximately 7,000 students taught by 77 teachers in 66 high schools participated in this study, which was designed as a randomized clinical trial, considered to be the most rigorous of research designs.

Results of this evaluation were similar to those reported for other subject areas. Students who learned economics using PBL scored higher on a multiple-choice test of economics content knowledge, and—equally important—they were better able to reason and think critically about economic concepts than were the comparison students.

## A Cautionary Note

These various studies provide important proof points demonstrating PBL's efficacy as an instructional approach, but it's important to remember that PBL is not a silver bullet that works every time, in every classroom. PBL differs from school to school and teacher to teacher. Some projects last several days; others take a semester. Some are interdisciplinary; others drill down into a single subject. This diversity suggests that it's important to realize that just because PBL has been shown to be effective in multiple studies, this does not guarantee that it will be effective in every implementation. Much depends on the teacher, the project design, and the implementation.

---

### PBL + Deeper Learning = College and Career Ready

The American Institutes for Research in 2013–2014 studied a group of "Deeper Learning" schools known for their schoolwide attention to project based learning. Part of the Hewlett Foundation's "Deeper Learning" network, these schools were committed to developing "the skills and knowledge that students must possess to succeed in 21st century jobs and civic life" (http://www.hewlett.org/uploads/documents/Deeper_Learning_Defined__April_2013.pdf). In addition to emphasizing PBL, schools arranged internships to develop students' connections to the world outside school, emphasized group work and long-term assessments such as portfolios and exhibitions to develop collaboration and communication skills, and encouraged study groups and student participation in decision making to develop academic mindsets and "learning to learn" skills. Students at these schools

- achieved higher scores in reading, mathematics, and science on the OECD PISA-based Test for Schools (PBTS)—a test that assesses core content knowledge and complex problem-solving skills—than did similar students in comparison schools not committed to PBL and Deeper Learning. These students also earned higher scores on state-mandated English language arts and mathematics tests.
- reported higher levels of collaboration skills, academic engagement, motivation to learn, and self-efficacy.

**PBL + Deeper Learning = College and Career Ready—(*continued*)**

• were more likely to graduate from high school on time than were students from comparison schools. The graduation rate among Deeper Learning school students was estimated to be about 9 percentage points higher than the graduation rate among similar students in comparison schools.
• were more likely to enroll in four-year institutions (27 percent compared with 23 percent) and in selective institutions (4 percent compared with 3 percent).

For more information, see http://www.hewlett.org/sites/default/files/AIR%20 Deeper%20Learning%20Summary.pdf

## Teachers' Experiences Implementing PBL

FINDING: *Teachers vary in their initial and continuing effectiveness using PBL and often report that PBL is challenging to implement. Teachers can improve their implementation skills and confidence with the support of peers, mentors, and school leaders. Once they become competent with PBL, most teachers see its value and want to continue using it.*

The Buck Institute's own research has documented teachers' varying effectiveness in using PBL (Maxwell et al., 2005), and researchers have noted that PBL is often challenging with regard to content coverage, coordination with district standards and expectations, scheduling and time use, assessment, and team management (Marx et al., 1994; Marx et al., 1997; Thomas, 2000). Although teachers may experience challenges when they first use PBL, they typically become converts once they've had a chance to resolve their difficulties with the support of peers, school leaders, and resources. For example, after describing the challenges she confronted, a science teacher described her conversion to PBL:

> My experiences with project-based science have introduced me to new dimensions of student achievement. I can no longer be satisfied with "right" answers on tests, tidy well-run labs, or … congratulate myself [on] the approving oohs and aahs after my "Mr. Wizard" demonstrations… [Project based science] is of vastly more lasting

value for students [and enables them] to develop cognitive and social skills they can apply to ever-changing circumstances.... For me, project based science is a one-way street: having once turned onto it, I cannot imagine going in any other direction. (Scott, 1994, pp. 92–93)

This conversion is not an overnight process. It took two years for the teacher just quoted to feel confident using PBL:

Perhaps more noteworthy than the transformation of two or three units within a year-long curriculum is the transformation of my own attitude as I approach each day's objectives. Now, comfortably supported by the project-based framework, I find myself frequently putting the students in charge of achieving these objectives—a reflection of the dynamic process of project-based science as it continues for me. (p. 93)

This is typical of our experience. It takes a while to develop both the PBL perspective and the planning, management, and assessment skills that make PBL successful. PBL is not mastered in an afternoon workshop but requires trying out, problem solving with peers and mentors, reflecting upon what worked and what didn't, and trying it again.

Most teachers find the PBL journey worth the effort. When the 77 high school teachers participating in the Project Based Economics research described earlier were asked to rate their satisfaction with the economics curricula and resources they were using, the PBE teachers were much more satisfied than the teachers using traditional materials and approaches (Finkelstein et al., 2010).

## Students' Experiences with PBL

FINDING: *Although students are engaged by PBL, they need support and guidance, especially when new to PBL. Projects need to be carefully constructed with an eye to the requisite skills and knowledge students will need to have to be able to complete the project successfully.*

Most students enjoy project based learning, and teachers frequently comment about how much more engaged their students are when doing PBL. This is a good thing, for engagement can power student learning, but it's not the same as learning. Some very interesting PBL research illuminates how projects need to be planned with students' background knowledge and cognitive capability in mind, and orchestrated by a teacher ready to coach and scaffold student thinking and performance when necessary. For example, the massive Detroit middle school science study discussed earlier found that while students were good at developing research plans and carrying out pre-specified procedures, they had difficulty

> a) generating meaningful scientific questions, b) managing complexity and time, c) transforming data, and d) developing a logical argument to support claims. More specifically, students tended to pursue questions… based on personal preference rather than questions that were warranted by the scientific content of the project, they had difficulty understanding the concept of controlled environments, they created research designs that were inadequate given their research questions, they developed incomplete plans for data collection, they often failed to carry out their plans systematically, they tended to present data and state conclusions without describing the link between the two, and they often did not use all of their data in drawing conclusions. (Thomas, 2000, p. 24)

Middle school students are not alone. Researchers have observed high school students in earth science classes who had difficulty maintaining their motivation and planning and conducting systematic inquiry activities. Part of their difficulty stemmed from the lack of background knowledge necessary to complete the expected inquiry activities (Edelson, Gordon, & Pea, 1999).

Both of these studies show the importance of preparing students for PBL, and the need to design projects that both build on the knowledge students already possess and enable them to fill in their knowledge gaps as the project unfolds. In addition to teacher interaction and scaffolding, other students can be engaged in peer tutoring and discussion, and technology can be used to structure student inquiry (Kim, Hannafin, & Bryan, 2007). Projects that require specialized procedures (such as designing experiments, conducting interviews) or sophisticated cognitive operations (such as prioritizing questions, linking evidence and conclusions) must be planned with opportunities for students to learn these skills, preferably through instruction, modeling, and practice.

## PBL and Contemporary Conceptions of Learning

FINDING: *PBL is aligned with current thinking about the nature of human learning and the necessary conditions to help students learn with understanding, retain what they have learned, and apply their learning to new contexts and situations.*

PBL seeks to develop what cognitive scientists call "usable knowledge"—knowledge that's not just recalled for a test but that once learned, can be used in daily life and problem solving (Bransford et al., 2000). It fits well with the concept of "situated learning," the idea that learning is most effective when it involves knowledge generated by completing authentic tasks in familiar, everyday contexts (Lave & Wenger, 1991). Such knowledge is better organized and better integrated with prior knowledge, perceived as more meaningful to the learner, remembered longer, and applied more easily to new situations (Hung et al., 2007).

PBL's emphasis on students' understanding and the application of knowledge—in contrast to repetition and practice—as well as the active cognitive engagement of students in problem analysis and examination of relevant prior knowledge (*What do we know? What do we need to know?*) and problem solving, may explain the usability of knowledge gained through project based learning. PBL's focus on significant learning also encourages knowledge retention and reorganization. Surface (or rote) knowledge rarely transfers to new contexts and situations (Bransford et al., 2000).

The research by Jo Boaler in mathematics, described earlier, and the large body of research on the use of problem based learning in medical and professional schools provide examples of PBL's superiority in situations where students had to purposefully use their knowledge, not just remember it (Dochy, Segers, Van den Bossche, & Gijbels, 2003; Strobel & van Barneveld, 2009; Walker & Leary, 2009).

Researchers have also documented that students who learn in PBL environments remember what they've learned longer than those taught using traditional methods (Capon & Kuhn, 2004; Dochy et al., 2003; Martenson, Eriksson, & Ingelman-Sundberg, 1985; Wirkala & Kuhn, 2011). One study (Tans, Schmidt, Schade-Hoogeveen, & Gijse-laers, 1986) reported that PBL students' long-term retention rate was 60 percent higher than that of the students who learned the same material using traditional approaches!

## PBL and Student Motivation and Engagement

FINDING: *PBL is aligned with current thinking about maximizing student motivation and interest.*

When teachers talk about PBL, one of the first things they generally focus on is student engagement, and this is not surprising. Project based learning brings together a number of factors that have been shown to encourage motivation. First, PBL involves a collaborative group effort, and working with other students is usually motivating (Blumenfeld et al., 1991). Second, PBL allows students to have voice and choice, and such opportunities for self-expression and decision making are considered very powerful motivators among both students and adults (Brophy, 2013). Third, PBL emphasizes authenticity in the tasks that are completed and the public product that emerges from the project, and such authenticity encourages student engagement (Brophy, 2013; Seidel, 2011). Finally, PBL generally involves novelty in the nature of the questions addressed, the academic tasks completed, and the contexts in which the project unfolds. PBL is not school as usual, and this is a strong catalyst of student motivation and engagement (Blumenfeld et al., 1991; Thomas, 2000).

Not surprisingly, the conditions that motivate students to engage in PBL are also motivating to adults. Considerable research has been conducted on the factors underlying job satisfaction, and three factors have been identified as important in creating motivating, meaningful work. Motivating jobs (1) require workers to use a variety of skills, as opposed to repetitiously applying a single skill; (2) engage workers on a project from beginning to end, and enable them to experience completion and accomplishment, as opposed to being assigned one, limited part of a job isolated from the ongoing process; and (3) have an impact on other people, both in the workplace and beyond (Hackman & Oldham, 1980).

Good PBL—like a good job—engages students in authentic tasks from start to finish, working with peers and producing results that make a difference to the students working on the project and to the world beyond.

# 4 | Designing a Project

Are you ready? You know what PBL is and why it's a good idea for today's students. You've been inspired by learning about Gold Standard Project Based Learning and hearing about great projects in which young people are fully engaged in their learning, understand content more deeply, work in ways that prepare them for college and careers, and perhaps even benefit their communities. You've wondered if you could do something like that with your students. Yes, you can; and we're going to take you through a project design process that will result in a well-thought-out project that has a good chance of succeeding—and surprising you and your students with what they're able to accomplish. We'll begin by building some background knowledge.

## General Notes on Designing Projects

Designing a project is not like planning a lesson; it's more like planning a unit. In fact, some people think of projects as curriculum units updated for the 21st century. A project, like a unit, lasts for at least a week, usually two or more, not just a day or two. A project has several learning goals, not just one or two like a typical lesson. A project contains within it multiple lessons, activities, tasks, and student assignments, and it requires a variety of resources. And although a lesson follows certain steps that include a beginning, a middle, and an end, a project moves through what are more like phases than steps, leading to a culminating activity—usually a presentation and an explanation of what has been learned. Finally, a teacher may decide during the course of a project to make additions or modifications more substantial than the typical minor adjustments made during some lessons.

Compared to planning a lesson, planning a project takes more time and more thought about how all the parts connect. The trick is to plan your project, again as Goldilocks might say, "just right." It can't be mapped out too tightly, or you'll take away student voice and choice, one of the essential elements of Gold Standard PBL. But it can't be too loose, either, or you'll risk the dangers of wasted time, misdirected student energy, and failure to meet learning goals.

How much structure you plan for your project also depends on how comfortable you are with teaching in a PBL environment. As we said in the discussion of project based teaching in Chapter 2, it's better for PBL rookies, generally speaking, to err on the side of overplanning. PBL veterans can allow for more student voice and choice and can involve students in developing project goals, deciding on products and how to make them public, and managing their own work.

Another note about designing a project: it's not a straightforward process. Typically, you start with some general ideas, then step back to reflect and, if possible, get some feedback from peers or an instructional coach. Feedback from colleagues  and helpful resources—can also be collected by posting your project idea online. We suggest joining the BIE PBL Google+ Community (https://plus.google.com/+-BIEPBL/posts) and using it to share and discuss your project ideas with other members; you can also find fellow travelers in the Edmodo PBL Community (https://www.edmodo.com/publisher/biepbl). After digesting the feedback, you either revise the idea or go ahead with planning the basic framework for the project—and again go through a process of critique and revision. (At Buck Institute workshops, we use a critique protocol called the "Tuning Protocol" in which teachers give and receive feedback on their project designs; a video that describes the process is available at http://bie.org/objects/cat/videos.) Once you've built the framework, you can work on nitty-gritty details such as creating rubrics and student handouts, arranging resources, and planning specific lessons.

## What Project Based Learning Is Not

When you're designing a project, keep in mind that project based learning is not the same as "doing a project." Here are some examples of assignments or activities that are sometimes called "projects" that, although they may have a legitimate place in the classroom, are not PBL:

• *"Dessert" projects.* At or near the end of a traditionally taught unit of instruction, a teacher sometimes serves up a dessert project to students, almost as if it were a reward for slogging through the material. These projects typically involve making something tangible: a model of the Egyptian pyramids, a video trailer about a novel, a tessellations art poster, a diorama of an Indian village, a board game about human physiology and health, a robot assembled by following directions from a kit. Dessert projects are typically seen as fun; the goal is not to teach the content or assess student learning, but to provide a "hands-on" experience.

• *"Side dish" projects.* This kind of project is similar to a dessert project but occurs during a traditionally taught unit or outside the bounds of units altogether. Students might be asked to do something at home: design and conduct a science experiment, create a family tree, observe the moon and record data, or pretend to invest money in the stock market. The teacher might ask students to choose a topic and conduct research, then (usually) present it to the class, to provide an "extension" of what is being covered in the class. Think of students making a tri-fold display or a PowerPoint presentation about a famous inventor, an aspect of life in Shakespeare's England, an endangered species, or a country in South America. The goals are similar to those of a dessert project, but with more emphasis on giving students a chance to study a topic in depth, with some degree of choice.

• *"Buffet" projects.* Some teachers design units in which students experience a number of varied activities, most of which are hands-on and fun as well as educational. The activities are united by a common theme, time, or place. Some of the activities may be called projects, and students sometimes get to choose which ones they do or what topics to pursue—much as they'd choose food items at a buffet dinner, except all the choices are desserts or side dishes! These "buffet" projects are often very impressive in their complexity and student engagement level. For example, imagine a 7th grade history unit about China. In addition to learning through lectures, textbooks, worksheets, and videos, students create maps of Marco Polo's journey and Genghis Khan's empire, make illustrated time line posters, write and perform skits about Chinese culture, learn to paint Chinese characters, play traditional Chinese games, and learn to cook Chinese food. Similar units are found in the early elementary grades, perhaps with themes such as "insects," "cultures," or "our community." The goals of buffet projects are similar to that of dessert and side dish projects: engage students and enrich the basic content of the unit.

• *End-of-unit performance assessments or applied learning tasks.* Teachers sometimes ask students to demonstrate what they have learned as the culmination of a unit and call the effort a "project." It could be an individual or a group task, and it could take many forms. Students might solve a problem or answer a question through a written product or a presentation; design and create a tangible object or a performance; or conduct a scientific investigation. The goal of such projects is mainly to assess student learning, and sometimes to allow students to experience a hands-on, enjoyable activity.

Why are these examples *not* project based learning? *Because they are not the main course.* They are not thought of as the method of instruction in the regular classroom or school program, but as an addition to it. They are not the primary vehicle for addressing content standards. They do not replace a traditional unit or act as a major part of a unit, but are supplemental to traditional units—or even completely separate from what happens in the regular academic course or classroom. See Figure 4.1 for a comparison of the key features of "doing projects" versus project based learning.

**Figure 4.1**    Projects Versus Project Based Learning

| Projects | Project Based Learning |
|---|---|
| Supplemental to a unit | The project is the unit, or a major vehicle for teaching content standards within a unit |
| Task is based on following directions from the teacher and is repeated year after year | Task is open-ended and involves student voice and choice; often differs from year to year |
| Typically done individually | Done in collaboration with a team |
| Done independently, often at home | Done with teacher guidance, much of it during school hours |
| Focused on the product; the product may even be called "the project" | The project includes a sustained inquiry process *and* the creation of a product |
| Not authentic to the real world or to students' lives | Authentic to the real world or to students' lives, or both |

*Note:* We are indebted to Amy Mayer, friEdTechnology.com, for some of these ideas.

### Senior Projects and Capstone Projects

Are these project based learning, or not?

In senior projects, students typically choose a topic of personal interest, do research, write a paper, and make a presentation. They may also conduct fieldwork, spend time in an internship or doing community service, or create something tangible—then write a report on it or assemble a portfolio, reflect on the experience, and make a presentation.

Capstone projects are similar to senior projects but culminate a particular course or program. The term is most often found at the postsecondary level, as a final step in a bachelor's or master's degree program, either along with or instead of writing a thesis. The College Board has recently developed an AP Capstone program for high school students, in which they analyze topics through multiple lenses, plan and conduct an investigation, communicate their findings in writing and discussions, and collaboratively solve a real-world problem. A few high schools have students complete a project, often multidisciplinary, at the end of a school year, and these resemble capstone projects. Students who have experienced PBL in their regular classes would be well prepared for the senior or capstone projects they do individually.

**Senior Projects and Capstone Projects—(*continued*)**

It's true that in both of these types of projects, students are learning by doing a project, which is the basic definition of PBL. And they are to some extent learning something of significance, which is not the case in many dessert or side dish projects. One key feature of Gold Standard PBL these projects might lack is collaboration (with the exception of AP Capstone), because the project and its products are typically done individually. There might be collaboration of a sort, if students meet occasionally with adult experts who give them feedback on their work. But they are not creating something together, as a team.

These are certainly worthwhile learning experiences that share most of the features of Gold Standard PBL. However, if a school said it uses PBL because it has senior projects, and that was the extent of it, we'd say, "Nice start, but...." To say you use PBL, you would have to use it as a common methodology in regular academic courses as well.

# Types of Projects

Projects come in many shapes and sizes. Some teachers might prefer one type, based on their own interests, teaching style, or approach to a discipline. Certain subject areas tend to see one type more than another. The students' age, needs, and interests can also be a factor in what type of project a teacher designs. However, all types of projects follow the same basic path and share the same essential elements.

The following sections cover five general types of projects, with examples. Note that some projects might be a combination of types.

## Solving a Real-World Problem

Students investigate a problem at their school, in their community, in the wider world, or one modeled after problems faced by people on the job or professionals in a particular discipline. They could simply propose solutions or actually put their solution into effect. Student products could include written proposals and other documents, artifacts, and presentations. This kind of project can be seen in any subject area but tends to occur less often in history, arts, or litera-ture-focused ELA courses. Here are some examples of problems stu-dents could tackle:

• The school has an ineffective waste management system. (See *Systems Thinkers* in Appendix A.)

• Behavior issues are being seen on school playgrounds and in restrooms. (See *Powerful Communities* in Appendix A.)

• A low-income community needs improvement through better land use, investments, and resources. (See *Reimagining South Central* in Appendix A.)

• A local business needs to attract young people to its website.

• Wild animal species are declining in numbers.

• National or state immigration issues need to be addressed.

The problem also could be framed in a fictitious (but still realistic) sce-nario, as in these examples:

• Investigators try to determine the location of a missing airplane that crashed in the ocean.

• Advisors to the president recommend a response to an interna-tional humanitarian crisis.

• Forensic teams determine the adequacy of DNA evidence found at a crime scene.

• Government experts develop a plan for reducing the level of *E. coli* bacteria in swimming areas.

## Meeting a Design Challenge

This is a broad category that could range from developing a proposal or plan, to actually creating or constructing something, to putting on a performance or an event. These projects can be found in any subject area but are typically the preferred type in math, sci-ence, career/technical subjects, world languages, physical education/health, and the arts. Here are some examples:

• Develop plans for a skate park.

• Build birdhouses to attract birds to the school campus. (See http://pblu.org/projects/schoolyard-habitat-project.)

• Produce podcasts about the history of a community.

• Write a field guide for a local natural area.

• Construct cardboard boats and test them in a pond with passengers aboard.

• Create a modern-day version of *Macbeth* using video and social media.

• Run a business or service, for real or as a simulation. (See http://pblu.org/projects/bizworld.)

• Host community visitors at a celebration in the classroom. (See *Farmer Appreciation Project* in Appendix A.)

• Design new habitats for the zoo. (See *Home Sweet Home* in Appendix A.)

• Draw blueprints for a home renovation. (See *House Hunters* in Appendix A.)

• Design holes for a miniature golf course. (See *Up to Par* in Appendix A.)

• Produce videos to help an exchange student integrate into a French community. (See *An American Student in France* in Appendix A.)

• Cook hard tack candy in the chemistry lab. (See *Sweet Solutions* in Appendix A.)

## Exploring an Abstract Question

In this kind of project, students are not focused on a concrete problem or product, but rather on intangible ideas and concepts. These projects are most often seen in English language arts, social studies/history, and sometimes science or the arts; they can also be explored from the perspective of multiple disciplines.

Students can express their answer to the question—which is open-ended, with several possible answers—in a variety of ways. They could create a written product such as a book, blog, letter, report, or magazine. They could create a video or make a presentation with visual aids, or put on a live performance such as a debate, play, speech, or poetry slam. Here are some examples of abstract questions for exploration:

• What happens when two cultures interact?
• Can torture be justified?
• When do we grow up?
• Are robots friends or foes?
• How can art reflect a community?
• Do any human beings ever realize life while they live it? (See *Global Happiness, Local Action* in Appendix A.)
• What makes people take a risk? (See http://pblu.org/projects/choose-your-own-adventure.)

It may seem at first glance that projects focusing on an abstract question are more appropriate for older students, but they can work even for primary-age children. Kindergartners at Heather School in San Carlos, California, considered the question "Should we kill spiders?" (see http://www.scsdk8.org/should-we-kill-spiders-a-kinder-garten-pbl-project/). In the *Pizza Shops and the World of Work* project at Mission Hill School in Boston, 2nd and 3rd graders explored the question "What does it mean to work?" by interviewing family and community members; they then created their own two-day pizza restaurant—an example of a project that combined the conceptual with a concrete design challenge.

## Conducting an Investigation

This kind of project involves students in answering a question that requires research, data collection, and analysis. It typically occurs in history or science and sometimes math, but it could work in other subjects, too. A report or other piece of writing, an exhibit, or a presentation are common products in these projects. The question could be about any intriguing topic, as long as the answer is complex—and not readily obtainable via an Internet search. Here are some examples:

• Could the British have avoided the revolt of the American colonies?
• What are the best household cleaning products?
• What was it like for my _____ (relative) to come here from _____ (other place)? (See http://pblu.org/projects/back-in-the-day.)

• What can we learn from other people's inspiring stories of resilience? (See http://pblu.org/projects/resilience-café.)

• How might global climate change affect native plant and animal species in our region?

• Do we really need to wear a bike helmet?

• Were the Dark Ages really dark?

• What is the process of owning a home, and what are the economic and social barriers that prevent many from pursuing home ownership? (See *The Home Ownership Project* in Appendix A.)

• How did these rocks get here?

• Why did our town grow the way it did?

• How did technology change the Civil War? (See *Civil War Technologies* in Appendix A.)

## Taking a Position on an Issue

Students in this type of project study a controversial or debatable issue, gather evidence, and make an argument. This type of project typically occurs in history, social studies, or science but can be found in other subjects, too, and is often multidisciplinary. Students might produce written documents, conduct a debate, deliver a speech, or make a presentation in these projects. Here are some examples:

• Do we have the right to capture and cage animals? (See *The One and Only Ivan Global Project* in Appendix A.)

• Was the Treaty of Versailles fair to the losers of World War I?

• Should we produce oil by the process of fracking?

• Should President Truman be found guilty of war crimes for dropping the atomic bomb?

• Do police have the right to search our cars?

• Should our county develop its open space and natural areas?

# Project Design Step 1: Considering Your Context

Just like designers of new products in the business world, teachers begin designing projects by thinking about their overall context: Who is this for and what are my goals? What's my time frame? Who am I working with? What are the parameters and constraints? Only after you've made some of these big-picture decisions will you be ready to dive into the innovation process. Let's take a closer look at the contextual questions you should consider.

## Which Students Will Be Involved?

If you're an elementary school teacher in a self-contained classroom, the answer to this question is usually "all of them." Additionally, your project could involve the whole grade level, students in other grades, or even students from other schools. We do not advocate using PBL only for, say, students in a gifted and talented program or those who are above a certain literacy-skill level.

Secondary school teachers answer this question by deciding which classes will be doing a project. Again, the answer could be "all of them." But if you have three different preps for the five classes you teach, it might be too much for you to conduct three different projects at the same time. If that's the case, spread them out over the calendar. Especially if you're a PBL rookie, consider trying out a new project with just one of your classes instead of all four of the periods when you teach a course. You'll need to factor in other considerations, such as the particular group of students in each class, the specific curriculum and goals for the course, and the availability of resources.

## When Will I Conduct the Project?

Teachers typically start thinking of projects in terms of the standards and curriculum to be taught over the course of a year. A history teacher might say, "I want to do a Civil War project," which means it will take place in January. Or an elementary teacher might say, "I'll wait until after I've gotten our math and literacy programs underway and we're ready for our first science unit," and start the first project in late September.

The timing issue gets more complicated if you're doing an interdisciplinary project with other teachers, or you're coordinating the schedule with school specialists or with outside experts and organizations (see the next section for more thoughts on how simple or complex you want the project to be). Then there are the usual parameters to think about: the overall school calendar, when major events are happening, and your district's testing, grading, and reporting cycles, pacing guides, and curriculum maps.

Some PBL teachers like to start the year off with a project, to engage students right away. If your school has a well-developed PBL program, your students may be ready to go; they know how to work in teams, conduct inquiry, make presentations, and generally function effectively in a PBL culture. But if your students are new to PBL, consider taking some time before launching the first project to familiarize them with the process, as we explain in Chapter 5.

And remember, Gold Standard Project Based Learning is ambitious, a target to shoot for, a way of maximizing PBL's effect. Some projects attain that goal, but others, although beneficial to students, do not. It's generally better to start small and try something that works, excites your students, and fosters learning, than to strike out with an overly ambitious project more closely matched to the Gold Standard design framework. The main task for PBL newbies is to try something, learn from it, and do it better the next time. Each iteration gets you closer to Gold Standard Project Based Learning.

## How Simple or Complex Will My Project Be?

This question might not be fully answered until after you've generated some ideas, but it's worth keeping in mind from the start. A project can range from simpler to more complex along a scale with several dimensions, as shown in Figure 4.2.

Projects that are "simple" aren't necessarily better or worse than more complex ones; and generally, especially for PBL newbies, it's easier to focus on the coaching and scaffolding necessary for PBL teaching if the project is simple. For some teachers, some students, or some purposes, a simple project is just fine—and we should really say *relatively* simple. Even a project at the "simple" end of the scale will present opportunities for practicing critical thinking and at least one of the other key success skills. And even a simple project should engage students deeply—and leave them wanting more!

**Figure 4.2**   Defining Features of Simpler Versus More Complex Projects

|  | Simpler Projects | More Complex Projects |
| --- | --- | --- |
| *Number of subject areas* | One subject | Multiple subjects |
| *Who is involved* | One teacher | Several teachers; outside experts and organizations; people in community or distant areas |
| *Where it takes place* | Classroom, school | On and off campus |
| *What products are being created* | One product that does not require too much time and advanced skills or tools | Multiple or elaborate products |
| *Technology to be used* | Fewer and familiar tech tools | Several tech tools that require new learning |

Whether you choose to design a simpler or more complex project depends on several factors. As we've said before, if you're new to PBL, it's probably wise to not be too ambitious until you get the hang of it. A multisubject project requires either one teacher to have expertise in several different subject areas or the involvement of two or more teachers, which requires coordinated planning, resources, and scheduling, plus shared students. A project that involves outside experts, organizations, or local or distant partners or that takes place away from school means you'll need to make contacts and arrangements.

Another factor is variety. Even veteran PBL teachers might decide they and their students are ready for a change (or a break). You can imagine why, after a couple of complex projects, a teacher might say, "Let's address that standard about the Vietnam War with a simpler debate project, rather than partner with the city and the local veterans association to design and build a monument in the park."

## How Long Will My Project Be?

This is another question that you might not be able to answer completely until you've generated an idea and done some planning, but it's good to keep this factor in mind as you start the design process. A project needs to be long enough to include, at least to some extent, time for student investigation into a topic, development of products and solutions, critique, and revision—and making student work public, which alone requires at least a day or two on a project calendar. A relatively simple project might take 8 to 10 hours of class time. More complex projects typically range from three to five weeks. Some very ambitious projects can take months, although not every minute of every class or day is devoted to project work.

If students are able to work on the project outside of class time—if a team can accomplish some tasks, for example, over the weekend—you may need fewer total days. The same goes for projects taking place in a "flipped classroom" in which students gain content knowledge for the project as their homework and use class time to apply what they learn.

Sometimes the subject matter dictates a project's length and complexity. A relatively concise and distinct content standard can be addressed in a short project with straightforward processes and products. Secondary math teachers, for example, may not feel they can spend much more than a week on a project that teaches only one major concept or process. (Secondary math teachers interested in projects that are relatively short can check out the projects at www. PBLU.org authored by Mathalicious.)

Some PBL teachers like to begin with a short project—lasting perhaps just three or four days—to get students ready for longer projects to come. The short project should include all the phases of a project (see Chapter 5) and all of the elements of Gold Standard PBL, but to a more limited extent.

## How Many Subject Areas Will Be Included?

The full power of PBL, many of its advocates would say, comes from investigating a topic from many different angles. Many real-world issues or problems cannot be addressed without the contributions of people from various fields. For example, if students are analyzing a ballot proposition about solar energy in a state election, they'll need to know something about government, economics, math, and physical science. Some project products cannot be created without drawing on knowledge and skills from different disciplines. For example, if students are creating a field guide to local native flora and fauna, they would need to know some biology as well as use writing and graphic design skills.

However, single-subject projects are totally appropriate in many cases. Single-subject projects provide an opportunity to "go deep" into the complexities of a topic or an issue. Some topics and issues only lend themselves to study from the point of view of one discipline. For example, having students decide which mobile phone plan best fits the needs of their family could be done solely as a math project. Or a project whose product is a debate about the Vietnam War might be contained within a history class. But few projects are truly single-subject, because most involve reading and writing. This is especially true in elementary schools, but also in secondary schools working to build literacy skills across the curriculum.

### A Caution on Multidisciplinary Projects

Be aware that multidisciplinary projects are more complicated to plan and manage. Elementary teachers, for example, might need to figure out how a social studies/art project can include literacy and math goals. Secondary teachers could go one of two ways to include multiple subjects in a project. You could do it all yourself—for example, by teaching writing as part of your history project, or by including some math in your biology project. Or a team of teachers who share the same group of students could take the more ambitious route and combine two, three, or more subjects in one project. They would need to find common planning time, coordinate schedules, and decide how to fit their own particular content goals into the project. (You'll find a good video example of this on the BIE website at https://www.youtube.com/watch?v=9VzhStQwQSI.)

It's also important for secondary teachers to not feel like their subject area is always "tagging along" with the main focus of the project. This happens most often for math and English teachers when they're part of a project whose topic is drawn from social studies or science. The math is often

**A Caution on Multidisciplinary Projects—(*continued*)**

statistics or arithmetic, not, say, algebra; the English teacher simply helps students with their writing assignments. To prevent this, make sure some of the multidisciplinary projects taught by a teaching team are rooted mainly in important math or ELA standards.

# Project Design Step 2:
# Generating an Idea for a Project

For most teachers, generating ideas for projects is fun. You get to be visionary, think creatively, and—ideally—work collaboratively with colleagues, because the process is more lively and productive when more than one person is involved. The process shares many traits with design thinking; it starts with brainstorming, when any idea can be considered, and only later do you home in on the best idea to develop.

There are two basic ways to arrive at a project that's right for you and your students. One is to adapt someone else's project to fit your needs. The other is to design your own project from scratch.

## Customizing Someone Else's Project

Coming up with a good idea and designing your own project does take time, not to mention a certain knack for it, so there's no shame in customizing the work of others. Especially if you're not experienced in planning your own curriculum units, adapting an existing project is a good way to get your feet wet in PBL. The Innovation Unit in the United Kingdom, for example, provides teachers with sample projects to jumpstart the planning process, using the term "tribute project" to honor the original creators (see http://www.realpbl.org/designing-projects/#tabs-1).

Finding a project to borrow and customize might be as simple as walking down the hallway to talk with a colleague about a project he has done. Schools, districts, or networks committed to PBL often create a library of projects to be shared. Or you might find projects designed by more distant colleagues and posted online. The Buck Institute for Education has collected hundreds of projects from various sources, available via its online Project Search tool (http://bie. org/project_search).

An ever-growing number of commercial publishers and other organizations today are also producing projects. Many publishers include "projects" in the teacher's edition of textbooks or in supplemental materials. This is especially true for STEM (science, technology, engineering, math) curriculum, where it's common to have students construct something—a robot, model car, or other device—simply by following directions. Lacking student voice and choice, and many of the other features of Gold Standard Project Based Learning, such so-called STEM projects are really just STEM activities. They can be used, however, within a redesigned project that includes an authentic purpose, has opportunities for critique and revision, and concludes with making student work public. Such redesigns will move them away from being mere activities toward the characteristics defining Gold Standard PBL.

When you find a project you might like to customize, evaluate it by asking the following questions:

- Does it address the standards/content I need to target?
- Is it main-course PBL, or only a "dessert" project?
- Does it reflect Gold Standard PBL design criteria?
- Will my students find it engaging?
- Is the length and level of complexity appropriate for my students and for me?
- Can I conduct this, given my own expertise and the resources available to me?
- How much would I need to do to adapt this project so it will work for my students and me?

## Generating Your Own Idea

Many teachers gravitate toward generating their own idea because curriculum planning around a topic of interest is often a favorite part of the job—and you know your students best. Also, you may have a lesson, an activity, or a unit from the past that you could turn into a full-blown project by revising or expanding it using the Gold Standard design criteria as your guide.

There's no set formula for coming up with ideas for projects. Some teachers start by analyzing their content standards. Others start by thinking of real-world applications for the material they want students to learn. Sometimes an idea jumps out at you from the news or a conversation with your students. Here are some sources of inspiration:

• *Issues in your school or community.* Identify issues or problems in your school or community—or better yet, have students find them—that could be addressed in a project. For example, in the *Powerful Communities* project, 1st graders developed solutions to problems of playground misbehavior at their school. In the *Reimagine South Central* project, 9th graders designed an online game to bring residents of South Central Los Angeles into a conversation about their community's future. (See Appendix A for descriptions of both projects.)

• *Current events.* Capitalize on what's happening locally, nationally, or globally to create a timely project. For example, the *Home Sweet Home* project (see Appendix A) began when teachers heard about the Detroit Zoo's plans to build a penguin conservation center. A government/economics teacher a few years ago designed a project called *Rebuilding Afghanistan* about what form of government and economic investments were best for that nation. (As of this writing, there are no doubt many biology teachers designing projects about the ebola virus.) Elections are an especially fertile ground for projects, as demonstrated by the *Propositions Project* (see http://bie.org/results/search&keywords=propositions&category=388+397).

• *Real-world problems.* Think of the kinds of problems people solve while on the job or in their lives, or the challenges people in government or the private sector might face. For example, in the *House Hunters* project, 7th graders learned math by planning renovations for a house. In the *Sweet Solutions* project, high school students acted as chemists making hard tack candy. (See Appendix A for descriptions of both projects.)

• *Content standards.* Analyze the standards you need to teach—whether it's the Common Core, your state's, or another set for a particular subject area—and look for the ones you could envision students exploring in depth. Think about how a standard might be employed in an authentic real-world context. For example, in the *Civil War Technologies* project (see Appendix A), teachers wanted students to understand the lasting effects of the Civil War on the United States, an important history standard.

• *Your students' lives and interests.* Draw from your students' interests, such as pop culture, fashion, food, sports, and social media; or what's important in their lives, such as family, friendship, relationships, personal identity and growth, and (for older students) their future. These subjects often lead to the most engaging projects for young people. For example, the *My Cheezy Fingers* project (http://mycheezyfingers.com/) focused on junk food favored by the 4th graders at Katherine Smith Elementary School. In *The Waiting Game*, a project created by Mathalicious (http://www.mathalicious.com/lessons), students use probability to come up with a rule to try to maximize their happiness in a romantic relationship.

## Project Design Step 3: Building the Framework

As we noted earlier, designing a project is an organic process, not a mechanistic, linear one. Teachers often go back and forth, focusing first on one part of the project and then on another. Changes made to one part often necessitate changes elsewhere as well. While generating ideas, you may already have thought of some of your project's goals and features, but now it's time to give it more structure by doing the following:

• Setting learning goals
• Selecting major products
• Deciding how products will be made public
• Writing a driving question

## Setting Learning Goals

A project should be designed to teach two types of learning goals: (1) key knowledge and understanding and (2) key success skills.

*Significant Content.* In theory, it might seem logical to start by analyzing the standards you need to follow for the grade level or course you teach, and then design a project accordingly. But many teachers think of an idea for a project first, then go back and specify which standards it will address. Whichever way you go, be very clear and specific about what you intend for students to learn, to avoid the common pitfall of being unfocused in terms of outcomes. This point is especially important should a project, once underway, begin to take off in an unexpected direction or expand due to students' interests or ambitions. Be sure it still focuses on important learning goals.

Keep two criteria in mind when using standards to define key knowledge and understanding: consider which content standards are most *important* and which standards are most *appropriate* for a project. Your state or district may have already identified some standards as more important than others, because they're considered fundamental to the subject or are targeted by a high number of items on high-stakes tests. Your school or department may have also prioritized certain standards. If neither of these situations is the case, make those judgments yourself, based on your own professional knowledge. The high-priority standards are the ones to specify for projects; if your students are going to spend weeks on a project, it had better be worth their time.

To decide if a content standard is appropriate to learn via a project, consider whether it calls for in-depth understanding rather than simply knowing a set of facts or procedures. For example, a science standard about laboratory safety procedures is probably not a good choice as the central focus for a project, nor is an ELA standard about pronouns. Those kinds of standards could still be included in a project, but they don't have the scope and depth to be the main reason for doing the project. In contrast, the following example from the *Next Generation Science Standards* for middle school is more appropriate for an in-depth project: "Construct a scientific explanation based on evidence from rock strata for how the geologic time scale is used to organize Earth's 4.6-billion-year-old history."

A caution is needed here, regarding how many content standards to include in a project. There should certainly be enough to justify the time spent, but avoid the temptation to wedge in too many. Remember, content standards are what need to actually be *taught and learned*, not items to "cover" on a checklist.

Depending on how specifically worded the standards are, focusing on two or three content standards per subject area per project is generally a good rule of thumb. If you have too many standards, it's impossible to teach and assess them well. Note that we said "focusing on" because there could be additional standards that are reviewed or revisited but not explicitly targeted in every project. For example, reading and writing standards are likely to be threaded throughout projects and in other learning activities during a school year.

*Key Success Skills.* Although there are many competencies needed for success in college, career, citizenship, and life, you may remember from Chapter 2 that Gold Standard Project Based Learning prioritizes three: critical thinking/problem solving, collaboration, and self-management. While all projects should provide opportunities for students to develop and practice these skills, it might be too much to try to explicitly teach and assess them all in one project. Some PBL teachers pick one or two to focus on, and target others for the next project.

## Selecting Major Products

In Chapter 2 we noted that a defining aspect of PBL is that students *produce* something, as opposed to just studying and remembering. And showing that product publicly is important. Products provide a means to demonstrate and discuss what students have learned. Products are what parents and community members see; they *are* the project in viewers' eyes. So the selection of the major products is a big decision when designing a project.

What students produce in a project can vary widely. A product can range from a physical artifact to an event or performance to the presentation of a solution to a problem. A typical project includes one or two major public products—for example, a written report and an oral presentation with multimedia. Several additional products—which are often for purposes of formative assessment or reflection—could also be part of a project, such as a video storyboard, research notes, or a learning log/reflective journal. (We'll say more about these various kinds of products in Chapter 5.)

Given the many options for products, it's easy to be overwhelmed by the possibilities. To help winnow down the choices, ask yourself the following questions when you're selecting the major products for a project:

• *Does the product provide enough evidence that students have met the targeted goals for learning, or will I need a combination of products?* In some projects, the major product can provide direct evidence of student progress toward content standards. For example, in the *Global Happiness, Local Action* project mentioned earlier, students wrote nonfiction narratives about local history and published them on the class website. This product provides evidence that students have met an English/language arts content standard for writing "narratives to develop real or imagined experiences" (CCSS 6–12, Writing 3). In *The Cancer Project*, students created exhibits and made presentations based on their research. But in a math project in which students design new containers, physical models would provide only partial evidence that students have learned the targeted standard. The project would have to require at least one other product, such as a set of drawings with a written mathematical model analysis, where students create a function that compares the dimensions of a container and its volume or surface area. The analysis would also represent the function in graphical, numerical, algebraic, and verbal form. The chemistry students doing the *Sweet Solutions* project wrote a series of blog posts in addition to making hard tack candy for holiday gifts. The 8th grade history students in the *Civil War Technologies* project wrote research papers along with creating an artifact as the centerpiece of a presentation.

• *Is the product as authentic as possible?* As we said in Chapter 2, authenticity is one of the essential elements of Gold Standard PBL, so think about how "real-world" your project's major products will be. Consider what people do in the world outside school. If they were solving the problem, addressing the issue, or meeting the need that is the focus of your project, what product would they create? For example, lobbyists for an environmental group would not create a brochure for a member of Congress; instead, they would write a persuasive letter or make a presentation at a meeting. Similarly, a chef creates a menu, an architect a set of plans, a civil engineer a scale model, a legislator a law; none of them writes a five-paragraph essay.

• *Is the product feasible?* This is a more practical consideration. Given the limits of your own expertise, what your students can do at their age, and the time and resources available, can the product be created? For example, you or your students might be feeling ambitious and decide to write and stage a two-hour play in a community theater; but you have only two months left in the school year and other things to teach, and your students have never done this before. Maybe a few scenes would be a better idea. Or perhaps you envision your 5th graders designing and building robots, but the cost, materials, and advanced engineering required are prohibitive; so try simple electronic toys instead.

• *What products will be created by individual students or done as a team?* To ensure accountability and allow you to assess each student's learning, you'll need some products, or important parts of them, to be created by individuals. For example, if a team is making a multimedia presentation, require each student to write part of the report on the topic or write his or her own answer to the driving question. If a team builds an electronic sculpture, ask each member to submit an explanation of the process used and what he or she learned. (In Chapter 5 we'll say more about the need to assess individual students on a project and not give only "group grades.")

• *Will student teams all create the same product or different products?* The answer to this question depends on the nature of the project, the degree to which students have voice and choice, and practical considerations for managing the project. Some projects by their nature are going to have the same product. For example, if students are staging a poetry slam for the community, the product is going to have to be a poem—but the topic of the poems could vary. If you decide to let students choose the products they create, be aware that it gets more complicated logistically if you—or even a team of teachers—try to manage the production of videos, website pages, letters to Congress, illustrated calendars, and a mural. (See Figure 4.3 for a matrix of options for products and focus.)

| **Figure 4.3**   Matrix of Options for Products and Focus | |
|---|---|
| **Same product, same focus** <br> *Example:* Presentation on water quality in our region | **Different product, same focus** <br> *Example:* Presentation or photo essay on water quality in our region |
| **Same product, different focus** <br> *Example:* Presentation on water quality in various parts of our region | **Different product, different focus** <br> *Example:* Presentation or photo essay on water quality in various parts of our region |

Once you've considered these questions, you'll find it easier to decide on the products you'll ask students to develop. A project could have one or more of the following types of products or include a combination of them.

*Presentations* include any kind of live performance:

- Speech
- Debate
- Oral presentation/defense
- Live newscast
- Panel discussion
- Play/dramatic presentation
- Poetry slam/storytelling
- Musical piece or dance
- Lesson
- Public event
- Sales pitch

*Written products* include some traditional academic kinds of writing, but in a project the writing is for a particular audience or authentic purpose, not just for a school assignment:

- Research report
- Letter
- Brochure
- Script
- Book review
- Training manual
- Mathematical/engineering analysis

- Blog
- Editorial

- Scientific study/experiment report
- Field guide

*Media and technology products* include all old and new media:

- Audio recording/podcast
- Slideshow
- Drawing/painting
- Collage/scrapbook
- Photo essay

- Video/animation
- Website/page(s) for website
- Computer program/app
- Digital story/comic

*Constructed products* include anything that is built by students, although it could be a model rather than an actual, full-scale structure or working device:

- Small-scale model
- Consumer product
- Device/machine
- Vehicle
- Invention

- Scientific instrument
- Museum exhibit
- Structure
- Garden

*Planning products* include various types of proposals or plans for doing something, but not the actual construction or enactment of it. Creating such products can be a demanding, rigorous task by itself, and they should be detailed and prepared the way a professional would:

- Proposal
- Business plan
- Design
- Bid or estimate

- Blueprint
- Time line
- Flow chart

## Deciding How Products Will Be Made Public

In the next chapter we'll discuss the details of how to conduct project presentations and exhibitions of student work. As you design your project's framework, you need only make some general decisions about the format. There are a variety of ways students could make their products public:

• *Put it to use in the real world.* In some projects, the product students create is inherently "public" because it is created for actual use in the real world. In the *Powerful Communities* project, for example, the 1st graders' posters about proper behavior were placed in school restrooms. In the *Reimagine South Central* project, various stakeholders in the community were recruited to play the video game students had created. (See Appendix A for descriptions of these projects.)

• *Give presentations to an audience, live or online.* The audience should be anyone beyond the students' classmates and teacher: other students, school staff and administrators, parents and community members, people from the business world, or experts from nonprofit organizations and academia. The 7th graders in the *House Hunters* project, for example, made presentations to an audience that included a friend of the teacher's who worked on housing renovation projects. Audience members can be asked to play a role if the "real people" are not available (e.g., ask the school principal to play the role of the president of the United States). If students are creating a product for particular end users, those people should be in the audience. For example, 5th grade students in the *Systems Thinkers* project presented proposals for improved campus waste management to members of a parent committee and school administrators. (See Appendix A for descriptions of these projects.)

• *Conduct an event.* Similar to making a presentation, students can plan and execute an event to which the general public or a particular group is invited. The possibilities are many, depending on the nature of the project: a film/video festival, poetry slam, art exhibition, speech, panel discussion or debate, mock trial, school assembly, author's book talk, trade show, or a community celebration. In the *Farmer Appreciation Project*, K–1 students hosted visitors from the community in their classroom. In *The Cancer Project*, students conducted a fund-raising spaghetti dinner with presentations and exhibits. The students involved in *An American Student in France* held a public screening of films they made. (See Appendix A for descriptions of these projects.)

• *Display it in a public space.* Certain kinds of products are appropriate for public display, such as murals on the school wall, museum exhibits at the community center, devices or models in the lobby of a local science-oriented corporation, or photo essays and artwork at the town library. In the *Freedom Fighters* project (see Appendix A), 9th graders created museum-quality exhibits that they took into various settings in the community.

• *Publish it, post it, or send it to someone.* Students can share their work with readers by making it available as a hard-copy or digital book, magazine, or other written product. In the *One and Only Ivan Global Project*, students from 15 classrooms around the world collected their writing in a 250-page digital book, published it using iTunes, and distributed it via the iTunes store. In the *Global Happiness, Local Action* project, the students posted their nonfiction narratives about local history on their class website, then put QR code links to them on signs at each location they wrote about. In the *Up to Par* project, high school geometry students e-mailed their design proposals and a persuasive pitch letter to the owner of a miniature golf course. (See Appendix A for descriptions of these projects.)

## Writing a Driving Question

Gold Standard Project Based Learning begins with a challenging problem or question. A *driving question* is a statement in student-friendly language of the challenging problem or question at the heart of the project. It reminds students why they are completing the project. It's crafted to incite students' interest and focus their attention on the key ideas, questions, and knowledge at the heart of the project. It guides teachers when they're planning, helping them think through the activities students will need to complete to answer the driving question. Teachers should take advantage of the driving question by posting it on the classroom wall during the project and revisiting it regularly with students as the project unfolds and they're gaining new knowledge and understanding.

Driving questions can also be called "essential questions" or "problem statements." Writing one can sometimes be tricky, depending on the nature of the project. Some teachers, for some projects, write the driving question during the planning process, as we suggest here. But many PBL teachers prefer to write the driving question *with* their students near the start of a project, to build a sense of ownership.

To be effective, a driving question should meet three criteria. It should be (1) engaging for students, (2) open-ended, and (3) aligned with learning goals.

To be *engaging for students*, the driving question should have the following attributes:

• Students can understand it.

• It is appropriate for students of the project's intended age, demographic background, community, and so on.

• It does not sound like a typical question from a teacher or a textbook.

• It is provocative or intriguing, leading students to ask further questions that begin the inquiry process.

• Depending on the project, it might have a local context or a charge to take action, making it even more engaging.

• When applicable, it uses the words *I*, *we*, or *us*—not *you* or *students*—to help create a sense of ownership in students.

A question that is *open-ended* has the following attributes:

• It has several possible "right answers."

• The answer will be original; it is not "Google-able" by students.

• The answer is complex and requires in-depth research and investigation.

• It may be a question with a yes or no answer, but if so, the answer must require a detailed explanation or justification.

A question that is *aligned with learning goals* has the following attributes:

• Students will need to learn the project's content standards and practice key success skills to answer it.

• It does not restate the content standard but may contain language from the standard if it does not make the question too lengthy or uninviting to students.

• It is not too big, requiring more knowledge than can be learned in a reasonable amount of time (e.g., "Who was the best U.S. president?" or "How might global warming affect life on Earth?").

As we explained earlier in this chapter, we see five general types of projects. The driving question might be written a bit differently according to the type of project, but it still should meet the three criteria. We showed you some of the driving questions for the project ideas we suggested earlier, but let's look at more examples. Some of the following point clearly to the project, but for others we've added a note about what the project might be.

*Solving a Real-World Problem:*
• How can we, as entrepreneurs, develop a business plan that will attract investors?
• What should we do about the gophers in our soccer field?
• Could our school district develop a more efficient school bus system?
• How can we, as advisors to the London Investors group, plan a successful mission to settle the New World?
• How can we determine the validity of statistical data on climate change?
• Can a sports team win more games by spending more money? (See http://www.mathalicious.com/lessons/win-at-any-cost)

*Meeting a Design Challenge:*
• How can we raise funds to fight leukemia?
• What should we plant in our school garden?
• How can we hold an Olympic Games event for all the schools in our district?
• How can we design an appropriate Vietnam War memorial for our city?
• How can we plan and conduct walking tours of historic sites in our city?
• How can we produce a successful poetry slam?

• How can we start a viable laundry business for our school's sports teams and the local homeless shelter?

• How can we create a website that encourages others to read the books we like?

*Exploring an Abstract Question:*
• What is a healthy diet?

Students plan and conduct an awareness-raising campaign about nutrition in their community.

• What evidence is needed to believe a scientific claim?

Students evaluate various claims about consumer products and create a Consumer Guide website.

• Who is a hero?

Students create of a book of stories about important people in their lives who meet the criteria for a hero.

• Why do people move?

Students read stories and compare national and local data, then produce videos that answer the driving question with examples from their community.

*Conducting an Investigation:*
• How good is our drinking water?

Students conduct experiments, do field work, and interview experts to prepare a presentation to the community.

• Did birds evolve from dinosaurs?

Students act as teams of scientists weighing the evidence in a panel discussion and written report.

• What national events and developments were most influential in our community's history?

Students interview members of the community and study historical documents to create digital scrapbooks.

• What was life like for children in the past?

Students study evidence that historians use to learn about everyday life from recent centuries to ancient civilizations, and create multimedia displays for museum exhibits.

*Taking a Position on an Issue:*
  • Are GMO foods harmful or beneficial?
Students evaluate the evidence on both sides and stage a debate before an audience of community members, including experts on the issue.
  • Should we kill spiders?
Students study the benefits as well as potential dangers of spiders and create videos expressing their answer to the question.
  • Should some books be censored?
Students read various books that have been censored in the past and learn about censorship laws and court decisions, then write letters to the National School Board Association expressing their views.
  • Does Kashmir rightfully belong to India or Pakistan?
Students conduct a mock trial at the International Court of Justice.

---

**Multiple Driving Questions in One Project**

Some projects—longer and more complex ones—might need more than one driving question or at least some subquestions. For example, imagine a science project with this overall driving question: *Why do extinctions happen and what are their effects?* This is a big question, so it could be tackled by having students focus on more specific subquestions such as *What caused the Permian-Triassic extinction? What killed the dinosaurs? How do extinctions make room for new species to evolve? How does what's happening now compare to previous mass extinctions?*

---

Sometimes a first attempt at writing a driving question misses the mark. Let's look at some examples of driving questions and see how they can be refined to better meet the three criteria.

*From:* What trees grow in our city?
*To:* How can we inform people about what trees grow in our city?
*Why it's better:* The first question had a single right answer, and the answer might even be readily available via an Internet search. The second question is open-ended; there are many ways to inform people, including a written field guide, a Google Map tour, a podcast, or a "live" walking tour. If students are creating the product

for an authentic purpose—such as being asked by a city agency to create a field guide for actual use—that authenticity also makes the question engaging.

*From:* What are healthy foods?
*To:* Does it matter what food we eat?
*Why it's better:* Students would still need to learn the same content to answer the second question, but the second one is more open-ended. It also has a critical-thinking component, because students have to take a stand and defend it with evidence. It sounds provocative and more engaging—with a bit of an edge—for elementary-age students.

*From:* Which buildings in our county should be classified as historic and protected by law because they represent important pieces of our past?
*To:* Should our county save its old buildings?
*Why it's better:* Even though it's open-ended and locally focused, the first question "sounds like a teacher" who wanted to pack in several terms and concepts as well as a rationale. The second one is more engaging because it's shorter and has simpler vocabulary—and students would come to their own understanding of why it might be important to save pieces of our past, rather than being told that it is.

*From:* How is math used when calculating basketball statistics?
*To:* Who's the better player, Kobe Bryant or LeBron James?
*Why it's better:* The first question sounds like one of those "special feature" pages in a math textbook. The second question is much more engaging because it's open-ended and relevant to students' interests. To answer it, students will still learn plenty about how math is used to calculate stats in basketball. It also requires critical thinking, because students need to evaluate evidence and use criteria for making a judgment (Bailin, Case, Coombs, & Daniels, 1999).

*From:* How can knowledge of diffraction and how light is transmitted help determine the best uses of low-pressure and high-pressure sodium vapor streetlights?
*To:* How can we create the best lighting plan for a city block with mixed uses?
*Why it's better:* Again, the teacher was trying to include a bunch of content-related terms in the first question. The second one is more student-friendly yet aligned with the same learning goals, without stating them explicitly. As a bonus, the second question is made

more engaging by its focus on an authentic challenge to take action locally. Adding the word *best* to the question emphasizes the need for critical thinking, because students would need to establish criteria for making a judgment.

## Pause and Reflect

Once you've designed a project's basic framework—you've set learning goals, selected major products and decided how they'll be shared publicly, and written a driving question—it's a good idea to step back a moment for some critique and revision.

Consider your project from the perspective of Gold Standard Project Based Learning. Does it reflect the design features described in Chapter 2? Do you want to modify anything based on that model?

Consider your project design from the perspective of your students. Will they be engaged by it? Will they find it challenging but not overwhelming?

Consider the project from the perspective of a colleague or administrator. Is the content to be learned important enough to spend this much time on? Do the project idea, the learning goals, the major products, and the driving question hang together? Does the project seem appropriate and feasible, given your context and constraints?

The best way to reflect on your project's design is to show it to other people and invite their feedback. You could do this informally, during prep time with a colleague. Or consider asking a team of colleagues to join you in a structured process, such as the Tuning Protocol Protocol (http://bie.org/objects/cat/videos). You could even run your project design past a focus group of students, if they're mature enough and have sufficient experience or guidance.

In the next chapter, we'll look at how to take your project from design to implementation in the classroom.

# 5  Managing a Project

In this chapter we'll look at what to consider before launching a project with students and how to manage it once it's underway. We conclude with some notes on using technology in PBL.

After a teacher designs a project, the often more challenging task is to make it work with students. There are a lot of implementation details to plan. And what looks good on paper might not—make that *will* not—work perfectly in the reality of the classroom, so it's important to stay flexible. Because no two projects roll out exactly the same way, it's impossible to give universal advice about managing projects. Projects also vary in the amount of student input, direction, and voice and choice they allow. The description we present here is general and generic—your project will probably look different.

We've also chosen to describe how to manage "teacher-guided" projects, rather than "teacher-facilitated" projects. The latter are more typical for teachers and students who have experience in Gold Standard Project Based Learning, and they feature substantially more independent student work and greater student voice and choice.

Finally, we should note that much of the advice we give here is more applicable to teachers of upper-elementary and secondary students. For younger students who are not able to work as independently, teachers will need to make adjustments accordingly.

## Are Your Students Ready for PBL, or Should You Lay a Foundation First?

As we mentioned in Chapter 4, in schools where all or most teachers use PBL and the model for designing and guiding projects is fairly consistent, projects can be launched without spending a lot of time to prepare students. They know how to work effectively in teams, how to approach an open-ended question or task, find and use resources, manage their time and tasks, talk with adult experts, and meet the other demands of a PBL culture. But if your students are new to PBL, or if you're not sure about their prior experience with projects, you'll need to spend some time gathering data and preparing them.

If you know your students have done projects before, talk with them about what it was like. Find out what projects they did, what went well, and what challenges they faced. If they're old enough, ask students to reflect on what skills or habits of mind they'd like to work on this year, perhaps by giving them a survey or asking them to write about it. You might also want to know what technology tools they're familiar with, what special skills they have, whether they're a good artist or leader, and any other strengths they can bring to project work.

If all or most of your students are new to PBL or have only done a few projects that did not reflect Gold Standard PBL, you can go two ways. One is to launch a first, relatively simple, project in which you build students' PBL skills. Another approach, perhaps the safer one, is to plan some skill- and culture-building lessons in the days and weeks before launching your first project. Think about what students might need to be prepared to do by asking yourself these questions:

• *Are your students able to work well in teams?* This is often a big hurdle to get over, especially if students have had bad experiences with "group assignments" in the past. Have an honest conversation with students about typical challenges that arise when working in teams and how to overcome them. If necessary, have students do low-stakes team-building activities that allow the class to discuss what it means to work together as a team. Prepare students for teamwork by practicing collaborative discussion skills such as active listening, sharing and building on ideas, and respecting diverse viewpoints. Teach students how to make decisions by consensus, how to develop a plan to complete a complex task, and how to divide up the work fairly. Give them opportunities to practice with short activities or "miniprojects" that last only a day or two.

• *Are your students used to instructional methods that mostly involve teacher-directed tasks, lectures, textbooks, worksheets, and "getting the right answer"?* This issue is more about building a PBL culture than teaching students new skills, but it's very important. Talk with students about the goals of PBL and why they're important in today's world. Share examples of student work from past projects, bring in former students as guest speakers, or watch videos of PBL in action to show how exciting and educational PBL can be. You could tell a story about a successful project and discuss how it was different from traditional schoolwork. Or you could ask students in the class who've done successful projects before to talk about their experience.

One tool in project based teaching is modeling, so demonstrate what it means to think about an open-ended question, using examples, and arrive at your own answer to it. Teach students how to ask good questions to guide an inquiry process by walking them through a few examples. Let them know it's OK to struggle a bit on their own and that you're not going to tell them what to do every step of the way, but you are there to support them when needed. Tell them it's OK to be wrong at first and to go back and learn more, start over, or revise what they're doing.

• *Will your students be able to think critically, solve problems, find and evaluate information, brainstorm ideas, give and receive critique, and perform other complex cognitive tasks?* Some of this will need to be taught during a project, in its particular context, but you can do some skill building ahead of time. For example, have students do some activities that require critical thinking, then debrief to create a shared understanding of what it means. Teach them how to use a process for problem solving (see, e.g., http://www.mindtools.com/pages/article/newCT_10.htm) and idea generating (see, https://openideo.com/blog/seven-tips-on-better-brainstorming). Provide lessons on

Internet searches and how students should decide if they're finding high-quality, useful information. Practice any critique protocols you plan to use (such as the ones available at http://elschools.org/sites/default/files/Protocols_EL_120313.pdf).

• *Do your students know how to use a particular technology tool you intend for the project, contact and interview an expert, and make a presentation?* Again, you could teach some of these skills during a project, but doing so would take some time, so consider whether you can make the project run more smoothly by practicing in advance. In particular, learning how to use technology can eat up time in a project, so if you or your students want to use a new tool for online collaboration or creating a product, consider allowing time to learn how to use it before launching the project.

One of the distinguishing features of many projects is the involvement of adult experts, mentors, or others from the world outside school. Contacting and interacting with adults can be a major hurdle for young people. Reduce their stress and build their skills with low-stakes practice activities. Ditto for public speaking. It comes naturally to most teachers, but organizing a presentation and speaking effectively in front of an audience is a big deal for students. (You can find help in Erik Palmer's book *Well Spoken* or his ASCD webinar: http://www.ascd.org/professional-development/webinars/erik-palmer-webinar.aspx.)

## Creating a Project Calendar and Arranging Resources

Just as you map out a unit before it starts, you should create a day-to-day plan for a project. Many teachers new to PBL can envision the beginning of a project and its culmination, but the middle part is cloudy. Some stereotypes about PBL make it seem like you can just set the goals, then step back and let students work independently all the time. It's true that the more experienced you and your students are with PBL, the more autonomy they should have, given their age. But independent work time—monitored and coached by the teacher—is only part of the picture.

Generally speaking, a project calendar should include a mix of lessons and other teacher-provided experiences, field work or contact with other adults (in some projects), and work time for students. Some days may be almost all work time, especially toward the end when students are finishing their products and preparing to make them public. Other days, especially near the beginning, will feature more knowledge- and skill-building activities. The calendar should also have regular checkpoints with students and plenty of time for formative assessment, critique, and revision. To decide what details to fill in on your project calendar, see the information in the next section on guiding each phase of a project. You can find a project calendar template at the Buck Institute website (http://bie.org/object/document/project_calendar) along with completed samples.

Another important step before launching a project is arranging any necessary resources. If you plan to involve outside experts, mentors, or organizations, be sure to contact them well in advance to coordinate schedules. Also arrange for any necessary equipment, technology, school/community facilities, or student travel off campus. In addition to the coaching that you'll provide students on the fly during the project, you may need to build special scaffolds and handouts that will enable all the students in your class to be successful with the project. For example, English language learners may need materials that will help them with project vocabulary. Students who do not read at grade level may need a variety of texts in order to do research.

## Phases of a Project

When you design a project, the Gold Standard Project Based Learning design framework (as described in detail in Chapter 4) gives you a structure upon which to build. Your task now is to plan how to help all students answer the driving question and create high-quality products. Figure 5.1 shows the basic path of a project. A typical project moves through four phases, following a process of inquiry and product development. The rest of this chapter provides suggestions and tips for managing each phase.

**Figure 5.1** Project Path

| What Students Think About | PROJECT PATH | How Teachers Support Inquiry |
|---|---|---|
| ‣ What is the project asking me to do?<br>‣ What do I need to know?<br>‣ Why is this important?<br>‣ Who will I be sharing my work with? | **Phase 1**<br>Launch Project: Entry Event and Driving Question | ‣ Conduct entry event and present/co-construct driving question<br>‣ Facilitate process for generating student questions |
| ‣ What resources can and should I use?<br>‣ Can I trust the information I am finding?<br>‣ What is my role in the process? | **Phase 2**<br>Build Knowledge, Understanding, and Skills to Answer Driving Question | ‣ Facilitate use and evaluation of resources<br>‣ Provide lessons, scaffolds, and guidance in response to student needs |
| ‣ How can I apply what I have learned to the project?<br>‣ What new questions do I have?<br>‣ Do I need more information?<br>‣ Is my work on the right track? | **Phase 3**<br>Develop and Critique Products and Answers to the Driving Question | ‣ Help students apply learning to project tasks<br>‣ Provide additional experiences to generate new knowledge and questions<br>‣ Facilitate processes for feedback |
| ‣ What should I explain about my work?<br>‣ How can I best share this with others?<br>‣ What have I learned and what should I do in the next project? | **Phase 4**<br>Present Products and Answers to the Driving Question | ‣ Help students evaluate their work<br>‣ Facilitate student reflection on process and learning |

REVISION

Copyright © 2014 Buck Institute for Education. Used with permission.

## Phase 1: Launching the Project

The project is launched when the teacher conducts an entry event that lets students know this is not just another assignment. The event engages their interest in the project and sparks questions about the topic and the process. After the teacher presents the driving question (or creates one with students), a list of student questions is generated, which will guide the inquiry process. This phase is usually when the project's major products are defined, student teams are formed, other logistical details are discussed, and groundwork is laid for project tasks.

## Phase 2: Building Knowledge, Understanding, and Skills

Now the work really begins. Students gain the knowledge and skills required for the project by a combination of teacher-provided lessons and resources, independent investigation, and perhaps contact with experts and mentors. Students ask deeper questions as they learn more.

## Phase 3: Developing, Critiquing, and Revising Products

In this phase, students apply what they're learning to develop possible answers to the driving question. The teacher may provide a new experience—a twist in the problem, an activity, additional readings, a guest speaker, a field study, a resource—that leads students to ask further questions. Initial drafts, prototypes, and ideas for products are submitted for critique by peers, the teacher, and experts or users of a product or service. Students then decide if they need to revise their work or learn more, and the process repeats.

## Phase 4: Presenting Products

Students arrive at their answer to the driving question and finish creating their product or products. They make their work public and explain the process they used to complete the project. The teacher facilitates students' self-evaluation of their work and reflection on what they learned in the project.

## Managing Phase 1

The first phase of a project typically lasts two or three class periods or hours for upper-elementary and secondary students. For younger students, who might need more time to explore a topic and gain some context before focusing on a project, the first phase may take multiple days, depending on how much time per day is devoted to it.

The entry event, driving question, and list of student questions always come first. These elements begin the inquiry process but also create engagement and a sense of ownership for students. Giving too many logistical details at once, such as due dates, point values, a reading list, and homework assignments, sends the wrong message: it's all been planned and students have no voice and choice. But after the first three bullets in the following list, the activities and their order can vary.

Here's what typically happens in Phase 1 of a project:

- Entry event is conducted.
- Driving question is introduced.
- List of student questions to be investigated is generated.
- Major product(s) is discussed.
- Project calendar is explained.
- Initial team meetings are held, with team-building activities.
- Norms for teamwork and team contracts are discussed and written.
- Preliminary task lists are written.
- Individual activity logs or project journals are begun.
- Research, reading, or other content-related work is begun.

### Conducting an Entry Event

To maximize the engaging aspects of PBL and initiate the inquiry process, a project should not begin like any other assignment or activity. Some sort of activity or call to action should get students excited and curious. We call this an "entry event," a term borrowed originally from problem-based learning.

An entry event is not a simple "hook" like what you would find in traditional lesson planning. It's more in-depth and usually longer, and it's meant to get students thinking, not just get their attention. A good entry event encourages students to access their prior knowledge about the challenging problem or question that's the focus of the project. An entry event could range from 10 or 15 minutes to a whole class period. For very young students, it may be spread over several days in order to introduce them to an unfamiliar topic.

An entry event could be any one of the following:

- Field trip
- Guest speaker
- Video or scene from a film
- Provocative reading
- Simulation or activity
- Startling statistics
- Puzzling problem
- Real or mock correspondence
- Lively discussion
- Song, poem, art

The sample projects in this book (see Appendix A) feature a range of entry events. In the *Farmer Appreciation Project*, the 1st graders heard from guest speakers: former students who talked about making a difference in projects they had done. The *Home Sweet Home* project began with a letter to students from an expert at the Detroit Zoo. The *One and Only Ivan Global Project* began after students read an engaging novel. To launch the *Systems Thinkers* project, the teacher asked students to walk around campus and make observations. Students took a survey and compared their data to global results to start the *Global Happiness, Local Action* project.

## Introducing the Driving Question

There's no single rule about when and how to introduce a project's driving question to students. It depends on the project, the entry event, the students, and a teacher's judgment and style. For example, imagine a history/English project about the Holocaust. To launch it, the teachers might show a powerful scene from the film *Schindler's List* after a brief orientation to it. Following a class discussion of the scene, the teachers explain that students will be doing a project about the following driving question: *What does the Holocaust tell us about human nature, and why does genocide still happen?* The teachers could have stated the driving question before showing the scene from the film, but the question would have had less of an impact on students. Once they see the scene and discuss it, students will have some context for the question. It carries more emotional weight and becomes a topic worthy of investigation. Hands will go up as students begin to ask their own questions about the Holocaust and more recent genocides.

Consider this example of how to introduce a driving question, as seen in the 4th grade project *Home Sweet Home* (see Appendix A). The project's entry event took the form of a letter from the Detroit Zoo to the students, asking them to design animal habitats that met certain criteria. The teacher presented the driving question immediately; it was fairly straightforward and readily accepted by students: *How can we design a habitat for the Detroit Zoo?*

Some PBL teachers elect to write a driving question with their students, which gives the students a greater sense of ownership. For example, after a field trip to a local park in need of an upgrade, a teacher talks with students about what they want to do about it. The class decides they want to do a combination of things: they want to undertake a short-term clean-up effort and also contact the city with a proposal for new landscaping and new playground equipment. They frame their project with the driving question *How can we make our park a better place to play in and visit?*

Discuss the driving question with the class. Be sure students understand it. Have them suggest possible answers to it. Add subquestions if you or your students think it makes sense. For example, the *Home Sweet Home* project generated these subquestions:

- What animals are we designing habitats for?
- What does a zoo habitat need?
- How much space do we have?
- Can we get plants, soil, and rocks from the place the animal came from?

• How much money can the zoo spend?
• Do we need to make models or drawings?

In all later phases of the project, revisit the driving question. Have students discuss emerging ideas about it and evaluate possible answers to it. In some projects, you and your students may even decide the driving question needs to be refined or changed. At the end of the project, ask students to explain their final answer to it and reflect on how they developed it (see more about this in the section on Managing Phase 4).

## Generating a List of Student Questions

Immediately after the entry event and the driving question, the teacher facilitates a process for students to ask questions about the topic and their task in the project. Some PBL teachers create a two-column chart with the headings "What do we know?" and "What do we need to know?" Other teachers, especially in the elementary grades, are familiar with the KWL Chart (Know, Wonder, Learn) and use it to track students' questions and learning in a project. Students find these techniques useful because they organize the inquiry and provide guidelines for what they must learn and understand to answer the driving question. These techniques also activate students' prior knowledge about the topic, a process that researchers in problem based learning have found very important for future learning and effective use of what has been learned.

Help students effectively generate and organize questions by doing the following things:

• Remind students about any practice they had with this process when you were preparing them for PBL, and review the norms. (If they didn't get this opportunity, give them some examples now.)

• Allow students some time to think before creating a whole-class list. Have them write questions first by working in pairs or in teams, then share aloud. Remember the power of wait time!

• Capture questions in the students' own words, to create ownership.

• If you choose to allow a greater degree of voice and choice for each team, let each one have its own set of questions.

• After generating a list of questions, help students organize them into categories. This makes it easier for students to get their heads around what might otherwise seem like a daunting list. It might make sense for different students or teams to investigate certain questions.

Once the list of student questions is generated, use it as a tool to guide students throughout the project. (See the section on Guiding Student Inquiry later in this chapter.)

## Defining Major Products

Exactly when and how this step is accomplished is another "it depends" situation in PBL. You might describe the products student will create, or suggest the possibilities, during the entry event or when discussing the driving question. Sometimes you might want students to explore the topic a bit before discussing what they will produce. And in some projects, you might ask students to decide on the products themselves after they have investigated a topic to some extent. In any case, students' questions about the product and how they will create it should be added to the list that was begun at the project launch.

Help students understand what a high-quality product looks like with rubrics and exemplars. Each major product in a project should have a rubric. Rubrics can be written before a project (or reused from a previous project), or you may construct one with students during a project. A rubric should be written in student-friendly language. The best way to make sure students understand a rubric is to have them practice using it with an example of the kind of product they'll create in the project.

## Forming Student Teams

Collaboration, as we've noted before, is an essential element of Gold Standard PBL. However, the extent and nature of doing project work in teams depends on the age of your students. Much of the information we provide here applies more to students in the upper-elementary and secondary grades. If you teach younger students, whole-class projects may work better than having students do the bulk of the work in teams—but you should still provide short-term opportunities for children to learn how to work well with others.

Some projects may involve a combination of individual work and teamwork, or shifting teams for various purposes. For example, you could jigsaw the work so some students become "experts" by researching a particular topic or learning a particular skill, then return to their project teams bringing what they know.

How a PBL teacher forms student teams is another judgment call. Many teachers like to decide on teams before a project and announce them to students. Other teachers like to give students some voice and choice in the matter. Figure 5.2 shows some pros and cons related to various approaches.

No matter which team-forming approach you choose, we do not advise it be done randomly. Instead, establish criteria for assigning students to teams. The criteria could include leadership ability, academic skills, personality, language ability, gender, maturity, art skills, or tech skills. Another factor might be the nature of the project. For example, a project that involves a dramatic performance might require a different team makeup than a project in which students construct a model of a building. A heterogeneous mix of students on project teams is usually best. Heterogeneous teams bring different strengths to the task and teach all students valuable lessons about working with diverse people.

To help make decisions about teaming, especially if you don't yet know your students well, find out about their interests, skills, or special needs. Very young students may not be able to describe themselves in these terms, so you'll need to rely on your own observations and other data. For older students, give them a survey or a short writing assignment, or conduct a class discussion.

The size of a project team can vary. Four-member teams are generally best for sharing the workload and for optimal group dynamics. This number also allows for doing some tasks in pairs. Some projects might require a five-member team, depending on the products and tasks, but having more than five on a team can be problematic. It's harder to conduct team meetings and communicate about project tasks, some students may not have enough to do, and the team may fracture into subgroups. Doing a complex project in a team of only two or three might not be effective, either, in terms of generating ideas and getting the work done. Class size is also a consideration. If you have 34 students working in pairs, that's 17 teams, 17 products, and 17 presentations to manage!

**Figure 5.2**   Pros and Cons of Various Approaches to Forming Teams

| Approach to Forming Teams | Pros | Cons |
| --- | --- | --- |
| **Teacher decides** | • Saves time.<br>• Reduces disagreements and hurt feelings.<br>• Allows teacher to balance teams for student growth and maximum effectiveness.<br>• Is authentic; most real-world teams do not get to self-select. | • Some students may be disgruntled about their team.<br>• Students may lose sense of ownership and buy-in.<br>• Students do not have opportunity to learn how to choose teammates wisely. |
| **Teacher decides, with student input** | • Minimizes disagreements and hurt feelings.<br>• Still allows teacher to balance teams for student growth and maximum effectiveness.<br>• Students have some sense of ownership and buy-in.<br>• Students have some opportunity to learn how to choose teammates wisely. | • Takes more teacher time.<br>• Can be difficult to honor all students' preferences.<br>• Some students may still be disgruntled about their team. |
| **Teacher manages process for students to decide** | • Almost eliminates disagreements.<br>• Students have sense of ownership and buy-in.<br>• Students have opportunity to learn how to choose teammates wisely. | • Potentially takes more time if students need to be taught how to choose teams.<br>• Classroom culture needs to be right, to prevent issues with cliques and socially marginalized students.<br>• There's some potential for hurt feelings.<br>• Is not advised for very young students.<br>• Students may not realize what capabilities are needed for the team to be effective. |

## Helping Student Teams Get Started

The first decision you need to make is in response to the question "Do my students need team-building activities before they start work?" The answer is usually yes, but the extent and nature of this depends on your students' prior experience with PBL and your own classroom culture. You could do fun activities like building a tower of spaghetti and marshmallows, conducting a scavenger hunt, or playing a low-stakes game of some sort. You could have students come up with a team name and mascot, slogan, or symbol. You can also use these activities to teach lessons about effective collaboration, communication, critical thinking, or problem solving.

At the first team meeting or two, have students focus on the process they'll use for project work. They should focus on tasks such as these:

• Telling each other about strengths they can bring to the team.

• Agreeing on what it means to work well together; this could be done by each team or with a whole-class discussion. Have students look at a rubric for collaboration (see examples online at http://bie.org/objects/cat/rubrics) or make their own list of criteria.

• Writing a team contract to hold each other accountable (see an example online at http://bie.org/object/document-project_team_contract).

• Assigning team roles, if you or they choose to have them.

• Exchanging contact information and agreeing on how to stay in touch.

• Beginning a list of project tasks and planning how to accomplish them, using a Team Task Log or some sort of planning tool that sets out the what, who, and by when.

## Starting a Project Journal or Log

Not all PBL teachers use a project journal or log, but it's a useful tool. The basic idea is to have a place where individual students—and teams, if you choose—can keep track of what they do, what they're learning, new questions that emerge, and other reflections. Students can document their use of time, thoughts about the project, and evolving answers to a driving question in a journal. They can describe how they solve problems and use critical thinking, creativity, collaboration skills, and other competencies. This information can be used for formative and summative assessment.

## Managing Phase 2

The second phase of a project—Building Knowledge, Understanding, and Skills—can last from a few days to several weeks, depending on the project. Note that students may go back and forth between this phase and the next, when they apply what they're learning to project tasks. Students may realize—or be coached to see—that they need to go back for more information, better skills, or deeper understanding. And keep in mind that not all students or teams will necessarily be at the same point in a project; some will be ready to move on, while others need to go back.

In this phase, a PBL teacher's main job is twofold: (1) help students answer their questions by finding and using resources as independently as possible, and (2) provide them with scaffolding—including direct instruction—if and when needed. One additional job that begins in this phase but continues throughout the project is to monitor student teams as they work, and coach them or intervene as necessary.

### Guiding Student Inquiry

How much you guide your students' inquiry process depends, once again, on their age and experience with PBL. For older and very experienced students, a teacher may only need to monitor the process and offer feedback or guidance when necessary. For younger and less experienced students, the teacher should direct the process more, provide scaffolds, and model what it means to think critically and solve problems. Teachers can provide a combination of support for the inquiry process, using elements such as these:

- Lessons on how to find and evaluate sources of information
- Readings and other texts

• Research logs and note-taking guides

• Reader's workshops, literature circles, and other discussions of texts, to connect them to students' questions

• Field work and contact with experts and mentors

• Structured opportunities for students to share information, compare notes, and discuss what they're learning and how it applies to the project

It's important to actively use the list of student-generated questions during the inquiry process. After you've launched a project with the entry event and the driving question, don't simply post the list of student-generated questions on the classroom wall as an inert artifact. You and your students should decide how to approach the process of finding answers to their questions. For example, the list could be divided among student teams or "jigsawed" expert groups. Some questions might be answered through student research, whereas others might be answered by teacher-provided lessons.

Revisit the list of student questions frequently. As questions are answered, check them off the list. Add more to the list as students dig deeper into the project and come to understand more about the topic and task. Near the end of the project, revisit the list to make sure students feel as though they've gained what they need to successfully complete their tasks and answer the driving question.

## Scaffolding Student Learning

Scaffolding, or support for student learning, can take many forms in a project. As should be evident, Gold Standard PBL does not simply "turn students loose"; it includes plenty of room for teacher-provided lessons and materials, even lectures and direct instruction if warranted.

We recommend a scaffolding planning process that starts with the project's major products. (Some people call this "backward planning.") When designing the project, you made sure these products would provide evidence that students have learned the standards and other goals set for the project. Now it's time to unpack the products and determine exactly what knowledge, understanding, and skills are needed to complete them.

The project planning tool *Project Design: Student Learning Guide* (http://bie.org/object/document/project_design_overview_and_student_learning_guide) maps out the scaffolding required for each major product in a project. Let's look at the completed example in Figure 5.3 for a 5th grade project involving a scenario in which students diagnose a sick patient.

Here's how the teacher of this project constructed the *Student Learning Guide*:

1. In the left column, she listed final products with an "anchor learning target" based on a Common Core standard.

2. In the second column, she specified the learning outcomes/targets needed to complete the product.

3. In the third column, she listed the checkpoints/formative assessments (we say more about assessment later in this chapter).

4. In the right column, she specified instructional strategies. The strategies include a combination of teacher-provided lessons and resources, contact with outside experts, and activities. Plans for meeting the needs of all students through differentiation are also noted.

We've found that interactive coaching and scaffolding in PBL is best provided on a "just in time" basis. A teacher may be tempted to frontload a lot of support for students, but a key feature of PBL is that it creates an authentic "need to know" in students. They have more motivation to pay attention and retain information when they see an immediate purpose for learning. If a project begins with a series of lectures and textbook assignments, it's not going to feel like an immediate need is being met; students will feel like it's just another situation in which they're told "you'll need to know this later." To put it another way, if students are made to wait before doing much in the way of independent investigation, it takes a lot away from the engaging power of PBL.

Although teachers may create written scaffolds as they design and plan their projects, they also need to engage with students and make judgments about when students need support and are ready to receive it. Ideally, teachers catch that moment when students recognize they need help and ask for it. Teachers can also contextualize the help and scaffolds they provide students by emphasizing what's needed to complete the project rather than any failings by the student. For example, the teacher can point to a new question on the students' "What do we need to know?" list and say, "Today I'm going to give you some material that will help answer this question." Younger students who might not know when or how to ask for support should still get the sense that the teacher is responding to their needs for the project, not just teaching something whose immediate purpose is not apparent.

You can plan the timing of some scaffolding in advance. For example, you might know that students will need some content information or a skill-building lesson to get started on a project. You might also be able to anticipate that at, say, the beginning of the second week they're going to need a lesson on X or resource Y.

Your project calendar should have some flexibility built into it, because projects aren't completely predictable. Students may come up with questions you hadn't anticipated. They may decide to go in a new direction that you find productive. Some needs will arise that require on the spot support.

## Monitoring and Coaching Student Teams

This task begins in Phase 2 but is ongoing in all phases of a project. After project teams are formed and the work is underway, you need to establish processes for teams to check in with each other and with you. Once again, if students are older and experienced with PBL, they may need less oversight but should still be guided in monitoring their own work.

At the first team meeting, students should agree to some norms for working together effectively, or create and sign a team contract (see an example at www.bie.org/objects/cat/student_handouts). It's also useful for students to read or write a collaboration rubric. Then, in future team meetings, ask them to revisit their norms and agreements. Set regular checkpoints for this throughout the project. Students can be asked to write about their teamwork in their project journals, make comments on daily or weekly exit slips, or provide data via quick surveys or by using an online system.

**Figure 5.3**    Project Design: Student Learning Guide (Sample)

| Project Design: Student Learning Guide | | | |
|---|---|---|---|
| **Project:** Medical Interns | | | |
| **Driving question:** How can we, as medical interns, recommend the best treatment for a sick patient? | | | |
| **Final Products(s)** Presentations, Performances, Products, and/or Services | **Learning Outcomes/Targets** Content and 21st century competencies needed by students to successfully complete products | **Checkpoints/Formative Assessments** To check for learning and ensure students are on track | **Instructional Strategies for All Learners** Provided by teacher, other staff, experts; includes scaffolds, materials, lessons aligned to learning outcomes, and formative assessments |
| Medical Report (individual) Anchor learning target: I can conduct short research projects using several sources to diagnose and treat a sick patient. (W5.7—Research to Build and Present Knowledge) | I can identify the parts of the circulatory system. (Life Sciences—Circulatory System) | 1. Summary of resources 2. Exit tickets following lessons 3. Lab notes/science journal 4. Quiz | • Teacher model of summary writing/note taking • Science labs on circulation • Interview with MD • Textbook lesson; video |
| | I can write a report to inform a patient of his/her diagnosis. (Writing 5.4—Informational Text Writing) | 1. Outline of report 2. Reflective journal writing 3. Drafts of report (peer/teacher feedback) 4. Charrette | • Examination of exemplar papers to determine structure, teacher model • Interview with MD • Writer's workshop, fishbowl modeling of peer critique • Review probing questions; model of charrette |

| | Learning Target | Evidence | Activities |
|---|---|---|---|
| | I can explain my diagnosis using evidence with facts, details, and quotations. (Writing 5.2b—Informational Text Writing) | 1. Summary of resources<br>2. Drafts of report (peer/teacher feedback)<br>3. Teacher conference | • Teacher model of summary writing/note taking<br>• Writer's workshop (differentiate for gifted/struggling writers) |
| | I can summarize or paraphrase information from my research. (Writing 5.8—Research to Build and Present Knowledge) | 1. Summary of resources<br>2. Quick-write assessment<br>3. Summary sentences on exit tickets | • Teacher model of summary writing/note taking<br>• Writer's workshop (differentiate for gifted/struggling writers)<br>• Small-group activity on summary sentences (with EL students) |
| Diagnosis Presentation (team) Anchor learning target: I can report on a topic in a logical way, using details to support my ideas. (S.L. 5.4) | I can use visual aids to enhance the content and message of my presentation.<br>I can respond to audience questions accurately and clearly. (Presentation Skills—Speaking and Listening 5.5) | 1. Draft of visual aids (peer/teacher feedback)<br>2. Fishbowl<br>3. Charrette | • Examination of exemplar visual aids; watch a student presentation with visual aids on video<br>• Questioning-techniques lesson with partner practice; interview with MD<br>• Review probing questions; model of charrette |
| | I can evaluate multiple sources on my topic and integrate valid sources into my report and presentation to speak knowledgeably about the topic. (Critical Thinking/Reading Informational Text 5.7) | 1. Summary of resources<br>2. Outline of report<br>3. Charrette<br>4. Practice presentation (peer/teacher feedback) | • Internet search lesson on finding valid sources; small-group support<br>• Align evidence and claims in teams; examine exemplar papers<br>• Review probing questions; model of charrette |

Copyright ©2014 Buck Institute for Education. Used with permission.

Another management strategy is, of course, to walk around the classroom listening to and observing teams as they work. Sit with each team periodically for a closer look. Collect data by making notes or using a checklist based on your collaboration rubric.

Students should be expected to manage their team on their own as much as possible, if they're old enough, or to do so with coaching from the teacher. Use any data you've collected to identify signs of trouble and prompt the team to take action. Intervene with teams that are unable to resolve difficulties themselves. Suggest how they might think about the problem, and if necessary offer them possible ways to handle it, but make decisions for them only as a last resort.

---

**Troubleshooting Common Team Issues**

When students work in teams, great things can happen, but there might be a few bumps in the road. Rest assured that as students become more experienced with PBL, the bumps tend to smooth out. But until then, here are some tips on how to handle the most common issues:

• *Team members are not getting along well or acting as a team.* If you didn't do team-building activities at the beginning of the project, pause to do some now—or if you did, do some more. Have discussions early and often about what it means to work effectively as a team. Refer students to team contracts, rubrics, or other criteria the class has discussed.

• *A high-achieving student is concerned about "doing all the work" or getting a bad grade because of what the team is doing.* Make each team member accountable for completing some pieces of project work. Be sure your grading system relies mostly or entirely on individual work, not a team-created product. (See textbox on grading on pages 125–126.)

• *Some team members are not doing their fair share of the work.* Find out what the cause is. Have the team members divided their tasks appropriately? Provide coaching and scaffolding, such as a process or form they can use. Do all members know what they're supposed to be doing? Coach the team to clearly communicate about tasks and deadlines. Does one member or more feel left out? Coach the team to talk with each other and find ways for everyone to contribute.

**Troubleshooting Common Team Issues—(*continued*)**

As a general rule, have student teams try to address their issues themselves, before calling in support from the teacher. Their team contract should have processes for dealing with issues as they arise. Remind them to communicate often and honestly, to prevent issues from growing larger.

# Managing Phase 3

The third phase, Developing, Critiquing, and Revising Products, is the heart of a project. It can last from a few days to several weeks, depending on the project. Like Phase 2, this phase is not totally distinct and separate. Students often go back and forth between this phase and the previous one, if they find they need to revise their work and gain more knowledge, understanding, and skills. In this phase, the project calendar includes more and more work time, as students create and refine products, develop their answer to a driving question, and prepare to make their work public.

## Providing Formative Assessment

Our earlier description of Gold Standard PBL pointed out that formative assessment is one of the most powerful ways to improve student performance. Its role in PBL is central and crucial. In a project, students must not only learn content but also create high-quality products. They also must learn how to think critically, solve problems, and collaborate with other students. To do all this well, students need to be given feedback and opportunities to improve their performance and revise their work.

Let's take a closer look at the checkpoints and formative assessments the teacher planned for the *Medical Interns* project described in Figure 5.3. The assessment-planning process started with the final, major products of the project: a written "medical report" and an oral presentation. These act as summative assessments of knowledge and skills. (Note: Some PBL teachers also might use a test as an additional summative assessment.)

Figure 5.4 shows how the teacher unpacked the knowledge and skills students would need to successfully write the medical report: how the human circulatory system works, how to write informative texts, and how to summarize research. In the next column, the teacher listed the formative assessments used to ensure students were on the right track. Once these have been determined, they can be entered at appropriate checkpoints on the project calendar.

**Figure 5.4**    Plan for Formative Assessments Tied to Learning Outcomes/Targets

| **Learning Outcomes/Targets**<br>Content and 21st century competencies needed by students to successfully complete products | **Checkpoints/Formative Assessments**<br>To check for learning and ensure students are on track |
| --- | --- |
| I can identify the parts of the circulatory system.<br>(Life Sciences—Circulatory System) | 1. Summary of resources<br>2. Exit tickets following lessons<br>3. Lab notes/science journal<br>4. Quiz |
| I can write a report to inform a patient of his/her diagnosis.<br>(Writing 5.4—Informational Text Writing) | 1. Outline of report<br>2. Reflective journal writing<br>3. Drafts of report (peer/teacher feedback)<br>4. Charrette |
| I can explain my diagnosis using evidence with facts, details, and quotations.<br>(Writing 5.2b—Informational Text Writing) | 1. Summary of resources<br>2. Drafts of report (peer/teacher feedback)<br>3. Teacher conference |
| I can summarize or paraphrase information from my research.<br>(Writing 5.8—Research to Build and Present Knowledge) | 1. Summary of resources<br>2. Quick-write assessment<br>3. Summary sentence on exit tickets |

For this project, the teacher used a variety of formative assessments, most of which are commonly found in traditional instructional practice. But let's take a closer look at a formative assessment practice that's especially noteworthy in PBL.

## Using Protocols for Peer Critique

One of the Gold Standard design elements is critique and revision. This process enables students to create high-quality products. Some of the feedback students receive, of course, should come from the teacher. And in some projects, other adults review students' work and critique emerging ideas, rough drafts, or prototypes. But having students critique each other's work in PBL is valuable for several reasons:

- It helps students learn how to work independently.
- It takes some of the burden off the time-crunched teacher.
- It serves an instructional purpose by helping students internalize the criteria for high-quality work.
- It promotes critical thinking, collaboration, and communication skills.

Effective peer critique requires the use of norms and protocols. Without them, students will flounder and the critique will not be helpful. Ron Berger, chief learning officer at Expeditionary Learning, offers a simple set of norms for peer critique: "Be helpful, specific, and kind" (Berger, 2003). A popular video by Berger called "Austin's Butterfly" captures the process and power of peer critique (see http://elschools org/node/36970).

You can use many potential protocols for peer critique. One example, a "charrette," is listed in Figure 5.3. In this protocol, which originated in the field of architecture, students form pairs or triads and take turns sharing a piece of work-in-progress or an idea they're developing. They might be asked to state a question or two they'd like help thinking about; then peers offer feedback or ideas of their own. Other examples of protocols include the Gallery Walk, Tuning Protocol, and Consultancy; many more can be found online, including an exhaustive list from the National School Reform Faculty (see http://www.nsrfharmony.org/free-resources/protocols/a-z).

In addition to norms, two keys to an effective protocol are (1) a structured process, with a time frame for each step, and (2) criteria on which to base the critique, often captured in a rubric or a checklist for a particular product. Some protocols feature a facilitator who is not part of the critique process, and others may be self-monitored by the participants. For example, the Tuning Protocol is often moderated by a facilitator who keeps time and reminds participants about the process and norms. A Gallery Walk, once everyone knows the drill, does not typically require a facilitator because it does not feature various steps with exact timing.

## Assessing Success Skills

Teachers know how to assess a student's knowledge of content, whether it's in PBL or in other instructional methods. In the *Medical Interns* project described earlier, for example, a student's knowledge of science was assessed through exit tickets following lessons; lab notes; quizzes; and an outline, rough draft, and final draft of a written report. Traditional tools for assessment definitely have a place in PBL.

Assessing a competency such as critical thinking, however, may be unfamiliar territory for a teacher. The same goes for problem solving, collaboration, and self-management—the other success skills we discussed in Chapter 2. Entire books have been written about teaching and assessing "21st century skills," but here are some tips and guidelines for assessing the success skills in the context of a project:

• Use a rubric or other set of indicators to clarify what the skill looks like, and use this to guide student assessment and reflection. (For examples, see http://bie.org/objects/cat/rubrics.)

• Use a combination of self-report, peer report, and teacher observation to collect data for assessment. For example, ask students to reflect on how well they're working as a member of a team and tell you how well their team as a whole is functioning. Older students, prepared by the right classroom culture, can report on their peers' collaboration skills as well as their own. Compare these data with your own observations to make an accurate judgment.

• Have students document in their project journals—or tell you, if they're very young—the ways in which they're demonstrating success skills.

• When students make presentations and at the end of the project, ask them to reflect on their growth in the success skills.

• Remember the goal of assessment is to guide improvement, not to assign a grade or score. Whether to grade students in the success skills is a call each teacher needs to make.

**Assessing Creativity**

Whether a teacher should assess creativity is controversial. Focus on how well students follow a process for innovation if you don't feel comfortable assessing creativity per se. The purpose of assessment is primarily to guide students in improving, not to evaluate, so you don't have to give students a score for "how creative they are." Assess and give feedback on their work, not them. You can find a rubric for creativity and innovation in PBL at bie.org (http://bie.org/objects/cat/rubrics).

## Managing Phase 4

The fourth phase, Presenting Products, is the big finish for a project. It's typically a very busy time, as students polish up their work and make it public. It closes with some time for you and your students to look back and think about what was accomplished.

But be aware that the last phase of a project can be make-or-break time. You need to plan this phase carefully, because it might seem like a project is going well until you realize students are not creating high-quality products or have not met key learning goals. Most projects are still going to see last-minute preparations and a rush to meet deadlines, but managing this phase well will avoid disaster.

**Grading in PBL**

Grading is a touchy topic for most teachers. Except in a few schools, teachers have their own system and their own criteria. Grading in PBL can appear complicated because it involves multiple products and multiple standards, and some of the work is done in teams. We would not be so bold as to suggest one "silver bullet" for grading in PBL, but here are some suggestions:

**Grading in PBL—(*continued*)**

• Use the same grading system for projects as you would use for "regular" assignments and units.

• Do not give one grade for the entire project. Doing so would give a huge amount of weight to one grade, and also mask a student's strengths and weaknesses in particular areas. Assign a grade or score to each assignment or product.

• Consider *not* grading a team-created final product or presentation. Doing so can raise issues of fairness, and in the case of a presentation, it puts a lot of weight into one event. You could grade only individual work.

## Presentations and Exhibitions

Students can make their work public in a variety of ways, depending on the nature of the project. They can make formal presentations to a live audience or to an audience reached online. They can post their work online or display it in a physical space. They can distribute a product to users or distribute written work to readers.

As we've said before, some schools using PBL have exhibitions for parents and the community, usually after school or in the evening. These can be tied to other events on the calendar, such as the spring open house or a holiday gathering, or they can be stand-alone events to showcase project work. A public exhibition is a great way to help parents and the community understand PBL and build support for it.

Here are some general recommendations for managing student presentations to an audience:

• Allow plenty of time on your project calendar for students to plan and practice their presentations. Have students present to other teams and give each other feedback, or consider recording practice presentations on video and having student teams watch and critique themselves.

• Teach students public speaking skills, if necessary. Provide scaffolds to help them organize a presentation, such as the Presentation

Plan handout available at bie.org (http://bie.org/object/document/ presentation_plan).

• Involve students in planning for the event.

• Be sure the logistics are all set, including the time, place, equipment, people, and materials needed.

• Invite audiences well in advance. If you plan on having audience members play a role, assess students, or provide feedback, decide if they need advance preparation or explanatory materials.

• Have students do dress rehearsals in the space where they will present, with all the technology, materials, appropriate attire, and other elements in place.

• If presentations involve technology, do a final tech check on the day of presentations and have tech support ready.


## Evaluation, Reflection, and Celebration

After the big finish, allow a day or two on your project calendar to process what you and your students have been through. It's important to pause for reflection and consolidation of learning before moving on to the next unit or project. Here are some ideas to consider.

• *Begin by debriefing the project.* Discuss what happened in each phase. Take note of the ups and downs, what worked and what didn't, the challenges and how they were met. Record student suggestions for improving this project or for improving the next project.

• *Take a last look at the list of student-generated questions and the project's driving question.* Ask students, Were all our questions answered? Did some turn out to be not important or relevant? Did we arrive at a satisfactory answer to the driving question, and how did our thinking about it evolve? Was our final product of high quality or our solution to the problem a good one? What questions remain, or what new issues have emerged?

• *Ask students to evaluate their performance.* Have them look back over their project journal or log, if you used one, and write about or discuss their growth in terms of understanding of content and the use of success skills. Have student teams use a rubric to make a final assessment of how well they worked together. Ask students to reflect on how they used critical thinking, solved problems, and demonstrated self-management skills.

• *Ask students to identify areas for growth.* Have them reflect on and answer questions such as, What did I learn? What more do I want to learn? What can I improve on? What do I want to do differently in the next project? How can I apply what I have gained to future situations?

• *Reteach or reinforce any key understandings or concepts that students might not have fully grasped.* During the last phase of the project, in students' presentations and final products, or when reflecting on the project, you may have noticed some gaps in students' understanding or knowledge. Now is a good time, while they're primed to listen, to (briefly) review important material—or plan how to reteach it later.

• *Celebrate success.* Have a reception for students and guests at a presentation day or exhibition. Back in the classroom, have a ceremony, an activity, or a party. Ask students to record thoughts about the project on a poster, make a scrapbook, or collect project artifacts to display and perhaps keep for next year.

## Technology and Gold Standard PBL

Back in the early days of introducing technology to the classroom, projects were often designed to introduce specific tools or applications. Many of those first digital projects were little more than dessert-style activities (such as making PowerPoint presentations). Technology may have added an element of novelty, but it was no guarantee of sustained inquiry.

Times have changed. Today's connected learners are more apt to use a range of digital tools during PBL to accomplish authentic tasks, from researching to collaborating to publishing original content. Gold Standard PBL doesn't specifically call for technology integration. Look closely at exemplary projects, however, and you're apt to see effective use of digital tools embedded all along the project path. In some instances, technology gives projects the equivalent of a turbo boost, taking learners places they couldn't otherwise go (Boss & Krauss,

2014). Let's consider just a few examples of tech tools that you and your students might want to incorporate during the different phases of PBL.

In Phase 1, when projects are launched, compelling video clips or photos from digital archives can provide the spark needed to ignite curiosity. Consider using primary source repositories such as the American Memory Project at the Library of Congress (http://memory.loc.gov/ammem), or share videos from TED Ed (http://ed.ted.com), TeacherTube (www.teachertube.com), or SchoolTube (www.schooltube.com). A guest speaker offers another option for an entry event. If you can't arrange a face-to-face visit, take advantage of Skype in the Classroom (https://education.skype.com) or Google Hangouts (https://plus.google.com/hangouts) for a virtual meet-up.

In Phase 2, when students are building understanding and background knowledge, teachers scaffold their learning by curating content. Newsela (https://newsela.com) is a platform that adjusts current news stories to five different reading levels. Pearltrees (www.pearltrees.com) is a tool for organizing and sharing online resources. Diigo (www.diigo.com/education), a social bookmarking tool, enables users to share and annotate online resources. Evernote (http://evernote.com) allows for collaborative note taking.

Digital tools can help you check student understanding. Tools for formative assessment include TodaysMeet (http://todaysmeet.com), which opens a "back channel" for student conversations. Padlet (http://padlet.com) allows you to create virtual bulletin boards where students can post reflections, photos, exit tickets, and more.

Students may want to conduct surveys or polls to gather data that will help them answer their driving question. Tools to help include Poll Everywhere (www.polleverywhere.com), Google Forms (www.google.com/forms/about), and SurveyMonkey (www.surveymonkey.com).

Blogs offer a platform for students to reflect on their learning throughout projects and also comment on each other's posts. Popular student blogging platforms include Edublogs (http://edublogs.org), Kidblog (www.kidblog.org), and Weebly (www.weebly.com). In addition, education sites such as Edmodo (www.edmodo.com) enable teachers to add student blogs to online classroom spaces.

*In Phase 3,* when students are developing and critiquing products and answers to driving questions, collaborative tools are useful. SketchUp (www.sketchup.com) is an online tool for 3-D modeling. Skitch (http://evernote.com/skitch) lets users mark up (and share) anything from a rough sketch to a screenshot, photo, or map. Google Docs (http://docs.google.com) allows for anywhere, anytime collaboration.

*In Phase 4,* when students are preparing to share their learning with audiences, they can choose from a range of tools for creating original content, presenting information, and publishing online. This is an opportunity to encourage student voice and choice in how they present their product or share findings.

To make data more understandable, students might use Lucidchart (www.lucidchart.com) or FlowingData (http://flowingdata.com) to create infographics. Glogster (www.glogster.com) is a tool for producing online, interactive media posters. Storybird (https://storybird.com) enables even young students to turn an image into an interactive story. Screencasting tools such as Jing (www.techsmith.com/jing.html) and Screencast-O-Matic (www.screencast-o-matic.com) allow students to combine voice-over narration with imagery. For projects that call for documentary-style products, students can take advantage of tools for podcasting, video production, and online publishing.

## Project Management Tools

All along the project path, take advantage of technology tools to assist with project management. Use online calendars, class websites, wikis, or LiveBinders (www.livebinders.com) to keep important project details and deadlines accessible to everyone. Use task trackers such as Trello (http://trello.com) to help students manage teamwork. Take advantage of platforms like Project Foundry (www.projectfoundry.org) or Edmodo (www.edmodo.com) to keep all the components of PBL in one place so that you can keep learning on track.

## Questions Worth Considering

As you consider which technologies to integrate into PBL, here are some questions to guide your planning:

• *What are the key learning goals you want students to achieve?* Focus on learning goals first, rather than planning a project around the latest tech tool.

• *Do your students have ready access to technology?* If your school has a one-to-one laptop program or has adopted bring-your-own-device policies, you might assume students will have equal access to digital tools. But if tech access is more limited or if some students do not have Internet access at home, be careful about making digital tools a requirement for a successful project.

• *What is your own comfort level with technology?* If you're new to digital-age learning, think about potential partners. Can you collaborate on PBL with a media specialist, technology integration specialist, or classroom colleague who has tech experience? (Don't overlook online opportunities to connect with colleagues.) Who else is available to help you and your students deepen your digital literacy together?

• *Are you taking advantage of your students' digital skills?* Consider surveying students to find out about their expertise when it comes to making videos, coding, 3-D printing, digital gaming, or publishing online. Engage knowledgeable students as peer experts.

## Moving from the Classroom to the School and District

Individual teachers can have a significant influence on students' lives through PBL. But imagine how much more powerful PBL can be if every teacher in a school is doing it! The next chapter looks at some of the districts that have decided to make PBL a school and district priority to maximize the effect on teachers and students.

# 6  Leading a PBL Implementation Effort

Veteran PBL teachers understand the wisdom of starting with the end in mind. When designing a project, they set the learning goals and envision how students will demonstrate they have met them. It's equally important for educational leaders to have a clearly defined vision for the use of PBL in the classrooms of their school or district.

In this chapter we suggest field-tested strategies for leaders who are considering widespread PBL efforts. The end goal for such initiatives can vary widely. Some leaders want to see wall-to-wall PBL, with students learning mainly through projects in every subject, which is an ambitious but challenging task. For others, a more realistic goal is for students to take part in projects at least a few times during the school year. For strategic reasons, some leaders choose to concentrate PBL, at least at first, in certain subject areas, such as STEM, or at specific grade levels.

Whether your goal is for projects to happen occasionally or every day, in one building or across an entire school system, lasting results will require thoughtful leadership.

## First Question: Why PBL in Your School or District?

Why do you want to see project based learning take hold in your school system? How do your values and current vision as an institution align with the student-centered learning and professional collaboration that are at the heart of high-quality PBL? What would a successful implementation of PBL accomplish for your students, your teachers, and your broader community?

Those big questions demand frank discussion if you're considering a shift to PBL. Alignment to mission, vision, and values is all-important when assessing a school system's readiness for PBL. That's where conversations need to begin, according to Jennifer Cruz, director of implementation for the Buck Institute for Education, who works with administrative teams to design PBL initiatives. Whether the institution is a single school, a district, or a larger system of education, she says, the opening question remains the same: "What has brought you to PBL?"

Many school leaders anticipate that PBL will be the catalyst for school improvement. Indeed, introducing the project-based approach to teaching and learning is likely to cause ripples throughout a system, affecting everyone from administrators to students themselves. Because PBL involves active learning, students gain a greater voice in their education and more opportunities to create their own understanding. Educators need to get comfortable with instructional practices to support student inquiry. This may mean more time for professional development and expanded opportunities for collaboration with colleagues. PBL will likely be unfamiliar territory for many parents, school boards, and other community stakeholders. It's a safe bet that most of them "did school" in more traditional ways when they were younger, and they may be skeptical about an instructional method that they haven't experienced firsthand.

## Preparing for a Serious Effort

If teachers and students are going to experience high-quality PBL, "conditions have to be created that will support them," Jennifer Cruz explains. "Those conditions extend throughout the system, involving teacher development, leadership development, and organizational development. It's everybody," she says. If school leaders are indeed ready to move forward, she adds, "they need to be *all in* at all those levels."

In answering the "Why PBL?" question for your school system, you can build momentum for change by bringing stakeholders into discussions at the early stages. Cris Waldfogel, systemic partnership coach for BIE, encourages the districts she works with to consider, "Is the decision to move forward with PBL widely shared? Who's on your bus?" If the vision for PBL isn't widely shared among stakeholders, then implementation efforts will be difficult to sustain, she cautions.

As you evaluate your system's readiness for PBL, it may be helpful for stakeholders to see it in action elsewhere. Recruiting a team of teachers and instructional leaders to join these observations will allow them to build shared understanding of PBL, while also prompting them to examine their own teaching beliefs and practices. One school leader, for example, recruited a team of interested teachers to survey the research on PBL, conduct site visits, and report back on their findings. Their recommendations shaped the next stages of implementation, and their enthusiasm built grassroots support for PBL across the entire school system.

As you develop a shared vision for PBL that suits your local context, consider any potential barriers to success. What are you prepared to change if you encounter obstacles when it comes to school culture, scheduling, professional development, assessment, or engagement with your community?

In a research project that involved extensive interviews with PBL principals, Rody Boonchouy, director of professional services for BIE, concluded that the professional learning necessary for PBL success needs to be ongoing "and takes time to evolve as a cohesive staff practice" (Boonchouy, 2014, p. 133). Regular opportunities for reflection and dialogue, supported by protocols that encourage collegial learning, can help teachers and school leaders make sense of PBL in the context of their work. Boonchouy also found value in practices that "de-privatize" the act of teaching, such as having teachers examine student work together or offer each other critical feedback on project plans.

"If you truly believe that PBL is valuable enough to pursue, then everything you do as a leader needs to focus on promoting this initiative," says Superintendent Eric Williams, who has guided a

12,000-student school division through a multiyear PBL implementation effort. (For a close-up look at that initiative, see the case study about York County School Division later in this chapter.)

Whether you're a school principal or a district administrator, here are some questions you will want to consider as you build a foundation for PBL success.

*At the district or regional level—*

• Does your mission, vision, and strategic plan reflect goals related to PBL? Does your school board endorse PBL as a necessary instructional shift?

• How well does your district culture reflect PBL principles, such as shared decision making, inquiry, and authentic assessment? How might you improve the alignment?

• As an educational leader, how do you model PBL practices such as collaboration, consensus building, problem solving, and effective communication?

• What are your district goals, time lines, and resources for PBL implementation? How are you engaging others in setting and communicating these goals districtwide?

• Are district policies inconsistent with, or even at odds with, PBL? Are you prepared to rethink policies about scheduling, grading, or teacher evaluation to remove potential barriers to PBL implementation?

*At the individual school level—*

• How will you honor the positive aspects of existing school culture and teachers' beliefs while leading change, if needed, to better align them with PBL practices?

• How will you create time for teachers to collaborate on project planning?

• How will you use structures such as professional learning communities and peer-led professional development to support teachers' ongoing learning?

• Do you encourage the use of protocols with faculty that support PBL and "de-privatize" classroom practice (such as critical-friend critiques, post-project reflections, or examining student work samples together)?

• Do classroom observations focus on evidence of high-quality PBL?

• How will you help to connect your students and teachers with community experts and resources to support PBL efforts?

• How will you share stories of PBL success, both within your school and with the larger community?

## Start Small or Go Big?

As a school or district leader who is "sold" on PBL, you might wish you could implement it systemwide right from the start. Be cautious. Moving too far, too fast can lead to failure. Because PBL represents a serious change for many teachers, students, parents, and school leaders, it's wise to start small to create success stories, build enthusiasm and expertise—and work out some of the bugs before a wider launch.

Another reason for starting small is to create a local success model of PBL practice, to show it can work in your context. When investigating the potential for PBL in their school or community, some people may see it in action elsewhere and say, "It's different here; I'm not sure it will work." It's true that many of the more well-known examples of schools where PBL is used extensively, which people may visit, read about, or see videos about, are special places which could create the impression that PBL can work for "those students" but not for "our students."

Accordingly, we suggest starting with a pilot PBL program before expanding the initiative. Some districts, for example, begin with one school. Some schools begin with one grade level, department, or academy. These exemplars provide opportunities for other teachers to observe and learn from what their colleagues are experiencing. When taking this approach, however, make sure it's part of a wider implementation plan so PBL is not seen as something to be done only by a small group of early-adopter types. Everyone should know from the start what the plan is: In Year 1, PBL will begin there; but in Year 2, it will begin here.

## Connecting PBL to Other Initiatives

Teachers and administrators often have concerns about how compatible project based learning is with other practices in curriculum and instruction. A common stereotype promotes the idea that adopting PBL means all former practices are abandoned as students work on their own with minimal guidance—but, as we explained in Chapter 2, this isn't true. In our model of PBL, teachers play a very active role in planning and delivering instruction, even using appropriate and effective traditional tools if they wish.

Teachers may also be justly concerned about their workload if they're asked to do PBL on top of, say, Response to Intervention, Understanding by Design, and differentiated instruction—or other practices in which they may have recently received extensive professional development.

In fact, projects allow room for many other practices. Think of the project as the toolbox into which teachers can place a variety of good instructional tools. Consider these examples:

- *Response to Intervention (RTI).* Projects are flexible enough to allow for the individually targeted assessment and interventions of an RTI program.

- *Differentiated instruction.* Projects provide natural differentiation when students grapple with a question or problem that has more than one possible answer or solution, and when students have voice and choice in how they work and the products they create. Projects also involve a variety of tasks, thus meeting the needs of students with different learning styles. When students are working in teams during a project, teachers can monitor individual and team needs better than they can from the front of the room, and provide differentiated support.

- *Framework for Teaching (Charlotte Danielson).* Because the framework is grounded in a constructivist view of teaching and learning, its "four domains of teaching responsibility" align well with PBL.

- *Understanding by Design (UbD).* UbD emphasizes teaching for deep understanding and transfer, performance-based assessment, and building a curriculum around essential questions and big ideas—all hallmarks of PBL as well. Projects can be the vehicle for delivering instruction based on UbD principles.

**Connecting PBL to Other Initiatives—(*continued*)**

- *The Workshop Model.* During a project, teachers can build students' content knowledge and skills using the components typical of reader's or writer's workshops: minilesson, application, formative assessment, debriefing.

# Case Study:
# A Transformative Vision for York County Schools

Early in his tenure at the helm of York County School Division in Virginia, then-Superintendent Eric Williams invited principals, teacher leaders, and others in the community to help shape a vision of learning for the school system's 12,000 students. As the result of their shared readings, research, and discussions, they agreed upon an ambitious goal that the superintendent calls "transformative learning. It's about giving students the opportunity to make a difference in the world—locally, nationally, or globally—as they learn the content and competencies of the curriculum."

With that end in mind, they searched for strategies to increase student engagement and also to help students build the expanded set of competencies needed for 21st century success. Academic rigor was certainly important, especially in a district that takes pride in its reputation for high-performing schools. So was an emphasis on authentic work, which they saw as a strategy "to lead kids to own their learning," Williams says. At the same time, the superintendent adds, "we had conversations about giving ourselves permission to experience the joy of teaching and learning."

Eventually, district stakeholders came to consensus about the core instructional strategy that would help them realize their vision. "PBL became the means by which we would provide students with these transformative learning opportunities," he says. They also recognized that a districtwide shift to PBL would not happen overnight.

As PBL efforts were getting off the ground, Williams made an effort to find early adopters of the project-based approach within the school district. Using social media—including his blog and Twitter account—he shined a spotlight on examples of high-quality projects.

A 3rd grade class, for instance, was tackling this globally relevant question: *How can we improve the soil quality of villages in developing nations?* Students had to recommend whether to invest charitable donations in fertilizer or compost to improve soil quality. As part of their inquiry, they Skyped with experts and designed experiments to compare the two methods. Then they made arguments, backed by evidence, to sway donors to a charitable organization. "Teachers found that kids' engagement was so much higher—and so were the results on standardized tests," Williams says. "An authentic question produced better learning." In a middle school class, the superintendent found students who were producing book trailers and posting them on YouTube to persuade their peers to read. Having an authentic audience and purpose motivated them to produce high-quality work. High school students, meanwhile, were engaged in an ambitious environmental science project to improve water quality and restore oyster beds in the Chesapeake Bay.

"These projects are all content-rich. They all lead to higher student engagement. And just as importantly," Williams adds, "they lead to higher teacher engagement. It turns out that PBL is incredibly invigorating for teachers."

In hindsight, Williams can see how sharing examples of PBL success helped to build buy-in and overcome skepticism within his district. "When it's a project happening in your own school or district, there's no reaction that, 'Yes, but we can't do that here because....' This is your school, your district, your colleague. There's real power in tuning in to what's happening locally. That helped to open some eyes about what's possible."

At this writing, York County is midway through a multiyear PBL implementation effort, developed in partnership with BIE, that involves extensive professional development and instructional coaching to help teachers get off to a good start with projects. The district also is building the capacity of teacher leaders who will sustain PBL efforts for the long term. Williams was able to identify the following key strategies that are continuing to build momentum for PBL across the school system:

• *Lay a foundation.* Even before York County embarked on a PBL implementation plan, educators across the district were building a collaborative culture and experiencing shared leadership. Teachers worked together, for example, to define high-quality assessment. Teacher cohorts designed sample performance tasks and rubrics and analyzed student work samples together. They also made regular use of protocols for collegial conversations developed by the National School Reform Faculty.

"That earlier work was helpful for laying a foundation for PBL," Williams says. "Even before starting our work on PBL, we had shifted our professional learning." Rather than relying on outsiders for professional development, for instance, the district increasingly turned to its own staff for expertise. That helped to build internal capacity to lead change. "Once we started working on PBL, we had the culture and skills to move more quickly."

• *Build teacher ownership.* If the goal had been to implement PBL as quickly as possible, the district could have taken a top-down approach. "We could have recruited a handful of our best teachers and paid them to develop great project plans over the summer," Williams says. Instead, York County has allowed time for project ideas to emerge more organically while teachers go through professional development in cohorts to develop their understanding of PBL. He expects the initial rollout to take three years. "It's a patient process that puts more emphasis on teacher ownership," the superintendent says.

Eventually, Williams expects students to take part in projects, for at least part of the year, in every grade level and content area. As teachers go through professional development, they're building a resource library of high-quality, classroom-tested projects that their colleagues will be able to borrow, customize, and modify to suit their needs. "This approach is about giving teachers autonomy to flourish, while also having common expectations. We're all going to do this," Williams says, "but we're still giving teachers voice and choice." Additionally, building-level leaders have a say in how their schools implement PBL. Some have started with grade-level or content-area teams; others have decided to go "all in," all at once.

• *Share success.* As PBL has started to spread across York County, the district has cultivated a culture of sharing. "We started with teachers doing gallery walks, exhibiting student work, and having conversations with their peers. That was a way to start scaling up these practices and foster a culture of teacher leadership. Now that PBL is becoming more common, we've moved into exhibitions of project work," Williams explains, with students sharing their results with public audiences.

Exhibitions offer opportunities for parents and other community stakeholders to build their understanding of PBL. To go even deeper, school board members and some parent leaders have taken part in PBL workshops. "We've looked at student work together and have wrestled with the concept of transformative learning," the superintendent says. One parent organization has shown its support for PBL by providing minigrants to fund project resources and PBL-related field trips.

Sharing projects also helps to extend PBL efforts beyond the classroom. Parents and other community members are stepping up to support projects as experts, audience members, and collaborators. "Those connections all improve student engagement," Williams says, "and help to build community advocates."

• *Stay patient.* Williams is convinced that slow, steady, grassroots change has been the right choice for the district. Still, he admits, "patience is difficult." If a reasonable time frame for a PBL rollout takes several years, then that means some students may graduate without getting a chance to experience transformative learning.

While giving PBL time to take hold, a school leader needs to maintain a clear focus on the work at hand. "If you believe there's a big bang for your buck in using PBL to achieve your vision for teaching and learning, then you need to be all in on that," Williams says. "That may mean not pursuing other strategies which offer potential benefits. It may mean making choices about great ideas you'll have to say 'no' to." If you do pursue other initiatives, he adds, "you'll need to show how they connect to PBL." As York County adopted a new literacy model, for example, Williams was careful to emphasize how the approach in language arts is consistent with PBL and not a change of direction.

Eventually, Williams predicts, the slow-and-steady approach will build advocates for PBL so that the instructional strategy will be sustained for the long term. "We're at the threshold now," he says, "of having enough teachers who say, 'We buy into this' and will keep it going." During the 2014–15 school year, Williams moved on to new challenges as superintendent of the Loudon County (Virginia) School Division, serving 70,000 students. Will he introduce PBL there? It's too soon to tell. "We need to have stakeholder conversations," he says, "about how best to engage students in deep, meaningful learning."

## Creating Space for Teacher Change

Although school leaders play a critical role in shaping the vision for PBL, it's teachers who will engage in the day-to-day work of bringing this vision to life in the classroom. For many teachers, a shift to PBL involves learning new instructional strategies as well as new ways of collaborating with colleagues and, perhaps, engaging with experts and other community members.

As a school or district leader, how will you support and encourage teachers through the challenging process of change? How will you honor teachers' existing beliefs while encouraging them to consider new ways of engaging with students? How will you create a safe space for risk taking? How will you model the ways of thinking and acting that you want to see both students and teachers develop? For example, how can you use driving questions and generate "need to know" questions at meetings, and use protocols for critique and revision to improve plans, policies, or events?

## What Do Teachers Want from PBL Leaders?

As a thought-provoking exercise, consider the topic of school leadership from your teachers' perspective. If your staff is heading into a PBL initiative, how will teachers want to be supported and encouraged by their principal, superintendent, and other administrators? How will leaders coach teachers to improve their practice of PBL? How will they create time for collaboration and build a transparent culture?

A team of teachers in the Los Angeles Unified School District recently had the opportunity to consider the qualities they want in a school leader to guide changes in instructional practice. To expand educational options in South Central Los Angeles, they collaborated with community members on a pilot project to design a new career academy focused on digital gaming and design. The small high school, which opened in 2012, shares a campus with two other career academies at Augustus Hawkins Schools for Community Action. At capacity, total enrollment among the three academies will be 1,500 students.

"We knew that we wanted a core value of our school to be student-centered learning," explains Mark Gomez, a founding teacher of the Critical Design and Gaming School at Hawkins. That led them to PBL as a key instructional strategy. Early on, they identified a need for professional development "to help teachers understand what PBL is and what it isn't."

As part of the school start-up process, teachers were tasked with interviewing candidates for the principal's job. They had in mind an administrator who would empower them as they worked collaboratively to realize their PBL vision. They knew that a leader who could forge partnerships would be critical to the school's success at building community alliances. Other qualities emerged, too, as they thought about their criteria for an effective PBL leader. As Gomez explains, "We realized we want a leader who can push innovation. We need someone who will be engaged with our community, our parents. And sometimes, we need someone who will back us up."

Although still new, the school is making progress with both projects and partnerships. Relationships with local organizations have led to a number of impressive projects in the community. (See an example, *Reimagine South Central*, in Appendix A, pages 216–218.) "We've had a lot of PBL moments that go way beyond anyone's idea of what a traditional project can accomplish," Gomez says. Communication between staff and administration has been open. "It's a pretty flat structure," he says, which sets the stage for shared leadership in a small school setting. "So far, so good."

## How Leaders Pave the Way

Leaders can help pave the way for smoother PBL implementation by building a collaborative culture, anticipating challenges, and removing potential barriers. It helps to think through each decision, one superintendent advises, "through the lens of PBL." That advice applies to big issues, such as grading policies, as well as day-to-day considerations, such as which field trip requests to approve.

What's more, leaders play an important role as PBL "cheerleaders." That's how teachers at one high-performing school describe their principal, who is a regular visitor to classrooms whenever projects are underway. He attends project exhibitions and creates opportunities for students to speak with community groups about their PBL experiences. His enthusiasm is visible—and contagious.

As you start down the PBL path, consider how these strategies will support your teachers through the process of change:

• *Share leadership responsibilities.* Collaboration, a critical component for effective PBL, is equally important as a leadership practice to help PBL take hold. Building a culture of shared leadership helps to build and sustain PBL initiatives, expanding the circle of supporters and deepening institutional capacity to lead change. And just as students often need to learn how to work effectively on a team, adults may also benefit from professional learning experiences that deepen their capacity to collaborate.

Whether leaders are working at the site level or across a district, "they need to engage a team to move forward with PBL," recommends Cris Waldfogel, systemic partnership coach for BIE. "One person alone can't effectively carry this kind of initiative forward." In her work with school systems, she has seen the best results with PBL initiatives when leaders empower a PBL task force. "You need to think about who's on that shared leadership team. What assets do they bring? How will you leverage those assets?"

Waldfogel encourages leaders to be strategic about sharing responsibilities with team members. "You're not just handing down a decision, but pressing the team to make better decisions. That means using a decision-making model that requires input from a number of people," she says, "and providing the necessary support so that they can move forward within a shared leadership paradigm."

Exactly how PBL teams work together can vary widely from one system to the next. Across diverse contexts, however, a clear purpose is a good starting point. "Without a purpose, your team might meet weekly but not accomplish meaningful work," Waldfogel cautions. "The gift of PBL is that it gives your team an authentic purpose from the start. How will the team move the PBL initiative forward?" Just as a good driving question brings focus to students' learning activities in PBL, a clear purpose for leadership teams enables them to advance the PBL agenda and use their shared wisdom to troubleshoot barriers.

• *Create time for ongoing professional development.* Learning how to design, manage, and assess Gold Standard projects takes time. Teachers' professional development needs don't stop once they've taken part in an introductory workshop. Having a project plan in hand—even one that has been carefully designed to attend to the Essential Project Design Elements—is just the start. Once students enter the picture, teachers can anticipate more "need to knows" about effective instructional strategies.

Schools that emphasize PBL as a core strategy dedicate time for ongoing professional development that's closely tied to the classroom. In settings such as High Tech High in San Diego or New Tech Network schools across the United States, teachers have regularly scheduled time with their colleagues to take part in project-design tunings and debriefs. In staff meetings, they examine student work together as part of ongoing conversations about assessment. The instructional leadership team frequently takes part in these collegial conversations. In addition, teachers use summer planning time to design new projects for the coming school year.

### New PD For PBL

When considering what kind of professional development teachers might need in order to be successful with PBL, think "real-world." Teachers can gain ideas for authentic projects and learn what it's like to work in the authentic ways called for in Gold Standard PBL by spending time talking with—or even working alongside—professionals in a variety of fields and settings. School and district leaders can support teachers by finding professionals from the community, business and industry, and academia who could be contacted, and by making arrangements for meetings, visits, field work, and other ways for teachers to connect with the world outside school. The Metro Nashville Public Schools put teachers in touch with local experts by leveraging partnerships with civic organizations—see more on this story below.

According to Helen Soulé, executive director of the Partnership for 21st Century Skills, "The push for project- and problem-based learning in many states' K12 curricula will result in big changes in PD. There is a lot more focus on making instruction and professional development more connected to the real world, such as through internships for teachers so they can connect their practice more to what the real world looks like" (District Administration, 2014).

What about schools that do not do PBL wall-to-wall? School leaders need to carefully—and creatively—consider how they use professional development time so that their teachers have the opportunities they need for just-in-time support, learning, and collegial conversations. This may mean rethinking existing structures, such as professional learning communities, to focus on PBL. Arranging for late openings or early dismissals once or twice monthly can create more pockets of time for teacher collaboration. Informally, a principal or an instructional coach might offer to cover a classroom for a period so that a teacher can observe a colleague's project in action. To work around persistent scheduling challenges, you may want to use online platforms for teacher collaboration and professional learning.

"There's no shortcut," says one superintendent, "and it's an ongoing challenge with all the other pressures on our schedule. But we know that teachers need time throughout the PBL process to plan, troubleshoot, reflect, and identify what worked and what didn't so they can continually improve projects. If you want teachers to succeed with PBL, you have to make time for that to happen."

• *Look for evidence of active learning.* When you walk into a class-room when a project is underway, what do you look for as evidence of effective teaching and learning? If classroom observations are part of teacher evaluation, which criteria are informing your evaluation?

One principal who was new to PBL made a revealing comment at the end of a workshop: "Last week, I walked into a classroom to do an observation. It was somewhat noisy. I noticed that some students were doing online research while others appeared to be working on editing a video. The teacher was working in a corner with a small group. Instead of sitting down to watch PBL in action, I made the mis-take of telling the teacher, 'Oh, I'll come back to observe sometime when you're teaching.' Now I'm starting to realize just how wrong I was! There was so much thoughtful teaching and learning underway, and I missed it. I was still defining good teaching as the teacher in front of the room, giving a lecture."

School leaders who are more comfortable with PBL tend to sit down alongside students and ask them about their projects. They might ask students to tell them about the driving question and explain how the activities they're working on today will help them answer that question. Similarly, school leaders who are familiar with PBL can be effective sounding boards if teachers need to troubleshoot challenges during projects.

*At the school level,* leaders should consider the following addi-tional questions about managing a PBL change process:

• How does your leadership style support teachers through the change process? For example, do you encourage teachers to take risks and improve projects through feedback? Do you share leadership responsibilities?

• How do you look for teachers who are early adopters of PBL and encourage them to become teacher leaders? (See the case study on Novi Schools later in this chapter.)

• Are you an effective "face to the world" for your school? Do you communicate the PBL vision to community members, potential partners, and decision makers in the district?

• Are you ready to stand behind your teachers as they introduce new ways of teaching and learning? How will you let them know that you "have their backs" when they take risks?

*At the district level,* leaders should consider these questions about supporting a PBL change process:

• How will you help school leaders learn what they need to know so they can guide PBL at the site level?

• How can you make district resources (including time) available for professional development?

• How can you encourage communication among principals to prevent isolation and support their PBL efforts at the site level?

### Are You Ready to Tackle Grading?

Schools and school networks that have been at the forefront of implementing PBL are also pioneers when it comes to rethinking assessment. Some have even updated the traditional report card to be more aligned to what students are learning through PBL. This is admittedly tricky territory. Changing traditional grading systems means schools have to be "willing to take on a sacred cow," according to Bob Lenz, cofounder and chief of innovation of Envision Education, a school change organization that manages three PBL-style charter high schools in the San Francisco Bay Area.

Yesterday's grading systems may well be due for a makeover. Listen to grading authority Thomas Guskey (2011), professor of educational psychology at the University of Kentucky:

> If someone proposed combining measures of height, weight, diet, and exercise into a single number or mark to represent a person's physical condition, we would consider it laughable. How could the combination of such diverse measures yield anything meaningful? Yet every day, teachers combine aspects of students' achievement, attitude, responsibility, effort, and behavior into a single grade that's recorded on a report card—and no one questions it. (p. 19)

## Are You Ready to Tackle Grading?—(*continued*)

More useful, he argues, are report cards that distinguish among product, process, and progress (Guskey & Bailey, 2010). Although such report cards are unusual in the United States, they're gaining traction internationally.

For the Envision network of schools, a new approach to assessment started by asking broad questions. "We started by asking, What do we want kids to know and be able to do? And how would we know they have achieved it?" Lenz says. Those questions have led to performance assessments and the use of portfolios to track student learning over time. "We also asked, How should we structure schools (including assessment and reporting systems) to help do this work?"

Meanwhile, the New Tech Network of more than 100 schools has redesigned its report cards to better reflect 21st century competencies. Instead of receiving a single letter grade for a course, each student receives a report that describes progress across several categories. Academic content mastery is assessed, but so are such competencies as work ethic, critical thinking, and communication.

To revise grading and assessment across a system, teachers may have to give up their attachment to individual grading practices. It may take consensus building and shared leadership to adopt schoolwide rubrics that use common language to define quality work. Teachers will need to come to agreement about what quality work looks like. "And that takes time," Lenz allows. As part of their ongoing professional learning, teachers need time to share, discuss, and calibrate their assessments of student work samples.

The upside of reinventing grading systems is the benefit for students. "It's a gift for kids," Lenz says. "If you have common rubrics, they don't have to figure out the rules for six different teachers." When students receive more nuanced progress reports, they have a clearer picture of where they are as learners—and where they want to go.

Courageous school leaders will likely be the ones driving discussions about grading. Guskey recommends that education leaders get familiar with the research on grading and what works best for students. Then they can propose "more meaningful policies and practices that support learning and enhance students' perceptions of themselves as learners" (Guskey, 2011, p. 21). Similarly, teachers might engage in action research about grading and share their findings with colleagues.

# Case Study:
# Peer Leadership in Novi Community Schools

Novi Community School District serves about 6,200 students in a community northwest of Detroit, Michigan. Since Superintendent Steve Matthews arrived in 2011, he has been guiding the district toward a vision of "engaging students in meaningful work." He recognizes PBL as a key instructional strategy to achieve that vision. "PBL is one of those approaches that helps students put their heart and soul into schoolwork," he says. "My goal has been to figure out how to bring PBL into our district consciousness so that more teachers begin to embrace it."

Rather than instituting a top-down mandate to implement projects, Matthews has deliberately encouraged grassroots change and teacher leadership. As a case in point, he describes the professional journey of veteran teacher Myla Lee (who is a member of the BIE National Faculty).

During his visits to Lee's elementary classroom, the superintendent says, "I could see that Myla had created an environment that was intentionally, and intensively, based on PBL. As I watched her work with her students, I started wondering, how might we expand her reach into the district? Could she create a cohort of teachers able to demonstrate the power of PBL across our district?"

In particular, the superintendent wanted to leverage peer leadership to "help teachers develop a clear appreciation for, and shared definition of, PBL. I thought it was important for us to appropriately define what we view as essential elements of PBL, starting with a driving question and continuing through to a presentation to an authentic audience—and everything in between," he says.

The superintendent had another reason for encouraging grassroots change. Recent education reforms at the state and federal level have exerted pressures on teachers from outside the district. "I didn't want to create another initiative where teachers would say, 'Here's somebody else trying to mandate what goes on in my classroom.' I wanted this to be more organic, more authentic. I wanted to point to real classrooms, real teachers in our district making an impact with

PBL. The power of student engagement with projects speaks to teachers. That's what will have staying power." Building teacher support "may take longer, but it's going to be more meaningful as we move forward," Matthews predicts.

Matthews demonstrated his commitment to PBL by budgeting existing resources for professional development toward a new initiative. He invited Lee to step out of the classroom for at least two years and shift from being a PBL teacher of children to being a PBL coach for her colleagues.

Lee recalls that career-changing opportunity, which happened in late summer 2013. "Dr. Matthews said to my colleagues, 'Myla's going on a journey. Does anyone want to come along with her? We'll support you as you learn about PBL.'"

Her first step was to host a workshop where her peers could learn more about the professional development opportunities ahead. That event resulted in the first cohort of 18 teachers volunteering to embark on their own PBL journeys. Each made a two-year commitment to learn about PBL, implement Common Core–aligned projects with Lee's coaching, and reflect on the experience.

Lee has discovered that adult learners are as diverse as students. "They're all in different places," she says. Teachers meet as a group for what Lee calls "digging deeper days," when they dive into specific aspects of PBL. Then she spends time in each of their classrooms, modeling PBL strategies and doing "whatever they need. I tell them that I'm here to support them during the first five days of a project, the last five days, and through the muddy middle."

Lee has taken care to be transparent about the professional learning that's emerging from this initiative, which also emphasizes technology integration. She set up a website to capture project highlights and teacher reflections, share resources, and build awareness across the district (and in the larger community) of what high-quality PBL looks like in action (see http://novipbl.net). On the home page, she highlights the driving question that has helped to focus the cohort's professional learning experience: "How can we, as NCSD teachers, develop a PBL culture and environment for our classrooms?"

Less than a year into the initiative, Lee and her colleagues were able to document evidence of cultural change. In one classroom, for example, an elementary teacher had just wrapped up her first successful project. She told students they were starting a new unit (which she did not intend to teach PBL-style). Lee describes what happened next: "When she said, 'OK, get out your social studies textbooks and let's start on the next chapter,' she could see the disappointment on her students' faces. They wanted to know, what's our driving question? Who's on our project team? She called me that night and said, 'I have to design another project. They won't let me go back to a traditional unit!'"

Of course, not every project has been a game-changer. "Are these first projects as authentic as we'd like them to be? Of course not," Lee says. "But we can see projects getting better over time." She estimates that, for about a third of the cohort, "PBL has caught on big-time. It's become a culture for them and their students." Another third now have a stronger "need to know" about building classroom practices to support and sustain PBL. For the rest, she says, "it's not yet a habit."

Meanwhile, interest in PBL is spreading well beyond the initial cohort. A larger cohort has already formed for Year 2, and Year 1 teachers will continue to receive just-in-time coaching and online support. Lee regularly fields requests from individual teachers and school principals who want to introduce PBL, and interest is spreading across all grade levels. As the initiative grows, Lee is strategically recruiting members of the Year 1 cohort to become teacher leaders. "They can become the go-to people in our district," she says, to continue the expansion of PBL.

From the superintendent's perspective, the grassroots approach is delivering the kind of results he hoped to see. During a recent visit to a 1st grade classroom, he sat down with a student and asked him about the current project. "He was able to tell me in great detail what he was working on, why it was important, and the positive impact it would have on the school. That was a powerful statement to me that this student is engaged," Matthews says. Similar observations in other classes have convinced him, he says. "Students can intuitively see the power of PBL. They want this in all their classes."

While eager to celebrate early successes, Matthews realizes that not all teachers are quite ready "to step back, relinquish some of their control, and trust that students will accept their responsibility in the learning process. Some are concerned about that," he acknowledges, "especially in an era when student growth is part of your evaluation as a teacher." It's going to take abundant examples of successful outcomes by PBL pioneers to show that "you can create a classroom that will engage students in ways they have not been engaged before. Not that we won't have bumps along the way," Matthews adds, "but we need to make these good examples visible and let teachers have conversations with each other. When teachers see the successes of their colleagues, they're going to want to be a part of that."

## Bringing Stakeholders Along

Whether you're leading a PBL initiative in a district or a single school, you can anticipate questions from stakeholders. Parents may wonder why you're changing the model of instruction that they remember from their own education. They may question grading policies that reflect team dynamics. Community members, including major employers in your region, may want to know whether this approach will prepare students for life after high school. Inevitably, given the current emphasis on accountability and initiatives like the Common Core State Standards, stakeholders will want to know how PBL will affect student achievement.

In your role as school or district leader, you need to be ready to communicate the "Why PBL?" message with a variety of stakeholders. Preparing an elevator pitch to answer that question is a good exercise, but that's just a small piece of a strategic communication plan. Work with your district experts in public relations and social media to shape a compelling message about why your students are engaging in projects and how research supports PBL. Share a consistent message in person and online. Look for opportunities to share positive stories about projects that have achieved compelling results, along with highlights from research about PBL's effectiveness. Leverage events such as project exhibitions to share your PBL story via media outlets. And don't forget to make sure other staff can communicate the PBL message, too, from office workers to board members, if they're answering questions from community members.

**Talking Points: Why Project Based Learning?**

*1. PBL makes school more engaging for students.* Today's students, more than ever, often find school to be boring and meaningless. In PBL, students are active, not passive; a project engages their hearts and minds, and provides real-world relevance for learning.

*2. PBL improves learning.* After completing a project, students remember what they learn and retain it longer than is often the case with traditional instruction. Because of this, students who gain content knowledge with PBL are better able to apply what they know and can do to new situations. Students learn content at a deeper level compared to superficial "coverage-based" approaches.

*3. PBL builds competencies for college and career readiness.* In the 21st century workplace, success requires more than basic knowledge and skills. In PBL, students not only understand content more deeply but also learn how to take responsibility and build confidence, solve problems, work collaboratively, communicate ideas, and manage themselves effectively.

*4. PBL helps address standards.* The Common Core and other present-day standards emphasize real-world application of knowledge and skills, and the development of 21st century success skills such as critical thinking, communication in a variety of media, speaking and presentation skills, and collaboration with others. PBL is an effective way to meet these goals.

*5. PBL provides opportunities for students to use technology.* Modern technology—which students use so much in their lives—is a perfect fit with PBL. With technology, teachers and students can connect with experts, partners, and audiences around the world, and find resources and information, create products, and collaborate more effectively.

*6. PBL makes teaching more enjoyable and rewarding.* PBL allows teachers to work more closely with active, engaged students doing high-quality, meaningful work, and in many cases to rediscover the joy of learning alongside their students. Compared to disappointing results they might see from traditional teaching methods, teachers using PBL see profound effects on their students.

> **Talking Points: Why Project Based Learning?—(*continued*)**
>
> *7. PBL connects students and schools with communities and the real world.*
> Projects provide students with empowering opportunities to make a differ-
> ence in their communities and the wider world, by solving real problems
> and addressing real issues. Students learn how to interact with adults and
> organizations, are exposed to workplaces and adult jobs, and can develop
> potential career interests. Parents and community members can be involved
> in projects.

Don't wait for end-of-project events to share your PBL story. Educate the public and the media about the benefits of PBL by offering
open houses and school tours—perhaps led by engaged students, who
tend to be passionate advocates for PBL.

Build more engagement by inviting community members to participate in projects as content-area experts. Invite a variety of stakeholders to share their expertise, including parents, representatives of
nonprofit and business organizations, faculty from local colleges and
community colleges, Chambers of Commerce or tourism bureaus, and
others with knowledge to share.

Encourage stakeholders to share problems or issues that could
benefit from student problem solving, too. For example, students might
use their critical-thinking and communication skills to help a nonprofit
organization develop public service announcements or create a social
media campaign to bring more visitors to their community.

# Case Study: Community Engagement in Nashville

Now several years into a large-scale PBL initiative, Metro Nashville
Public Schools has developed strategies to tackle a common PBL challenge: how to connect schools with experts and community partners.

The urban district, serving nearly 85,000 students, began introducing PBL as part of a school reform effort to create career academies
within all of its 12 comprehensive high schools. Academies focus on
diverse fields, including music recording, engineering, health careers,

cultural institutions, and automotive industries. That approach sets the stage for interdisciplinary projects related to a wide range of careers.

"Our teachers have had to figure out, who in the 'real' world does things with the content I'm teaching? And how can I make it real-world without losing focus on what I'm responsible for teaching?" says Todd Wigginton, a former social studies coordinator for the district who serves in a new role as coordinator of instructional projects. To ensure authenticity in projects, teachers may have to investigate real-world connections. "If teachers don't know who's using this content in the real world, we encourage them to seek out that information. Why are we teaching it? Why is it useful? Experts can help answer those questions," Wigginton adds. To connect experts with classrooms, the district has partnered with businesses and community organizations based in the Nashville area. Some partnerships are the result of old-fashioned networking by district leaders. Others have come about with help from Alignment Nashville, a nonprofit that enlists community organizations to support the city's youth, and the Pencil Foundation, which links community resources with public schools.

Established relationships make it easier to tap experts across the arc of projects, from the design stage all the way to culminating events. Experts typically offer critical feedback to teachers during project design workshops, for example, to ensure what Wigginton calls "authenticity in planning." They also help students troubleshoot challenges during the inquiry process and sometimes provide access to the tools of a particular profession. During project presentations, students can expect experts to ask questions that push their thinking, adding more real-world relevancy. Through the district partnerships, teachers also take part in short-term externships, giving them close-up looks at the workplaces where their students will soon be heading.

To build awareness of PBL in the community, Nashville ends each school year with a project exhibition that involves hundreds of students from district high schools and middle schools. "It's an opportunity to celebrate learning and publicly showcase student work," Wigginton says. Expert involvement means it's also an opportunity for deep learning. Judges are recruited from diverse disciplines and use a common rubric to score projects. Students go through three rounds of judging, honing their presentation skills before an authentic audience. "The students are so invigorated," Wigginton says. "The exhibition gets better every year."

## Being Smart About Achieving Scale

Once PBL takes hold in your school community, be sure to build on early successes. Celebrations of student and teacher accomplishments will help to build momentum.

At the same time, marshal your patience. Shifting instructional practice takes time. Be smart about achieving scale so that enthusiasm for PBL extends beyond the early adopters. Don't let your hard work to build support for PBL get eroded by new initiatives.

Here are a few final questions for PBL leaders to ponder:

• How will you encourage collaborative decision making across PBL leadership teams?

• How will you document and celebrate successful PBL to foster community awareness of the benefits?

• How can you build your staff capacity to provide ongoing, peer-led professional development related to PBL?

• How will you recruit PBL-ready teachers and instructional leaders?

• How will you help your staff avoid initiative burnout? How will you help them see how future initiatives—such as technology upgrades or new approaches in math, science, or literacy—are consistent with high-quality PBL?

# 7 | PBL in Informal Education and Summer Programs

What happens when project based learning takes place outside what we think of as "regular" school? Consider a few examples:

• High school students concerned about poor air quality in their community used their after-school-program hours to install monitoring devices in the neighborhood around their campus. Using the data they gathered and analyzed as evidence, they lobbied for stricter regulations on industrial polluters.

• Middle school students joined a school club to answer this intriguing driving question: How can we build a highly functional but low-cost prosthetic arm to improve the lives of children in the developing world who have been victims of war or accidents?

• Children taking part in an urban after-school program interviewed their relatives and published a cookbook celebrating world cultures and family stories.

Across a wide range of informal education settings—from after-school clubs and youth groups to summer enrichment programs—PBL is gaining traction as a strategy to enable children and teens to explore interests, build positive relationships, and engage in authentic problem solving. And although informal education may not always map neatly to standards, students can also be given opportunities to reinforce academic skills through projects in settings outside school time.

In some pioneering communities, PBL is transforming traditional after-school and summer programs. Instead of spending their free time on supervised homework or tutoring, with breaks for recreation, youth are now taking part in high-interest projects that may also benefit their communities.

In this chapter we explore the opportunities for PBL in informal education, along with strategies for making the most of these potentially rich learning experiences.

## Why PBL in Informal Education?

Learning that happens outside the regular school day is not constrained by a fixed school calendar or daily schedule. There's no predetermined curriculum and no grade-level expectation of what students should know. "There's no homework, no grades, no pressure," said a classroom teacher who also advises an after-school club. "It's all about what students want to do." Another advisor said that informal learning projects "give kids the chance to take an idea and just soar."

Despite the open-ended possibilities, informal learning programs do tend to have specific objectives. Some programs provide enrichment, exposing youth to opportunities they might not encounter during the regular school day. Others aim to build youth resiliency by connecting students with positive role models, reinforcing healthy decision making, or engaging participants in community service. School-based summer programs often aim to boost academic skills and increase engagement for struggling students.

Programs that extend learning beyond the four walls of the classroom and the traditional hours of the school day complement learning that happens at school and at home. Milton Chen, author of *Education Nation*, underscores the importance of these "third learning spaces," where students learn "in ways not bounded by the schedule of the school day, the limitations of the four classroom walls, or the location of one's home" (Chen, 2013, p. 108).

This observation is consistent with what researchers describe as "connected learning." During their free time, in public libraries, museums, community centers, and other spaces, youth are accessing technology and makerspaces to engage in discovery, creativity, critical thinking, and real-world problem solving. They're learning with peers and from mentors as they explore interests, create their own content, and sometimes take part in civic action. Spaces for connected learning are multiplying. YOUmedia, a model for connected learning that was piloted at the Chicago Public Library, is expanding to locations across the country with funding from the MacArthur Foundation.

Such programs have tremendous potential to extend and deepen student learning—if done well. The Afterschool Alliance, a leading voice in the out-of-school-time field, suggests that programs "must become known as important places of learning—more specifically, learning that excites young people in the building of new skills, the discovery of new interests, and opportunities to achieve a sense of mastery" (Piha, n.d., p. 1). After-school programs have advantages that perfectly position them to accomplish these things in ways that complement the learning that happens at school and home and offer valuable extended learning opportunities, according to the After-school Alliance.

Project based learning provides a fitting framework for addressing the goals of informal learning programs, or what one expert has dubbed "learning at not-school" (Sefton-Green, 2013). Student-driven inquiry and youth engagement—hallmarks of good PBL—are also quality indicators in out-of-school-time settings. What's more, well-designed projects often drive toward an action in which students apply what they've learned. Translated to informal learning, that may mean community service or youth leadership experiences. The PBL emphasis on learning by *doing* creates the expectation that students will, indeed, do something!

It's no wonder that PBL is getting a closer look from informal education programs promoted by a wide variety of stakeholders, including youth-serving organizations, museums, libraries, parks, and after-school and summer enrichment programs sponsored by school districts and partner organizations. Across these diverse contexts, there are natural connections between what's important for high-quality informal learning and what happens during PBL.

Learning in Afterschool and Summer (LIAS) is a project dedicated to promoting unified principles for after-school programs (see http://www.learninginafterschool.org/position.htm). The table in Figure 7.1 shows how the five core learning principles of LIAS align with the practices of PBL.

**Figure 7.1**    Alignment Between LIAS Informal-Learning Principles and PBL Practices

| What Matters for Informal Learning | What Happens in PBL |
| --- | --- |
| Learning that is active | Learning by doing, both hands on and minds on |
| Learning that is collaborative | Learning and creating products through teamwork, building the skills of effective collaboration |
| Learning that is meaningful | Learning through student-driven inquiry into important real-world questions and problems |
| Learning that supports mastery | Learning to deeply understand content and build success skills, with iterative cycles of feedback and revision leading to a product made public |
| Learning that expands horizons | Learning that allows for student voice and choice, with work presented to an authentic audience |

Focusing on what's essential for quality PBL can help to ensure that informal learning is time well spent. The essential project design elements that matter for Gold Standard PBL in the classroom are also important in informal learning, with slight modifications. For example, key knowledge and understanding in informal PBL isn't limited to academic learning goals and standards. What's "key" in an after-school or summer project is content that connects to students' interests and, often, has local context or personal relevance.

Among the other features of Gold Standard PBL, the ones that matter most for informal learning tend to be those that involve student engagement. After all, participation in out-of-school-time programs is not mandatory. To succeed during informal learning time, projects need to provide students with a strong sense of authenticity and allow for voice and choice. An engaging driving question helps to keep projects focused, while a public product provides additional motivation for students to do their best work.

Some communities are reimagining traditional out-of-school-time programs through the lens of PBL. Both summer school and after-school programs are getting a makeover by introducing students to engaging projects.

## The PBL Difference: Summer Learning

Convincing students to enroll in summer school can be a hard sell. Going back to school during summer vacation can feel like punishment for doing poorly or missing class time during the regular school year. On the positive side, for students who are behind academically, summer school does offer a chance to recover credit and, perhaps, strengthen academic skills. Well-designed summer programs offer students a chance to learn in a more relaxed setting, sometimes with smaller class sizes and differentiated instruction for diverse learners. Although many good programs exist, others continue to deliver worksheet-driven remediation. How can summer school providers keep students engaged and motivated during a time when many of their friends are not in school?

Project based learning can be especially useful in this situation. Through engaging project experiences, students can delve into their passions and strengthen academic skills, sometimes without even realizing they're "doing school." The short window of a typical summer program (often just a few weeks) makes for a perfect single focus on a project, with a culminating event to cap off the experience. In addition, the warmer weather and students' desire to be outdoors dovetail naturally with environmental and location-based projects that take students outside the classroom. What's more, for teachers interested in PBL, summer can offer an ideal season to "test-drive" this instructional approach. A few examples illustrate the possibilities.

Park County School District No. 6 in Cody, Wyoming, created a PBL Summer School that took 6th through 8th graders out of the school building with a variety of projects. One project was based on the students' belief that their town was boring, with not enough for young people to do. To address this concern, teams collaborated to create interactive maps (called RAFTS, or Recreational Activities for Teens) using Google Maps. They wrote accompanying text describing hiking trails, bike routes, and local parks. During the project, students developed writing and photography skills, used math to determine distances, and learned about marketing and communication. In another science/math project, students learned about a rare flower that was being trampled by visitors to a lookout spot on a nearby mountain, and built a viewing platform to protect its habitat.

In the iChallengeU program in Holland, Michigan, high school students can take a two-week intensive summer course that combines community college credit in a Business Innovations course with real projects for local businesses and nonprofits. Each team works with master teachers and local experts to research a problem, develop solutions, and prepare presentations. For example, students worked with a technology company to figure out how to attract top talent, helped a hospital devise a way to increase the number of underserved women in the county tested for breast cancer, and created a campaign to change perceptions of agriculture on behalf of a farm services organization.

An iChallengeU project team working for United Way of Ottawa County took up the following driving question: *Given that there is enough food in the county, how do we increase access to healthy meals so that one in four local residents no longer go hungry?* In their two weeks of work on the project, students visited food pantries and examined various food distribution systems. They developed a proposal for changing the food distribution model and presented it to a panel of judges.

# Summer School Case Study: A Fresh Approach for Katherine Smith Elementary

When Aaron Brengard, principal of Katherine Smith Elementary School, inherited the summer school program for the Evergreen School District in San Jose, California, he knew he had a challenge.

The program had been shelved the summer before and only recently reinstated. The district budget was being squeezed, which meant limited resources for the summer curriculum. He had 4th through 8th grade Title I students to teach and 15 days to fill. Having been a summer school teacher himself, Brengard wanted to make this experience richer and more meaningful than the usual combination of remediation and recess.

Brengard, along with Evergreen Director of Categorical Programs Denise Williams, were drawn to the career-tech movement in education and started investigating ways to connect what students do in summer school classrooms with the outside world. They reasoned that the short time frame would be perfect for short-term projects connecting school to career. They hoped the PBL approach would provide a purpose for student learning and a platform for igniting teacher passion. The administrative team incorporated project-planning skills into the application and training process for the teachers they hired.

Using Buck Institute materials for support, summer school teachers launched their projects. Students designed board games, created claymation movies, analyzed data gathered while playing sports, and created public service announcements. Many discovered they were learning more content and developing more skills than in "regular" school. As one 5th grader said, "We did a project about soccer. When we did math, we would go into the gym and take shots at the goals and collect data on the accuracy. We found out which angles have the best probability of making a goal." She compared that active, student-driven learning with the worksheets she did in a typical traditional math class. On those more traditional assignments, her motivation came not from curiosity about the content but from the chance to earn stars (by getting correct answers) to be able to take part in an ice cream party.

The summer program was so successful, it inspired an educational reform movement in the district. A little over a year after the summer school experiment, the district offered two new PBL programs: one at Katherine Smith Elementary School with Aaron Brengard as principal, and another at Bulldog Tech, which became a New Tech Network middle school.

## The PBL Difference: After-School Opportunities

After-school programs play an important role. For children of working parents, access to an after-school program means a safe, supervised place to go between school and home. More than 10 million children currently participate in after-school programs, and an additional 19 million would do so if a quality program were available locally, according to a fact sheet from the Afterschool Alliance (http://www.afterschoolalliance.org/documents/National_fact_sheet_10.07.14.pdf).

Programs typically offer homework help and tutoring, with some delivering specialized programming related to sports, arts, technology, and other interests. Researchers have found that high-quality after-school programs can boost student success during the regular school day, with participants showing improved school attendance and better academic results (Durlak, Weissberg, & Pachan, 2010; Vandell, 2013).

Despite the potential benefits, after-school programs face unique challenges. After-school staff often don't have the same training as classroom teachers. Turnover is high in some programs, many of which rely on part-time staff, creating a need for ongoing professional development. Access to technology and other resources may be limited. Finding time for innovative programs can be challenging, given the many agenda items that after-school staff already juggle: students' need to switch gears after the school day, making time for kids to have a quick snack and get homework done, the need for kids who've been sitting all day to get outside and move around—all this while keeping students safe and happy during those hours between the end of school and dinnertime.

Although PBL is not yet common in after-school settings, it's gaining a foothold. Implementing high-interest projects to replace unstructured after-school hours offers a strategy to increase youth engagement and elevate program quality. PBL strongly supports three quality indicators of out-of-school-time programs: staff engagement with youth, youth engagement, and high-quality, challenging activities (Schwalm & Tylek, 2012). For after-school providers, PBL offers "a model at once structured and flexible," according to a team from Philadelphia, Pennsylvania, that's responsible for implementing PBL across some 180 program sites (see the case study on Philadelphia in the next section).

The U.S. Department of Education has developed online resources and technical assistance to encourage PBL implementation in 21st Century Community Learning Centers, which provide after-school and summer programs for thousands of school-aged children across the country. (BIE consulted on development of the PBL training module for the related You for Youth website: www.y4y.ed.gov.)

In another example, middle school students in San Francisco can choose from a variety of Project Based Learning Clubs. Run by the Sunset Neighborhood Beacon Center, clubs meet four days a week for 90 minutes and use a variety of experiential and youth development approaches in a range of subjects based on student interest. Students have followed their interests to make movies and cartoons, design websites, and learn about urban dance. All clubs emphasize technology as well as English language arts standards for writing and research, complementing the learning that happens during the regular school day.

## After-School Case Study: The Philadelphia Story

The Public Health Management Corporation (PHMC) began introducing PBL through a network of more than 180 out-of-school-time programs in 2009. Thousands of children and teens have taken part in projects after school and during summer, and staff have documented improvements in program quality since the shift to PBL (Schwalm & Tylek, 2012).

"PBL gives a bigger purpose to each day's activities," according to a staff member. The structure of PBL helps after-school staff and youth focus on a shared goal, while the flexibility allows ample room for student voice and choice in project design.

To support its network of community organizations, PHMC has customized professional development for out-of-school-time staff. After initial training on PBL essentials was provided by BIE, PHMC developed its own capacity to train and coach staff. An online platform provides additional resources and also serves as a place to archive successful projects.

Students from K–12 settings have taken part in a wide range of projects. For example, K–5 students rewrote *Alice in Wonderland* into *Alice in Philadelphia* using storyboards and images and stories from local newspapers. Students first read (or listened to) the story of Alice and watched a movie version before creating their own stories. The final presentations included acting out one of the scenes they wrote at a "Mad Hatter Party." The students prepared all aspects of the party as well, crafting invitations, costumes, and decorations. Although the topic was fun and silly, students tackled valuable literacy skills during the afternoons four days a week.

Elementary-age students at Centro Nueva Creación were aware of the garbage-strewn streets on their way to their summer program at the community center. To create cleaner places to play, children took action in a three-pronged project. First, they organized a community clean-up to get trash off the streets. Then they wrote and performed a play about recycling to inform the community about the importance of reducing waste. Lastly, they converted a patch of vacant land into a garden.

High schoolers at the Bevilacqua Community Center learned through experience about the challenges of nonprofit fundraising. A team of boys attempted to organize a social dance that was not well advertised and did not work as well as they would have liked. An all-girl team learned from that experience and planned a carnival that successfully raised money to benefit local low-income families.

Despite these and other successful projects, Philadelphia providers have had to address a variety of challenges to grow their PBL program. The following strategies have helped to support systemwide change and build a high-quality program (Schwalm & Tylek, 2012):

• *Allow time for PBL, and more.* After-school providers recognize the importance of time for traditional activities, such as homework, snacks, and physical activity. Those things will always continue to have a place in the after-school schedule, even with the shift to PBL. PHMC set an expectation for participating programs to complete a minimum number of projects during the school year (four for elementary, three for high school) but left the calendar and daily schedule up to each site to determine. Elementary students typically spend a few weeks on a project, whereas teens may spend two or more months on more in-depth projects that often take place in the context of after-school clubs.

• *Build staff capacity.* PHMC has been strategic about providing ongoing professional development and technical support for after-school programs, many of which experience high turnover among part-time staff. Project planning and management resources, customized for out-of-school-time settings, are available citywide. These supports empower programs that, individually, may lack capacity for professional development.

• *Connect PBL to existing activities.* Many providers have found room for PBL by connecting projects with existing, high-interest programs, such as arts enrichment, dance, or sports. That way projects enhance rather than compete with core programming that has made programs successful in the past.

• *Communicate with parents.* Just as parents need to understand the value of PBL during the regular school day, the same holds true in after-school settings. Communicating with parents the "why PBL" message has helped program staff overcome initial concerns that projects would cut into homework time.

As a pioneer in bringing PBL to after-school settings on a large scale, PHMC has concluded that the benefits for students outweigh the challenges of managing tight schedules, building staff buy-in, and providing ongoing training (Schwalm & Tylek, 2012).

## Time for Exploration

The open-ended nature of PBL makes it an appropriate strategy for informal education programs that aim to expand students' horizons. In such programs, students may get their first chance to explore a field such as filmmaking or digital music recording, or use construction tools or 3-D printers in a makerspace. Others may be drawn to informal learning out of a desire to be of service; service-learning projects enable students to address local or global issues that matter to them.

Innovative educator Emily Pilloton, founder of a design/build program for the regular school year called Project H, has created a summer program geared specifically for girls age 9 through 12. Camp H introduces girls to design-and-build projects as a strategy to develop their creative confidence and spark their curiosity (see http://www. projecthdesign.org/programs/camp-h/). As one participant said, "I'm a 10-year-old girl and I know how to weld. What can't I do?"

Similarly, MESA USA (MESA stands for Mathematics, Engineering, and Science Achievement) is a national program that aims to attract underrepresented youth to the STEM fields. Although some states incorporate MESA into the regular school day, most sites engage with students in after-school clubs, with teachers serving as advisors.

The key strategy for reaching "educationally disadvantaged" youth, according to MESA USA President David Coronado, is through high-interest design challenges that give students an opportunity to help others. Students test their designs in competitions before a public audience. At the start of this chapter we cited a recent example of one such challenge: design a low-cost prosthetic arm that could improve the daily life of a child in the developing world who has been injured by war or an accident.

"We know that many young people become interested in STEM because they want to help people," said Coronado in an interview with *Edutopia*. "Many of these young people [served by MESA] have overcome obstacles themselves. Now they want to contribute back to their community. We want to connect to that sentiment" (Boss, 2014b).

Self-directed learning is a cornerstone of MESA, which incorporates PBL strategies. "You learn more if you figure it out for yourself," said a student named Melissa. "This is so much better than studying for a test."

Although the focus of MESA is squarely on students, it also offers a learning opportunity for teachers. "We want to create a sandbox for teachers to interact with students in a way that's fun, engaging, with no pressure. This creates room for teachers to be inventive, too,"

Coronado said, "and hone new skills. We want them to see that they can do many of the same things during regular class time." Teachers don't need expertise in engineering. "They need to be experts in fueling curiosity, helping students ask questions and find answers. We encourage teachers to learn together with their kids" (Boss, personal communication, Aug. 4, 2014).

Although there's little research to date about PBL in informal education, we know anecdotally that such programs can be opportunities to test-drive high-interest project ideas that may eventually migrate to the regular school day. For example, *World of Warcraft in School* is a popular project developed by teachers and media specialists who wanted to explore the potential of digital gaming in the language arts curriculum. As developers explain on the *WoW in School* wiki:

> The original focus of this project was to develop a curriculum for an after school program or "club" for at-risk students at the middle and/or high school level. This program would use the game, *World of Warcraft*, as a focal point for exploring Writing/Literacy, Mathematics, Digital Citizenship, Online Safety, and would have numerous projects/lessons intended to develop 21st-Century skills. Because of the success of the first year's implementation as an after school program, the program is now being implemented as a language arts elective for middle schoolers designed to provide enrichment for students at all levels. The program is spreading, too. To date, twelve schools in the U.S. and Canada have used our materials and have joined the adventure. (http://wowinschool. pbworks.com/w/page/5268731/FrontPage)

## Opportunities for Service

Service-learning projects have strong appeal for students who are motivated to improve their local community or want to tackle global challenges. Although service-learning projects frequently take place during the regular school day and connect to core content, many students are attracted to school clubs and other informal education programs because they offer more opportunities to engage with community issues.

For example, students from a science club at Roosevelt High School in Portland, Oregon, were moved to act when they learned that the air quality of their school ranks near the bottom of all schools in the country. Students used their out-of-school time to tackle the issue as citizen-scientists, lobbyists, and activists. As part of their ambitious project, they looked into NASA's research on plants' ability to clean the air and applied it to their classrooms and beyond. They used state-of-the-art measurement technology in collaboration with university scientists to test and monitor air quality. They raised attention by putting up neighborhood signs asking, "What's in our air?" With hard data in hand, they lobbied the state legislature to call for clean-up by major air polluters. (See http://chej.org/2013/04/teachers-and-students-that-inspire/.)

Service-learning projects provide important structures for collaboration and valuable time for reflection that help students develop other skills. The National Center for Learning and Citizenship at the Education Commission of the States reports that "high-quality service-learning has a statistically significant and positive relationship with students'... acquisition of 21st century skills" (Guilfoile & Ryan, 2013). Research also suggests that service-learning projects go beyond raising individual test scores and benefit the entire community (Berg, 2011).

## Strategies for PBL in Informal Education

Although PBL offers great potential for extending learning beyond the school day, this approach is not without challenges. For successful implementation, providers are wise to pay attention to the following key strategies that are emerging from the field:

• *Build staff capacity.* By nature, informal education jobs are often part-time, temporary, and seasonal. This situation creates high turnover, which makes training and consistency difficult. In addition, some staff might not be comfortable with or interested in shifting their practice for the sake of deeper learning. Staff members need to buy into PBL for it to be effective. Their doing so requires a shift in thinking from traditional programming approaches but doesn't mean staff should forget what they do well. Many people are adept at building positive relationships with youth, planning high-interest activities, and connecting with students' interests. These capabilities offer good starting points for PBL.

High-quality professional development that emphasizes PBL as a methodology rather than a discrete set of activities is crucial and can be done through direct professional development (face-to-face, online, or a combination of the two) or by training coaches who can continue to support practitioners. Similar to introducing PBL in the regular classroom, bringing this strategy to informal education requires not only initial workshops but also ongoing support. Access to resources, regular check-ins, documentation, and sharing what works all help to sustain the shift to PBL.

• *Consider timing, duration, and continuity.* Timing is a key consideration when it comes to introducing PBL to informal learning. Some programs last six hours a day during the summer, whereas others may occupy only an hour or two after school. Student attendance may also fluctuate widely. When planning projects, staff need to carefully consider their calendar and make room for competing agenda items that parents may expect (such as snack time and homework help). They may find that regular activities—such as art or recreation time—can be integrated into projects.

• *Build on students' interests and talents.* Informal education projects may attract students from across a community, which may mean more diversity of skills, interests, and background knowledge than occurs in a typical single-grade classroom. To leverage this diversity, it's a good idea for informal education staff to inventory students' interests and skills through surveys and casual discussions. Getting to know students and finding out about what matters to them helps to build relationships and ensure that projects reflect genuine student voice and choice.

• *Build a shared framework for PBL.* Similar to implementing PBL across a school or district, it helps if all informal education staff "speak the same language" and use the same basic framework for designing projects. Programs should agree on a shared definition and vision for

PBL, use a common project-planning form, and create shared rubrics and other documents. For example, the OST PBL blog from Philadelphia's out-of-school-time programs has common forms for project planning, group task lists, and debriefing for participants, plus assessment rubrics for staff. (See http://afterschoolinphilly.weebly.com.)

• *Foster collaboration.* The ability to work with and learn from each other is just as important for providers of informal education as it is for students. Providers need to be able to work with school staff, local businesses and programs, and their colleagues in order to plan and implement high-quality PBL. If projects offer potential for academic or service-learning credit, it's important to encourage frequent and clear communication between classroom teachers and informal education providers.

• *Emphasize student voice and choice.* Without student buy-in, informal education programs are often little more than childcare. As with all forms of PBL, student voice and choice should inform the focus and scope of project design.

## A Final Thought

Speaking about after-school and summer learning programs, Milton Chen (2013) aptly describes the potential of PBL across the informal education field:

> The rise of the afterschool and summer learning movement continues to be a bright spot in the new landscape of American education. Often delivered through school-community partnerships, the programs encompassed by this movement help to engage and broaden students' experiences from their lives in school or at home. This is a distinctly American invention, fueled by the commitment and perseverance of thousands of local educators and a broad spectrum of nonprofit, public, and private partners.
>
> Some may try to rein in this innovative movement to make learning look more like that offered during a typical 20th-century school day, but that would be a move in the wrong direction in light of global, social, and economic forces prevalent in the early 21st century. The afterschool and summer learning movement is a key driver of

break-the-mold efforts to provide children with any time, any place, any path, any pace learning opportunities and is thus on the leading edge of the future of education. (p. 109)

# Conclusion

After a project's culmination, teachers and students should take some time to reflect on where they've been and what they learned. Let's do the same here. We hope that readers of this book have understood some basic messages about Gold Standard PBL.

*Teachers,* you can do PBL with all students, in all grade levels and all subject areas. The number of projects you conduct each year, their type, and their complexity can vary according to your professional judgment and your school's or district's goals. The way in which the essential project design elements explained in Chapter 2 play out can likewise vary, but including them in every project you do, to the extent appropriate, will help ensure success. Likewise, how you manage a project depends on you and your classroom; but generally speaking, the more you can turn over to students, the better. If you're new to PBL, it can be a challenge at first, but give it a shot. You'll be pleased and maybe even amazed by what your students can do!

*School and district leaders,* you play a vital role in making PBL a success in your schools. Implementing PBL across a school or a system is a serious, long-term effort. Policies, practices, and perhaps even organizational culture will all need to change. Find ways to create time for teachers to collaboratively plan, critique and revise, and reflect on their projects. All stakeholders need to support a shared vision for PBL. Shared leadership will help make a PBL effort sustainable over the long haul. Together with your teachers, staff, and community, trust that with PBL you'll be better preparing your students for fulfilling education, work, and life in the 21st century.

*To everyone who wants the best for our students*—which means everyone who's reading this—even if you're not yet sure about PBL, we hope this book has defined it clearly and persuaded you of its benefits, or at least clarified your understanding. We believe the Gold Standard outlined in these pages will help ensure that PBL remains a lasting practice in classrooms around the world.

Although our model for Gold Standard PBL is set out in this book, it is not set in stone. We hope that PBL practitioners everywhere will contribute to our thinking and help us build a shared understanding of what it means to do high-quality project based learning as it grows more widespread over the years. We can foresee many ways to promote this understanding; a Gold Standard would be useful for individual teachers, for schools and districts, and for networks and organizations, to measure, calibrate, and improve their practice. So stay tuned for updates and further discussion.

Finally, stay in touch! There are number of PBL-oriented communities you can join, along with an ever-increasing number of resources available via the Buck Institute for Education website, www.bie.org. Best wishes for you, your students, and all your Gold Standard projects to come.

# Appendix A: Project Snapshots

## Elementary School

**Farmer Appreciation Project**

**Project Type:** Design Challenge (event)
**Driving Question:** *How can we honor local farmers?*
**Grade Level and Subject:** Early elementary (K–1); literacy and social studies

Leah Obach is a 1st grade teacher at Hamiota Elementary School, which serves an agricultural community in rural Manitoba, Canada. By listening for cues from her 1st graders, Obach designed a project in which students honored the contributions of local farmers.

Obach, who has taught at both high school and elementary levels, says she was doing PBL "before I knew that's what you would call it. Projects have always been part of my teaching." She's also a veteran collaborator. Obach routinely partners on projects with kindergarten teacher Devon Caldwell, whose school is about 45 minutes away. The two met when Obach was a student teacher in Caldwell's classroom and have been collaborating ever since.

The teachers often have their classes "meet" via a Skype videoconference. The interaction gives their young learners a reason to put their speaking and listening skills to good use, while also generating project ideas. "We'll have kids talk about issues or problems that they identify. We want to know, what interests them?" Obach says.

For inspiration about PBL ideas early in the school year, the teachers invited some former students to be guest speakers on a conference call. The older students described memorable projects that had made a difference, such as adopting polar bears or campaigning for litterless lunches. Their conversation not only gave the older students a chance to reflect on their learning, but also provided an engaging entry event for Obach's and Caldwell's students to think about how they might make a difference.

The teachers noticed that their current students were keen on talking about the weather and the effect it was having on farmers. "Kids noticed that their families were feeling stressed about getting their crops harvested. We'd had a good growing season, but all that rain was interfering with the harvest. The kids could tell that farmers were having a hard time," Obach relates.

The teaching partners then prompted students to brainstorm how they might help. That activity led to a range of possible solutions. Some students suggested helping to bring in the crops themselves; others imagined holding a fund-raising event to help farm families. After voting on a variety of student-generated ideas, the classes settled on the idea of hosting a Farmer Appreciation Day.

"It's amazing how perceptive students can be when you give them the opportunity to think about things affecting their community," Obach says, "and then ask how they want to respond. This is what makes for good citizens."

Between September, when the project idea emerged, and November, when the special day took place, students engaged in a variety of learning activities. Obach had no trouble mapping learning goals to the project. "In social studies, there are a lot of curricular connections about understanding our community. For language arts, I knew we would be reading procedural texts (such as recipes) and writing invitations (to an authentic audience)." Math problem-solving strategies would prove useful in a variety of ways, as well. Says Obach, "I knew I could address these goals in a meaningful way that would give students a need to know."

Planning for Farmer Appreciation Day also offered an opportunity to emphasize teamwork. "Sometimes that takes direct modeling—here's how you sit beside someone and work on something together. This is what sharing a job looks like," Obach says. "We'll also talk about what's happening if things aren't going well. Even though students are young, they usually know if something wasn't a good teamwork move. They can reflect on what they want to do differently next time. These collaboration and teamwork skills are just as important as the content knowledge that students are learning," she adds.

As she watched students work together to plan and prepare for Farmer Appreciation Day, Obach reflected on the difference between an authentic project such as this one and the thematic teaching that's common in the elementary grades. "With a project, the day-to-day learning activities tie together naturally. Students are directing a lot of their own learning. As the teacher, you're pulling in lessons and teaching skills in an authentic way." The teacher is actively teaching and assessing throughout a project, "but it's their work—they've taken ownership of it," Obach says. "It's not you saying, 'This month we're doing a farming theme,' and then trying to get them excited about it. That initial question—*How can we honor farmers?*—is coming from students themselves. That leads to more engagement. Your whole day just fits together so well."

As part of the *Farmer Appreciation Project*, for example, Obach assessed students' procedural writing individually. Each student chose a topic, used a graphic organizer to plan, wrote a rough draft, had an editing conference with the teacher, and then made improvements before producing a final version, which combined text and illustration.

When the big day finally arrived in November, students were ready to greet their honored guests. They had decorated their classroom with posters and artwork, prepared pumpkin cookies from scratch (starting with a giant pumpkin that was donated for the occasion), produced a video, and planned musical entertainment. Guests outnumbered their young hosts almost two to one.

"It was amazing how many farmers came," Obach says. "It was meaningful to them that our students took time to think about them and why their work is important to our community." Students were equally pleased by the adults' response, which reminded Obach why having an authentic audience is so essential to high-quality PBL. "It's powerful to know that someone is seeing the good work you're doing. You're not writing a story or an invitation because the teacher asked you to. You're doing it because you want someone else to enjoy what you're creating."

**How to extend this project:**

To expand literacy connections with older students, consider having them produce a book or video documentary to raise awareness about an issue of concern in their community. Look for opportunities to incorporate service learning, too, and have students reflect about what they learn by engaging with their community.

## Powerful Communities

**Project Type:** Solving a Real-World Problem
**Driving Question:** *How might we design a more peaceful community?*
**Grade Level and Subject:** Primary/early elementary; literacy, social studies

When minor conflicts between students started to migrate from the playground into the classroom, a team of 1st grade teachers turned a problem into an opportunity for inquiry.

Teachers Beth Lopez, Glenda Forgie, and Freny Dastur are the 1st grade team at the American School of Bombay in Mumbai, India. They designed the *Powerful Communities* project to engage students' problem-solving skills and also address grade-level learning goals for social studies that focus on the role of communities.

To scaffold the inquiry experience for young learners, teachers introduced students to the process of design thinking. The design-thinking process, used in a variety of industries as well as in education, typically starts with an empathy phase: understanding a problem by studying and engaging with those most affected by it. During this phase, students made observations about conflicts they noticed in and around campus—a community in microcosm. They analyzed the data they gathered to detect patterns and pinpoint where conflicts were most likely to occur, and then shared their findings by creating graphs. Through their analysis, students were able to group problems into types, such as small problems (that students should be able to resolve themselves) and big problems (that might need help from an adult).

Literacy skills also came into play. During read-alouds, students discussed conflicts in children's literature and noted how different literary characters responded to tensions. Students put their listening and speaking skills to good use, too. For example, they interviewed their school principal and other experts about the importance of a peaceful environment for learning.

When students were ready to generate possible solutions, they used a graphic organizer to capture their thinking. Three prompts asked students to describe (in words or pictures, or both)

- Our problem is...
- Why is this a problem?
- Ideas for solving the problem

With their ideas in this shareable format, students were ready to select solutions they wanted to prototype. Among the community-improvement ideas they tested were posters to ensure a conflict-free boys' bathroom, signed community agreements for peaceful playground behavior, and solutions to issues such as teasing or not sharing. The solutions they deemed most effective were adopted across the grade level to encourage a more positive learning community.

In a final reflection about the project, teachers noted heightened engagement for both students *and* teachers (Lopez, Forgie, Dastur, & Hoffman, 2014). Benefits were long-lasting, with improved classroom culture continuing long after the project concluded. During conferences, many parents remarked that their children were even becoming better problem-solvers at home.

### How to extend this project:

Use the design-thinking process to engage students in problem solving about an issue affecting their campus. For example, they might want to focus on strategies to reduce neighborhood traffic, expand school recycling efforts, increase parent involvement, or reduce the school's carbon footprint. Incorporate data gathering and statistical analysis to increase math content and build students' informational literacy during the research phase.

## Home Sweet Home

**Project Type:** Design Challenge
**Driving Question:** *How can we design a habitat for the Detroit Zoo?*
**Grade Level and Subject:** Upper elementary (grade 4); ELA, science

When the Detroit Zoo announced plans to build a $21 million conservation center dedicated to penguins—complete with an indoor viewing area where visitors will be able to watch the aquatic birds explore underwater—teachers at Village Oaks Elementary and Deerfield Elementary in Novi, Michigan, saw an opportunity for their 4th graders to dive into their own investigation of habitats.

They designed the *Home Sweet Home* project to address specific learning goals for reading and writing, along with science. Teachers saw opportunities for technology integration, as well, by having students use iPads to research and document their investigations with photos and video.

To add authenticity to the project, teachers contacted an education expert at the Detroit Zoo. Adam Dewey wrote a detailed letter to students that became the entry document for their project. In it, he invited students to collaborate with the zoo on designing models for animal habitats. He emphasized specific design criteria, such as considerations for animal welfare, positive guest experiences, and zookeeper safety. Student teams had the opportunity to choose a species that interested them, and then design a model habitat that would meet all criteria.

Myla Lee, PBL coordinator for the Novi Community School District, was impressed by students' depth of inquiry and critical thinking in the project. "They took this to another level. They were not only thinking about predator/prey relationships, life cycles, and survival, but also about the architecture of zoo exhibits," she says. Students learned about the behind-the-scenes features of zoos that separate predators from prey and help zookeepers stay safe. "There are trenches and barriers that animals can't get over, but you can't see those as a zoo visitor."

As students developed their habitat plans, Lee could see their critical thinking and creativity getting a workout. "They started asking questions like, 'If an animal can hop this far, how high would the fence or barrier need to be?'" Some students designed exhibits with an emphasis on accessibility for visitors with disabilities. One girl added a waterfall feature to her exhibit. "She designed it to be a water-purification feature to benefit animals, but also to be aesthetically pleasing to visitors. She realized that people are attracted to exhibits that look cool," Lee says.

During the revision process, teachers and outside experts gave students critical feedback to help them improve their plans. One student's aunt, for instance, happened to have experience working at the zoo and agreed to offer constructive feedback. Teachers challenged students to be true to animals' habitat needs but also go for the "wow!" factor that would attract human attention to their exhibits. That got students thinking about the use of color, artwork, and other elements. "They started thinking like architects and interior designers," Lee says. Students wrote informational texts about their habitat designs, explaining the scientific basis for their designs and demonstrating their in-depth understanding of ecosystems.

At the culminating event, the zoo's education director came to listen to students' presentations. He asked detailed follow-up questions about the thinking behind their design decisions. Parents had a chance to watch, even if they couldn't attend in person. Teachers livestreamed the presentations via Adobe Connect. Some teams also presented their work to the school's Parent Teacher Organization. "Parents said they didn't realize how creative their own kids are," Lee says. "They could see this was out-of-the-box thinking."

(You can read a case study about Novi Community School District's approach to building teacher leadership for PBL on page 150.)

## How to extend this project:

With older students, expand career exploration opportunities by having students interview technical experts (such as architects or zoologists) about their professions. Expand math content by having students produce detailed budgets about their proposals. Integrate geography by having students analyze habitat loss in the regions where endangered zoo species are native.

# Upper Elementary/Middle School

### The One and Only Ivan Global Project

**Project Type:** Taking a Position on an Issue
**Driving Question:** *Do we have the right to capture and cage animals?*
**Grade Level and Subject:** Upper elementary/middle (5th grade); ELA, social studies

Fifth grade teacher Heidi Hutchison from Friends School of Baltimore was attending an education conference when she hit on the idea for a collaborative project. What would happen, she wondered, if students from different communities read the same novel and then, by sharing their responses, created a new book together? She imagined a digital writing project that would incorporate technology and build students' global competency while also meeting learning goals for language arts.

The provocative novel that Hutchison chose as an anchor text for the project is *The One and Only Ivan* by Katherine Applegate. It tells a fictionalized story about a captive gorilla. Inspired by a real-life story, *Ivan* provides an emotional hook for readers to think critically about complex animal rights issues.

Hutchison set up a wiki describing the project (see http://global-classroom2013-14.wikispaces.com/The+One+and+Only+Ivan+-Global+PBL). She posted her idea on a collaborative site called the Global Classroom Project and shared the link with her personal learning network. Before long, teachers from five locations had joined the project (and many more expressed an interest). Participants agreed to have their students respond to the same driving question: *Do we have the right to capture and cage animals?* They also agreed to have their students read the same novel, write research-based responses, and share their writing with a public audience. What's more, students would have the opportunity to help animal rights organizations by donating any proceeds from the sale of their collaboratively written digital book.

"I wanted to make the project grow-able," Hutchison says, "to see if other classes would be interested in answering the same driving question." She mapped out the project that reflected the Gold Standard project design framework. She also identified videos and readings that would be useful for building students' background knowledge, such as a video interview with author Katherine Applegate and *National Geographic* content about endangered wildlife. To model best practices, she documented and shared her own students' need-to-know questions as they embarked on the project.

Hutchison also drew on her prior experiences with PBL, including an earlier global project involving the rights of girls to receive an education. "I knew that a project like this [Ivan] would teach writing," she says, "but I also wanted to include digital citizenship, global citizenship, and empathy among people from different backgrounds." Students discovered there are no clear right-or-wrong answers to many of their questions about animal rights, causing them to dig deeper into research and think critically about everything from pet ownership to loss of habitat.

Within the context of the Ivan project, Hutchison found ample room to differentiate instruction based on students' needs. "Students who were only ready for simple research could write about one specific species. But those who were ready to go deeper could get into more complex issues. PBL offers a natural fit for differentiation. There's room for all students to experience success."

By spring, all participating classes had finished drafting and polishing their content—enough original material for a 250-page digital book. Hutchison's husband, an instructional technology specialist, provided technical assistance with iBooks Author.

Hutchison acknowledges that the collaborative writing process "was sometimes messy. Students were constantly revising." But students were motivated to do their best work, she adds, because they knew their digital book would reach a public audience. "Students realized that their book was going to help educate the public about an important issue. That was a huge motivator." When the book was ready to publish electronically (via the iTunes Store), students from participating classes held a Skype discussion about which organization should benefit from book proceeds. They chose the World Wildlife Fund. Teacher Robin Farnsworth, based in Utah, created a Facebook page to help publicize the collaborative effort. "Then her students decided to make up a song to promote the book. This project has taken on a life of its own," Hutchison says. "It becomes so rich when students take ownership."

## How to extend this project:

Adapt the project for older students by choosing a different work of literature as a shared reading choice. To build global competency, consider having students from different geographic locations collaborate on the same project teams via Google Hangout, Skype, or another platform for connecting across distances.

**The Cancer Project**

**Project Types:** Conducting an Investigation; Design Challenge (event)
**Driving Question:** *How can we support cancer research?*
**Grade Level and Subject:** Upper elementary/middle (5th grade); science, ELA

The study of cells took a personal turn at Dupont Hadley Middle School in Nashville, Tennessee, when a 5th grade student shared her story of being a cancer survivor. CiCi Collins was first diagnosed with a form of brain cancer at age 3. By the time she entered middle school, she had endured surgery, six rounds of chemotherapy, 12 weeks of radiation treatments, and was cancer-free.

CiCi's courageous story made the study of human biology and medical research both relevant and compelling for her classmates. Teacher Pamela Newman leveraged student interest to design a project that aligned with academic standards in science, English, and technology. Through the project, Newman wanted students to research a real problem, identify possible solutions, and share their findings with an audience of parents and other community members. CiCi and her family agreed to share their story as part of the project.

Students took on the challenge, and then some. Along with educating others, they brought visibility and financial support to those on the front lines of cancer treatment.

As the project unfolded, students conducted in-depth research into plant and animal cells. To learn more about cancer cells and how they differ from normal cells, they connected with scientists through a program at Vanderbilt University. Experts from the Vanderbilt Center for Science Outreach provided students with access to equipment such as compound light microscopes.

For the culmination of the project, the entire 5th grade teamed up to plan a fund-raiser to benefit Monroe Carell Jr. Children's Hospital in Nashville. Using math, literacy, and collaboration for a genuine purpose, students calculated necessary ingredients for a massive spaghetti dinner and invited the school community. Guests learned about cancer research and treatments by exploring the exhibits and presentations that students created, based on their research. CiCi also shared her own story.

Results: $1,300 to benefit the children's hospital, plus enduring understandings of science and compassion for students and guests alike.

**How to extend this project:**

Look for opportunities for students to educate the public about the wide range of health issues that may be affecting members of the school community. For example, students might apply their research by hosting health fairs, promoting fitness events, producing public service announcements, or offering nutritional counseling in collaboration with healthcare providers.

## Champions of Change

**Project Types:** Solving a Real-World Problem; Design Challenge

**Driving Question:** *How can we, as filmmakers, encourage our community to recycle?*

**Grade Level and Subject:** Upper elementary/middle (grades 5/6); ELA, science

Residents of Elk Grove, California, are doing a better job of recycling and reusing household materials, thanks in large part to students from Foulks Ranch Elementary School. Through a series of video projects, students have educated their community about the ins and outs of recycling.

Teacher Jim Bentley, who "loops" with the same students from 5th to 6th grades, has discovered that video projects offer a powerful way for students to develop academic understanding while also taking an active role as citizens. He began introducing filmmaking several years ago as part of social studies projects focusing on government and citizenship. He found that making movies offers students an engaging way to develop their skills as writers and critical thinkers. Students also have reason to dive deeply into content to inform their productions. Such explorations can involve traditional research—including sometimes challenging nonfiction reading—and interviews with experts.

One such expert wound up inviting Bentley's students to produce an educational video for the city's integrated waste management department. At the time, Elk Grove was preparing to open a multimillion-dollar recycling facility and needed to teach the public how to safely dispose of hazardous household materials. The program manager had been talking with students about a different project idea they had investigated, which would have involved school-based recycling centers for batteries. She couldn't give the go-ahead for that proposal because of safety concerns. Instead, she invited students to produce an educational film with the city as their client.

That invitation turned into a long-term project. Students went through rounds of script revisions and hours of filming to meet exacting city requirements for the five-minute final cut. "Sixth-graders can sometimes move faster than government," Bentley says. The project was not completed during the school year, which meant that exiting 6th graders had to hand off their project to incoming 5th graders.

"They passed the torch," Bentley says. "I started the new school year with an entry event where I shared with the class, 'Last year's students got this far [with the film]. They need you to finish it.'" The project became a legacy, he says, "something handed on from kids to kids."

The success of that project has generated more requests from the city—and more film ideas from students themselves. Bentley's students continue to produce how-to videos on recycling that are published on the city website. They have more ideas in the works for public service announcements.

Bentley continues to incorporate film projects across the curriculum. Language arts are emphasized in each production. Students often need to read and analyze complex texts for projects that involve environmental science and behavior change. Critical thinking is important when students are assessing sources for reliability and accuracy. Writing comes into play during script writing and storyboarding. "It's hard to imagine teaching reading or writing in isolation," he says. Depending on the film topic, projects may also address science, math, or social studies standards.

Teaching in a self-contained classroom, Bentley is able to structure the day with large blocks of time that are well suited to integrated projects. Working on in-depth projects "is different from trying to cover a lot of content," he says. "I find that students do more deep thinking. They're more willing to question why, to have deep wonderings. They're not like stones skipping off the surface of a lake."

That's not to say that projects always proceed smoothly. "We've had some epic fails," the teacher admits. "I tell students early in the year that this is going to be hard. We talk about grit. I tell them that some of the project ideas they will come up with might involve reading complicated stuff—content written for adults, not for 6th graders. Yet even my most struggling students tell me they prefer learning this way to reading textbooks and doing worksheets. They're willing to be frustrated," he adds, "if they get a chance to do real things. And they love that adults take them seriously."

Meanwhile, students who want to go even deeper into the technical aspects of filmmaking can continue working on projects beyond the regular school day. Bentley and his students have formed the Foulks Ranch Film Academy, which meets after school. This gives interested students time to learn about editing and special effects, leaving the regular school day for the academic side of film projects. Students publish their videos on a YouTube channel, Curiosity Films, which provides yet another audience for their work (see (https://www.youtube.com/user/CuriosityFilms?feature=mhee).

**How to extend this project:**

If you teach in a single content area, look for grade-level collaborators who are willing to team up on cross-curricular projects like this one. Help high school students see how doing projects for authentic clients can help them meet service-learning requirements.

## Systems Thinkers

**Project Type:** Solving a Real-World Problem
**Driving Question:** *What is our school's waste management system, and how can we improve it?*
**Grade Level and Subject:** Upper elementary/middle; environmental science

Nathan Mulhearn, a year 5 teacher at St. Francis College in Crestmead, Australia, wants his 10-year-old students to realize that they have the potential to be tomorrow's change agents. To put their innovation strategies to work on a real-life challenge, he designed a project to upgrade the school's outdated waste management system.

As an entry event, students took a walk around their campus and made observations. Some students noticed litter, which prompted a discussion about the location of trash bins. When Mulhearn introduced the phrase "waste management system," students wondered what that meant. And so their investigation began.

Students took on the driving question, *What is our school's waste management system, and how can we improve it?* For Mulhearn, this question met several requirements: it addressed content standards in science and geography; it integrated 21st century competencies, including innovation and creativity; and it involved an authentic purpose and audience because the school was committed to upgrading its waste management system.

Working in teams, students began researching the current state of waste on their campus. They collected data about the amount of trash sent to the landfill daily and also investigated global waste issues. Then they expanded their research to learn about sustainability strategies that could reduce solid waste. A Skype call connected them with a sustainability expert from the United States.

Ready to apply their understanding, student teams moved into the idea-generation stage. Mulhearn and his teaching partner, Belinda Ciuffetelli, encouraged students to think critically and creatively about potential solutions. To encourage iterative rounds of testing and improving on ideas, teachers reminded students that commercially successful products such as the iPhone have gone through multiple versions. "They didn't get it perfect the first time," Mulhearn says.

With 56 students in their two classes, the teachers found tools like Google Docs helpful to keep the project organized and also to capture students' reflections throughout the project. When students were actively working on the project, the teachers opened a moveable wall between their classrooms to encourage real-time collaboration.

Students presented their proposed solutions to two rounds of audiences: first, to peers and teachers; next, to parents and school administrators at a celebration of learning. Students fielded a range of questions. They explained how they had arrived at their ideas, how specific ideas could be implemented, and how much their proposed solutions might cost to implement.

Mulhearn says the project was meaningful to students and fulfilled an educational purpose. At the end, there was no doubt in students' minds that they were tackling an authentic issue. The parent committee agreed to fund a new waste management system for the school.

**How to extend this project:**

Be on the alert for initiatives that have to do with the physical plant of your school and leverage the learning potential of future construction projects. For example, if your school is updating its heating system, have students investigate the potential for solar panels or other alternative energy sources. Worthy project ideas don't have to involve major expenditures. A geometry class, for example, might suggest how to restripe the parking lot to minimize the potential for fender benders. Elementary students might use words and pictures to document change over time of a construction project.

## House Hunters

**Project Type:** Design Challenge
**Driving Question:** *How can we, as mathematicians, calculate the materials needed for renovating a house?*
**Grade Level and Subject:** Middle school (grade 7); geometry, pre-algebra

Rosine Borello and Jennifer Lee team-teach 7th grade math at Bulldog Tech Middle School in San Jose, California. Their content is defined by the Common Core State Standards (indeed, their class was recently renamed Common Core Math 7). Yet these teachers find plenty of flexibility by designing projects with authentic problem solving in mind.

Their students have come to expect math class to relate to their lives, whether that means modifying a recipe or balancing a budget. Says Borello, "We never have students asking us, 'Why do we need to learn this?' We link everything we do to careers, to life skills, and to problems that they will have to solve in their lives. We hear them discussing math as if they are mini-architects, engineers, or chefs. It's exhilarating."

Renovating a home is one such problem their students have tackled through the lens of mathematics. Inspired by a friend who was featured on the television series *House Hunters*, they designed a project to calculate household renovations on a budget. Their friend, who happens to work at Google, provided an authentic public audience for students' final presentations (and also shared career insights from the tech sector).

For the project, student teams were tasked with preparing a blueprint and performing a series of calculations. Students took on different responsibilities, as if they were subcontractors bidding on a job. For instance, students assigned to install baseboards throughout the home had to calculate the perimeter of all rooms in linear feet. Those in charge of kitchen remodeling had to figure out the volume of cabinets that they planned to install. The painters had to accurately calculate the area of exterior and interior walls, allowing for window openings. "We taught everything—perimeter, area, volume—through the design of a home," Lee says. Each subcontractor prepared a separate bid and then collaborated with team members to write an overall project budget that had to stay within specific constraints.

The *House Hunters* project lasted several weeks and included a culminating presentation to a panel. The teachers alternate full-blown PBL with shorter-term problems, which may last for just a few days and usually don't involve an audience. For example, problems have focused on comparing the fuel efficiency of teachers' cars or modifying a favorite recipe to feed a crowd.

Regardless of scope, the day-to-day learning experience feels consistent. "We use problems to drive our curriculum," Borello explains. In longer projects, those problems all relate to the same driving question. "Longer projects are made up of a series of smaller, related problems."

The math teachers collaborate to design projects, following popular bloggers like Dan Meyer and Geoff Krall for inspiration (see http://blog.mrmeyer.com and http://emergentmath.com). They also work closely with the language arts team at their school. "We look to language arts teachers to help us scaffold the writing tasks in math," Lee says. "By working together, and also bringing in outside experts when we can, we try to make projects as rich as possible." Reimagining math with a PBL focus takes time, "but when you see students excited to be learning math, it's worth every bit of effort," says Borello.

### How to extend this project:

Adapt the *House Hunters* idea for high school students by incorporating an analysis of housing prices in specific neighborhoods and recommending which remodeling "fixes" would add the most value to a home. Or consider adding energy efficiency requirements to the remodeling task and having students calculate how long investments would take to pay off. Integrate technology by asking students to develop 3-D models of their design proposals, or challenge them to think bigger and redesign an entire neighborhood around specific constraints.

## Civil War Technologies

**Project Type:** Conducting an Investigation
**Driving Question:** *How did your technology change the Civil War?*
**Grade Level and Subject:** Middle (grade 8); U.S. history

History teachers Jody Passanisi and Shara Peters want their 8th graders to remember more than the key battles of the Civil War. "To me, what's important about the Civil War is how it has shaped the American psyche and culture. That might be a little much for 8th graders," says Passanisi, "but they can see how things that happened during the Civil War still matter today."

That's why these teaching and writing partners (known on social media as @21centuryteachr and on MiddleWeb as Jody&Shara) designed a project in which students trace the lasting effect of Civil War technologies. "Technology is tangible. Students can see the reverberations through time," says Passanisi. What's more, adds Peters, "Our kids are living in an age when things are invented every day. They appreciate how a technology can impact life. That's not a foreign concept to them."

To launch the Civil War project, which they have taught multiple times, the teachers have students make connections between today's technologies and inventions of the past. "We might have them brainstorm technologies that are used for war and defense today. They do a quick-write about the role of technology in war," explains Peters. Teachers also share a video clip from the History Channel's *Modern Marvels*, showing examples of diverse technologies that debuted during the Civil War. "They start to see that there are many ways of looking at war through the technology theme," Passanisi says.

The entry event sets the stage for teachers to introduce this driving question: *How did your technology change the Civil War?* As they begin the inquiry process, students form project teams based on shared interests, such as technologies relating to medicine, communication, transportation, or even food. "We added food as a category this year [spring 2014]," Passanisi says, "and that was very popular." Students were surprised to learn that tin cans—the precursor to today's meals ready to eat, or MREs—were among the innovations that kept soldiers nourished during the Civil War.

Students are expected to research their topic and reference both primary and secondary sources. As a culminating product, each team produces an artifact that represents its chosen technology. Teams present their work to an audience of peers, teaching each other jigsaw-style about the various influences of Civil War technologies. Students have wide latitude to determine their final product, but all teams are assessed by the same rubric. "They might choose to make a model of a ship or write a song or build a working telegraph," says Peters, "but whatever form their product takes, it needs to be beautiful, thoughtful, shareable, and relate to enduring understanding."

Advances in contemporary technologies have affected how students interpret the past. As students have gained access to tools such as Tinkercad and MakerBot, they've used 3-D printing to build mini-replicas of Civil War weaponry and warships. One team constructed its own working telegraph, capable of transmitting messages from classroom to classroom. That team impressed Passinisi with its grit—its capacity to overcome obstacles en route to success. Their experience is a good reminder that allowing time for iterative rounds of feedback and revision, learning through trial and error, is important in project design that emphasizes creativity and innovation.

Passanisi and Peters credit two educators for shaping their approach to PBL. Ron Berger, author of *An Ethic of Excellence* (2003), has been a key influence by encouraging projects that result in "beautiful work." Gary Stager, author and education consultant, helped to deepen their understanding of PBL during a workshop he led several years ago.

For Passanisi, a decade into her teaching career, the gradual shift to PBL has been a natural evolution. "When I began teaching, my main focus was constructivism. Back then, 'projects' weren't taken seriously. As I've learned more about PBL, I've found that it's very different from an activity. PBL provides a way to actualize constructivism. It provides a focus for student-driven learning," she says. "We're not telling students, "Here are the important things that happened during the Civil War. 'Instead, we're allowing for student discovery [of key knowledge and understanding]."

It's no accident that Peters shares a similar outlook. She did her student teaching in Passanisi's classroom. The two educators have been collaborating and stretching each other's thinking ever since. (Until recently, both taught at the same independent school in Southern California. Peters recently moved to a new job, but they plan to continue teaming up on projects.) Since her teacher-prep days, Peters says she has been drawn to many of the hallmarks of Gold Standard PBL, such as authenticity, critique and revision, and student-driven inquiry. "For me, those tenets were there from the beginning of forming my teacher identity."

The teaching team has used the same Civil War project idea multiple times, revising and updating it each year. "It gets better each time we do it," says Peters. The last time they did the project, several students used Twitter to connect with Civil War experts. The teachers hope to expand on the use of social media in the future and also are thinking about connecting their students with a wider audience through online publishing.

One recent modification has been adding more scaffolding to help students manage their learning. Passanisi has devised a simple checklist, for instance, to remind students of the process steps, from research and source evaluation to product development to crafting a presentation. She acknowledges a tension between "giving students parameters and guidelines, but not thwarting their creativity. I'm always trying to manage that tension between how slack, how taut in terms of autonomy." Simple project tools, such as due dates for milestone assignments, help students manage their own learning. "It's awesome to see them take charge of their own time. With the right scaffolding, they know they're in charge, but they also know what they need to do."

Passanisi is intentional about providing students with a wide range of learning experiences, not all of which are PBL. The unit before the technology project is a more traditional study of the causes of the Civil War. That builds students' background knowledge. By the time they move into the technology unit, she says, "they have some historical context. They're ready for this, and confident."

**How to extend this project:**

Connect the theme of technology's changing role to a wide range of other content areas, such as human geography, science, literature, or media literacy.

# High School

### Freedom Fighters Project

**Project Types:** Exploring an Abstract Question; Design Challenge
**Driving Question:** *How can we honor community members who stand up for justice?*
**Grade Level and Subject:** High school; humanities (interdisciplinary, ELA and history)

A student named Julio from Roosevelt High in Portland, Oregon, started his freshman year doing a project "as a class requirement I wasn't so excited about. By the end, it changed my life and opened my world" (Boss, 2014a).

Julio was describing the *Freedom Fighters Project*, which has become a tradition at his diverse urban school (see http://rooseveltroughwriters .org/our-programs/freedom-fighters-project/). An interdisciplinary humanities project, it challenges students to uncover stories of individuals in their community who have taken a stand for social justice. Students interview these unsung heroes, write essays about them, and compile their best work into a book. In the process, they hone their writing skills and learn about the history of the civil rights movement. Then they create museum-quality exhibits that they take into the community, sparking conversations about sometimes difficult topics and putting their communication skills to effective use.

The *Freedom Fighters Project* began as a summer writing experience to amplify student voice in the community. Two 9th grade teachers—history teacher George Bishop and English teacher Shawn Swanson—have taken up the *Freedom Fighters Project* in the humanities class that they teach together. They started with 90 students in 2012 and had 120 freshmen participate in the project a year later.

"I found a home for this project within the Common Core State Standards," Swanson explains. Students gain experience gathering information as they prepare to conduct interviews and put informational writing skills to use as they craft and revise essays.

The project doesn't stop there. "Students were inspired by the stories they heard, but inspiration isn't enough," Swanson explains. "I told them, 'You guys need to be the next Freedom Fighters.'" As the final phase of the project, he has students "pick an issue close to your hearts and write a speech about it." In the process, they learn to make compelling arguments and back up their words with evidence.

Julio, for example, wrote a powerful speech about immigration and race, which he has delivered to large community audiences. He was inspired by the Freedom Fighter he profiled, a local nonprofit leader who promotes intercultural communication and helps immigrant families understand their rights.

Julio not only found his confidence as a public speaker but also gained insights that will last long beyond his freshman year. Issues about immigration, race, and the achievement gap are complicated, he admits, "but it got simpler for me. I have a clearer view now. I have a better understanding of why things happen—cause and effect. I can see others' points of view. I understand what I'm doing, where I'm going."

Projects that emphasize service learning naturally encourage reflection. A student named Leticia, for instance, reflected on her own young life when she interviewed a community leader. The woman told Leticia that she was homeless during much of her childhood but managed to find her purpose in helping others. That resonated with Leticia, who has six younger siblings. "I try to guide them, to inspire them. I want the best for them," she says. Because students wanted to do justice to the stories they hear, they invested "so much time and effort," adds a student named Hannah. "This isn't like reading a textbook and taking notes. It's real life."

Having an authentic audience for their work has been key to the success of the *Freedom Fighters Project*. Since the project began, more than 3,000 people have seen the Freedom Fighter exhibits at settings ranging from the state historical society to churches to college campuses. That exposure gives the project visibility and helps to sustain it. Community members who have been recognized as Freedom Fighters have become supporters of the project, nominating others whose stories are worth telling and building stronger connections between school and community.

**How to extend this project:**

Look for opportunities to connect speaking and writing skills across the curriculum. For example, have your students present their scientific research to a public audience or produce a museum-style exhibit to educate community members about an issue they've investigated. Adapt the project for younger students or English learners by scaffolding the research process with suggested question starters or interviewing guidelines.

**Up to Par**

**Project Type:** Design Challenge

**Driving Question:** *How can we use geometry to design a challenging miniature golf course?*

**Grade Level and Subject:** High school; geometry, technology integration

At an indoor miniature golf course not far from Tech Valley High School in Rensselaer, New York, freshmen and sophomores walked the artificial greens with tape measures and protractors in hand. As they attempted various shots to maneuver golf balls over bridges and around obstacles, they paid attention to what was happening—mathematically speaking—when they attempted bank shots or double-bank shots. This was their entry event for a project in which they were asked to apply their understanding of geometry to design a challenging miniature golf course.

Math teacher Jason Irwin, a career-changer from engineering, regularly designs projects that help students make connections between math concepts and real-world applications. Those connections were hard to miss when students were asked to come up with their own miniature golf designs. To add authenticity to the challenge, the golf course owner took on the role of client. "He told them he's had the same basic golf course for 25 years. He wants some new designs to attract business," Irwin says. At the end of the project, students would be pitching their designs to him.

Back in class, Irwin and his students discussed the project in more detail and together developed a problem statement. In student language, the problem statement defines the role that students are taking on (in this case, mini–golf course designer) and the purpose for the assignment ("to help our client, the golf course owner, create great experiences for customers"). "It defines the what and the why of the project," Irwin explains. The teacher also shared his own driving question for the project, which focused clearly on math content goals: *How can we design a miniature golf course that incorporates the properties of triangles and transformations?*

Next, Irwin invited students to suggest possible golf course themes and then grouped them in teams based on common interests. As part of his team management, Irwin has students draw up team contracts that spell out norms and expectations. He also asks them to identify who will take on specific roles related to collaboration. For example, he typically asks one student to be the accountability manager, tracking process and time line, and another to manage documents and team organization. "These collaboration roles help ensure that team members are following the process and staying organized," he says.

Working through the design process, students started generating and sketching rough ideas. They critiqued each other's concepts and made several rounds of improvements. Because Irwin wanted to emphasize specific math concepts, he required students to make their first designs by hand. "Using graph paper leads to content in geometry that I need them to acquire," he explains.

Technology tools enabled them to move into 3-D design. Some students used SketchUp, while those with more technical fluency used computer-assisted design (CAD) software.

The project allowed ample room for creativity, along with specific math content. Students incorporated special effects to make their designs more appealing to specific audiences. One team, for instance, went with a Candyland theme, appealing to younger mini-golfers, while others pursued more futuristic or jungle-themed designs to attract different demographics. At the end of the project, students e-mailed their final designs in presentation format, along with a persuasive pitch letter, to the golf course owner.

The miniature golf design project is one that Irwin has used multiple times, but each year with a different community partner. Some golf course owners come to Tech Valley to hear pitches, and others prefer to review proposals in writing. "Every year is different," Irwin says, "with new ideas from students' creativity."

## How to extend this project:

Incorporate additional math content by having students calculate proposed costs of implementing their designs, projecting how much business would have to increase to pay for the remodel, or calculating different options for financing the improvements. If you have access to a makerspace or work area for making prototypes, have students produce 3-D models to scale.

## Global Happiness, Local Action

**Project Types:** Exploring an Abstract Question; Conducting an Investigation; Design Challenge

**Driving Question:** *How can we use data, creativity, and community to make the world a happier place?*

**Grade Level and Subject:** High school; English, digital media, social studies

English teacher Valerie Hoover was looking for a way to connect her students' reading of the classic American play *Our Town* with community service in their own hometown of Rochester, Indiana. Then she heard about the *Global Happiness Project*, an exploration of happiness that incorporates statistics, global awareness, and creative problem solving. "This became our springboard," she says, for a project that integrated literature study, digital media, and community service.

Hoover planned the project in collaboration with Rachel Haselby, who teaches digital media. They team up to teach a course called Digital Communication (better known as DigiCom) at Rochester High.

The *Global Happiness Project*, designed by the New Tech Network, took place during the 2013–14 school year. It engaged more than 200 classrooms from around the globe in answering this driving question: *How can we use data, creativity, and community to make the world a happier place?* The loosely structured project provides a framework of questions about happiness, along with resources to support students' investigations. It's left to each teacher, however, to determine how the project will meet specific learning goals and connect with students' interests.

Hoover set the stage for the project by having her students take a survey about happiness that was designed specifically for the *Global Happiness Project*. "Our kids took that survey right before spring break. When we all came back, we used the statistics [from the global survey results] to start our project." Results from around the world were compiled using an online platform for data analysis called Tuva Labs, which enabled Hoover's students to examine statistics by geographies, age levels, and other factors. They also were able to look at results for only their community. "We had class discussions and did some journaling about the differences in how people responded [to questions about happiness]. That brought the topic of happiness home," Hoover says.

Hoover organized the project in three phases: Defining Happiness, Connecting to the Community, and Giving Back.

*Defining Happiness.* The survey provided a natural entry point for having students define happiness. They also watched a documentary called *Happy*, exploring the science of happiness. Then, in readers' theater style, students read *Our Town* and analyzed playwright Thornton Wilder's take on happiness.

As a result of their research and literature study, Hoover says, students decided to focus their next steps on three factors that relate to happiness: to live in the moment, to give back, and to connect to your community. Their driving question for the project was a direct quote from the *Our Town* character named Emily. In the third act, she asks, "Do any human beings ever realize life while they live it?—every, every minute?"

*Connecting to the Community.* Rochester, like fictional Grover's Corners where *Our Town* is set, is a small town. "Students realized that if they were going to connect to their community, they needed to learn more about it," Hoover says. "Many students have lived here their whole lives but don't really know the history of the place. And it's a cool little town."

Students chose a place, a person, or an episode in history that interested them and then wrote short nonfiction narratives. Students went through the writer's workshop process, improving their essays. "They wanted their writing to be perfect," Hoover says, because the essays were intended for a public audience. Students posted their polished essays to their class website, along with photos, and then created QR codes that linked to each entry. Students then wrote a letter to each location they had written about, explaining the project and asking recipients to display the QR codes. "When people go around town, they can scan these codes and learn more about this place and what it used to be like," Hoover explains. Students produced about 60 essays, focusing on everything from the historic courthouse with lions carved from stone to forgotten graveyards to sites where the circus used to come to town.

*Giving Back.* Hoover says she stretched her own goals with PBL by asking students to choose a local community action for the final phase of the project. "I've never done anything quite so open-ended," she says. "There were no parameters of what they could do. I even left the group size up to them. Once they chose a community action, they would need to figure out how many people it would take to complete."

Student response exceeded the teacher's expectations. "They came up with the best ideas ever!" Six boys who were involved in 4-H activities decided to paint the horse barn at the county fairgrounds. Two students teamed up to clean up a local park. Others made presentations at the local elementary school on topics such as how to prevent bullying. One team, inspired by a TED talk, made a "Before I Die" board (see http://www.ted.com/talks/candy_chang_before_i_die_i_want_to). It's a place where community members can post their wishes for the city. It's posted at the school football field, a popular gathering spot. To encourage reflection about their service efforts, Hoover had students create photo journals to document their local action.

Although the project was ambitious, it took only about three weeks of actual class time, Hoover estimates. Community service was done during out-of-class time.

Now several years into teaching with PBL, Hoover says she has gotten more comfortable with meeting learning goals through engaging projects. "That was the hardest thing for me, as an English teacher, when I started doing PBL," she admits. "I realized that you don't have to change everything you did before." When students were reading *Our Town*, for example, she had them answer reading comprehension questions and gave a test at the end. "You can still incorporate a lot of traditional elements in PBL."

The benefit of teaching English via projects, she says, is that students "gain a deeper understanding of literature than they would just by answering my questions. I get more participation in the literature than I used to, because students can see that it's connected to the project."

In this project, students also got to participate in a global exploration of an interesting subject. Students from around the world who took part in the *Global Happiness Project* all tweeted out their reflections and insights on the same day.

**How to extend this project:**

Connect with a math teacher to expand on the opportunities for data gathering and statistical analysis in this project. For younger students, choose an appropriate literature selection that explores themes of happiness.

**An American Student in France (Un Lycéen Américain en France)**

**Project Type:** Design Challenge

**Driving Question:** *How can Nicolas and his friends help an American exchange student to their school integrate into their community and to French culture in general?*

**Grade Level and Subject:** High school; French language and culture, filmmaking

In his World Languages classes at Vintage High School in Napa, California, teacher Don Doehla looks for opportunities to create rich project experiences for language learners of all levels. When students are in the early years of language acquisition, projects are relatively brief by design. Nonetheless, Doehla wants even short-term projects to involve inquiry and reach an authentic audience. Novice speakers, for instance, might create a story in words and photographs that teaches others about life in a French-speaking country. They might design a menu for a restaurant that preserves the culinary heritage of a Francophone country of their choice and then share their work on a public website.

By the time students are in Year 3, they're ready for more extended inquiry experiences that require them to communicate almost exclusively in the target language. One example is a filmmaking project called *Un Lycéen Américain en France* (*An American Student in France*).

Doehla launches the project by presenting students with a request to produce a film about a popular French literary character, *Le Petit Nicolas*. In the *Nicolas* stories, the title character is a young boy. The challenge (purportedly from the book publisher) is to imagine him as a teenager. Students are asked to create a script and a film that portray Nicolas and his friends in high school.

Students start the inquiry process by considering their need to know questions in response to this driving question: *How can Nicolas and his friends help an American exchange student to their lycée (equivalent to an American high school) integrate into their community and to French culture in general?* The question is carefully worded, prompting students to think critically as they compare and contrast French and American teen cultures.

Working in teams of four, students take on the role of movie producers. They consult the *Nicolas* stories as source material, then put their own creativity to work developing characters and plot twists. Drawing on the rich tradition of French filmmaking, they make choices about shot selections and how to balance narration with dialogue. Research comes into play when they choose a specific French city as the setting and produce a storyboard that sets their idea against authentic landmarks. Through the critique-and-revision process, students improve their scripts and prepare for filming.

The project culminates with a public screening, to which students' families and members of the local French-speaking community are invited. There's also an online audience for the short films, which typically run about 8 to 10 minutes. Doehla has connected with French-speaking partner schools in Martinique, Marseille, and Paris, France, and students in those locations have the opportunity to view and critique the productions online.

Throughout the project, students collaborate and communicate nearly exclusively in the target language. They use Google Docs for collaborative writing and editing, and use French for nearly all team discussions. Doehla says students have enough technology fluency from previous projects so that very little class time is spent teaching the technical aspects of filmmaking. "Some students use their phones to shoot. Others have iMovie experience. Figuring out how to make the movie is part of their inquiry experience," the teacher explains. If students need specific instruction on video production, Doehla provides them with minilessons.

Doehla takes a multifaceted approach to assessment to ensure that he's tracking students' growth as speakers and writers of the French language. For example, along with the team assessment of the final film, students take part in an individual performance assessment that mimics a talk show. Students play the role of one of the characters in their film as they engage in an unscripted conversation. In another individual assessment, students respond to a prompt and write a letter or an e-mail response from one character to another.

Students are involved in their own assessment through peer and self-assessments. Doehla takes a creative approach to assessing the key success skill of critical thinking. As he explains, "I don't necessarily assess all criteria on the critical-thinking rubric. I give my students the complete rubric so they can see what critical thinking entails, and as we progress, we make a decision together about which two of the six criteria are of most interest to them, and those become the ones I assess with their help."

**How to extend this project:**

For similar projects in other languages, choose an appropriate literature selection that reflects the target language and culture. If students are not familiar with making videos, consider alternative ways for them to demonstrate understanding and use dialogue for a purpose, such as producing comic books.

## Sweet Solutions

**Project Types:** Conducting an Investigation; Design Challenge
**Driving Question:** *How can I use my understanding of chemistry to make hard tack candy?*
**Grade Level and Subject:** High school; chemistry

A team of teachers from Newberg High School in Newberg, Oregon, formed a professional learning community to support each other's explorations of project based learning during the 2013–14 school year. For veteran chemistry teacher Luann Lee, this was the opportunity she had been looking for to extend science inquiry labs into "a more open-ended adventure for students."

As her first project, she revised a traditionally popular lab activity—making hard tack candy—into a project. "This seemed like a good opportunity for students to see the real-world application of chemistry concepts," she says. She also hoped that, by taking something familiar and allowing themselves a little creativity, "students would have more confidence when we tackled more challenging work."

When she had done candy-making labs in the past, the learning experience was limited. "We used to simply hand students a recipe and let them bring sugar and flavoring to make candy. It was fun, but we would observe phenomena during the process of making the candy and generate questions that never quite got answered." Reconsidered as a project, candy making became a way for students to investigate the science of solutions as well as careers in chemistry.

Lee's overarching question for the project was broad: How can I use my experience in chemistry to learn to think and communicate clearly, logically, and critically in preparation for college and a career? More narrowly, she also wanted students to be able to demonstrate: *How can I use my understanding of chemistry to make hard tack candy?*

To encourage students to reflect on their learning throughout the project, Lee had them write a series of blog posts. Blogging was new for most students, although some had experience creating photo blogs for a photography class. "They quickly became our resident experts," she says. Specific assignments for blogs focused on students' preliminary research about solutions and solubility, candy making as data collection, and application of the science of solutions to other authentic situations. To encourage student voice in the project, Lee had students decide on the criteria for evaluating their posts.

To build student understanding of chemistry, Lee planned a series of learning activities related to solutions and solubility. For example, students modeled the solution process, graphed solubility of different ionic and molecular compounds at different temperatures, and used diagrams and modeling to explain unsaturated, saturated, and supersaturated solutions.

These activities led up to the day when students actually made hard tack candy, using Bunsen burners and other lab equipment. Instead of simply following a recipe, as they had done in the past, this time students approached the activity as food scientists would, making observations, gathering data, and justifying their results. "Safety issues are huge," Lee adds, and students also knew that they had to gear up with chemical splash goggles and lab aprons.

Because the project finale happened just before the winter break, students had the chance to take their product home as a holiday gift and share their candy-making experience with an authentic audience.

If Lee repeats the project in the future, she can imagine adding an entrepreneurship angle and having students market their wares for a holiday fair. Already, she's sold on the benefits of "showing students how chemistry relates to real life. We've done candy making for years," she adds, "but never with such a deliberate focus on connecting it to the science of solutions."

## How to extend this project:

Follow Lee's suggestion and add an entrepreneurship angle. Have students develop business plans for marketing their hard tack candy at a holiday fair. Have students interview a professional candy maker or other food scientists about the role of chemistry in their work.

**Reimagine South Central**

**Project Types:** Solving a Real-World Problem; Design Challenge
**Driving Question:** *How can we work together to reimagine our South Central (Los Angeles) neighborhood?*
**Grade Level and Subject:** High school; geography, digital gaming

What should the future look like for South Central Los Angeles, a 50-square-mile swath of Southern California? High school students from the Critical Design and Gaming School, part of Augustus Hawkins High School, are helping to answer this question through a project called *Reimagine South Central*.

During spring of the 2013–14 school year, 9th grade geography students used a digital gaming and strategic-planning platform called Community PlanIt to spark conversations, invite diverse perspectives, and start stakeholder dialogues about everything from land use to health care access to socially responsible enterprises.

For teacher Mark Gomez, the game-based project offered an opportunity for his students "to get a new understanding of what geography is. It's not just memorizing state capitals. Many students came away from this project with a deeper sense of the importance of geographic inquiry." They made and analyzed maps, for example, as part of their data analysis. They discovered that their community has no single identity. Some residents described their urban neighborhood as active, energetic, creative, and educational; others said they consider it dangerous, densely populated, and challenging.

Students also gained an introduction to the field of "serious games," in which game strategies focus on real-world issues and problem solving. "We're a game-design school, so it makes sense for our students to be designing their own games [as part of learning]," Gomez says. "Through the lens of serious games, they saw the uses that gaming can serve besides entertainment. They also understood that even a serious game has to have elements of fun." That meant thinking critically about what makes for a quality gaming experience.

For this project, students collaborated with game designers from the Engagement Lab at Emerson College in Boston, Massachusetts. These experts use games to design and research playful approaches to civic engagement. Gomez's students worked with them to customize Community PlanIt to invite residents of South Central LA into a conversation about their future.

Students were responsible for much of the content that players would see. "They came up with the challenge questions, themes, and media for the online game," Gomez explains. Students' contributions focused squarely on the driving question: *How can we work together to reimagine our South Central (Los Angeles) neighborhood?* As students investigated that question, they had a number of related need-to-know questions; for example, What is a healthy community? What's in the way of making South Central healthier? What's helping?

Meanwhile, game experts in Boston worked on the back end of the technology, programming the online platform where players could respond to challenge questions. Students and their Boston counterparts used collaborative tools such as Google Docs to communicate throughout the game design process. That connection to experts added to the relevance of the project. "Students knew that their work mattered beyond getting a grade," Gomez says.

Once the game was ready to launch, students were charged with recruiting diverse stakeholders to play. "It fell on them to promote the game beyond the walls of the classroom," Gomez says. Students produced flyers and extended personal invitations to church groups, clubs, friends from their previous schools, and other networks in the community.

For the three weeks that the game was live, students also took part as players. They responded creatively to game prompts (or "missions," in game lingo), such as, What's good about your 'hood? How does where you live affect how you live? How can we reclaim the corner stores? How do you cope? Where do you go for help?

"Once they started playing the game, students got a sense of what we had created," Gomez says. The game also afforded a novel way to gather survey data. "This was more engaging for them than writing survey questions in a Word doc. It was all done through the lens of the game."

Students will get a chance to return to the game when they take 10th grade World History, which Gomez also teaches. "We'll have a public event where we'll honor the players. Then we'll analyze the data and use it for action-based community projects," Gomez says. Games that quickly generate quantities of data have great potential for learning, he adds. "It can be hard to get kids out of hasty generalizations. They need to learn how to analyze data and make decisions based on that analysis. But that can take time," especially the data-gathering part. Using games to gather data "means we can spend more time on the analysis and action piece" and leverage their talents to make their community into the place they imagine.

**How to extend this project:**

With younger students, consider reframing the project as the design of a board game about communities. Incorporate literacy with age-appropriate reading selections that tell the stories of specific neighborhoods or communities.

**The Home Ownership Project**

**Project Type:** Conducting an Investigation

**Driving Question:** *What is the process of owning a home, and what are the economic and social barriers that prevent many from pursuing home ownership?*

**Grade Level and Subject:** High school (grade 12); economics, personal finance

For many families living in the neighborhood near Maplewood High School in Nashville, Tennessee, home ownership feels like an impossible dream. Teacher Danette McMillian wants to change that perception. "I have a personal interest in building wealth through home ownership," says McMillian, who teaches in the school's Academy of Business and Consumer Services. "Many people who live in this area don't know there is a correlation between the cycle of poverty and renting your home. They aren't aware what home ownership can do for your life."

That's why she designed *The Home Ownership Project* for her 12th grade economics students.

The project started to take shape during a weeklong externship that McMillian spent at Fifth Street Bank. Teacher externships are among the strategies that Metropolitan Nashville Public Schools uses to build partnerships between school and community. (You can read a case study about the district's PBL leadership on pages 155–157.) "My big idea was to help people see that home ownership is actually possible," McMillian says. "And I thought, why not have a group of students find out what you need to do to get a house?"

As an entry event, students pitched in on the construction site of a Habitat for Humanity home being built for a recent graduate of their high school. The occupant would be the first in her family to own a home. Her success story grabbed students' interest. The young woman agreed to come back to the high school to share her story and insights about personal finance.

After the entry event, McMillian introduced her driving question for the project: *What is the process of owning a home, and what are the economic and social barriers that prevent many from pursuing home ownership?* That got students asking more need-to-know questions, such as, "What can we do to spread awareness and encourage home ownership in our neighborhood?"

Their questions set the stage for research and analysis of economic trends related to housing and interest rates. Students also surveyed classmates to gather data about home ownership versus rental rates in their local community. For some, the topic got personal. "Some students went home and asked their families hard questions. They wanted to know, 'Why don't we own our home?'" the teacher said. When students realized that families may struggle with poor credit scores because of a lack of information, they were motivated to share what they were learning. "I realized, I'm teaching the kids, and the kids are teaching the parents!" McMillian says.

As the next phase of the project, students organized community education events. Staff from Fifth Street Bank agreed to take part in an open-house event for the community, and the Habitat for Humanity client shared her insights about home ownership.

To apply what they were learning, students also went through a simulation of buying a home. McMillian had them fill out loan applications, based on the projected income they would earn in the careers they planned to pursue. Students met with loan officers at Fifth Street Bank and went through the entire approval process.

Once students had loans pre-approved, "we were ready to go house shopping," McMillian says. She enlisted a real estate agent to work with students on selecting homes within their budgets. Students went through the entire sales process, learning about additional factors such as closing costs, amortization, and insurance. McMillian was able to connect the project with what students were learning in math. "There were good cross-curricular connections between math and economics." Students also produced a video to document the learning that happened throughout the three-week project.

"I like projects that have the potential to change students' lives," McMillian says. "It's real-world. When they graduate, they can look back and say, 'Now I understand how to do certain things because of a project I did in high school.'" Especially for students growing up in high-poverty neighborhoods, she adds, PBL experiences can connect them with experts and learning experiences they might otherwise miss. "I like the idea of PBL changing lives."

McMillian started teaching in 2004, then took two years away from the classroom to consult on a service-learning initiative. When she returned to teaching in 2008, she was quick to embrace PBL. Two of the elements that she considers key for deep learning are reflection and having a public audience for student work. "Those pieces are often missing from 'projects,'" she says, "but they're essential for PBL."

### How to extend this project:

Look for opportunities for students to provide relevant community education in other applications of economics and personal finance, such as navigating college loans, selecting health insurance, or avoiding credit card debt. With younger students, look for opportunities to connect math content with everyday life. Borrow McMillian's strategy of connecting with experts to reinforce the real-world applications of the content that students are learning.

# References

America Achieves. (n.d.). *The Global Learning Network: A learning community for OECD Test for Schools participants.* Available: http://www.americaachieves.org/oecd

American Management Association (AMA). (2012). AMA 2012 critical skills survey. Washington, DC: Author. Available: http://www.amanet.org/training/articles/AMA-2012-Critical-Skills-Survey.aspx

Arazm, G., & Sungur, S. (2007). Effectiveness of problem-based learning on academic performance in genetics. *Biochemistry and Molecular Biology Education, 35*(6), 448–451.

Aronson, E. (1978). *The jigsaw classroom.* Thousand Oaks, CA: Sage.

Bailin, S., Case, R., Coombs, J. R., & Daniels, L. B. (1999). Conceptualizing critical thinking. *Journal of Curriculum Studies, 31*(3), 285–302.

Balfanz, R. (2007, May). *What your community can do to end its drop-out crisis: Learnings from research and practice.* Baltimore, MD: Center for Social Organization of Schools, Johns Hopkins University. Available: http://web.jhu.edu/CSOS/images/Final_dropout_Balfanz.pdf

Barron, B. J., Schwartz, D. L., Vye, N. J., Moore, A., Petrosino, A., Zech, L., & Bransford, J. D. (1998). Doing with understanding: Lessons from research on problem- and project-based learning. *Journal of the Learning Sciences, 7*(3–4), 271–311.

Barrows, H. S. (1992). *The tutorial process* (Rev. ed.). Springfield: Southern Illinois University School of Medicine.

Berg, P. (2011, May 17). Service learning projects—Project based learning taken further [blog post]. Retrieved from: http://www.educationtransformation.org/2011/05/service-learning-projects-project-based.html

Berger, R. (2003). *An ethic of excellence: Building a culture of craftsmanship with students.* Portsmouth, NH: Heinemann.

Black, P. J., & Wiliam, D. (1998). Inside the black box: Raising standards through classroom assessment. *Phi Delta Kappan, 80*(2), 139–148.

Blumenfeld, P. C., Kempler, T., & Krajcik, J. S. (2006). Motivation and cognitive engagement in learning environments. In R. K. Sawyer (Ed.), *Cambridge handbook of the learning sciences*. New York: Cambridge University Press.

Blumenfeld, P. C., Mergendoller, J. R., & Swarthout, D. W. (1987). Tasks as heuristics for understanding student learning and motivation. *Journal of Curriculum Studies, 19*(2), 135–148.

Blumenfeld, P. C., Solloway, E., Marx, R. W., Krajcik, J. S., Guzdial, M., & Palincsar, A. (1991). Motivating project based learning: Sustaining the doing, supporting the learning. *Educational Psychologist, 26*(3&4), 369–398.

Boaler, J. (1998). Open and closed mathematics: Student experiences and understandings. *Journal for Research in Mathematics Education, 29*(1), 41–62.

Boonchouy, S. R. (2014). *Leadership for project based learning: Exploring how principals promote change, innovation, and professional learning*. (Unpublished doctoral dissertation). University of California, Davis.

Boss, S. (2014a, May 20). How to find a home for service-learning projects. *Edutopia. org*. Available: http://www.edutopia.org/blog/home-to-service-learning-how-to-suzie-boss

Boss, S. (2014b, Aug. 21). How to design right-sized challenges. *Edutopia*. Available: http.//www.edutopia.org/blog/how-design-right-sized-challenges-suzie-boss

Boss, S., & Krauss, J. (2014). *Reinventing project-based learning: Your field guide to real-world projects in the digital age* (2nd ed.). Eugene, OR: International Society for Technology in Education.

Bransford, J., Brown, A., & Cocking, R., Eds. (2000). *How people learn: Brain, mind, experience, and school*. Washington, DC: National Academy Press.

Bridgeland, J. M., Dilulio, J. J., Jr., & Morison, K. B. (2006). *The silent epidemic: Perspectives of high school dropouts* (Report by Civic Enterprises in association with Peter D. Hart Research Associates for the Bill & Melinda Gates Foundation). Available: https.//docs.gatesfoundation.org/Documents/TheSilentEpidemic3-06Final. pdf

Brophy, J. E. (2013). *Motivating students to learn*. New York: Routledge.

Brown, A. L., Bransford, J. D., Ferrara, R., & Campione, J. (1983). Learning, remembering and understanding. In J. H. Flavell & E. M. Markham (Eds.), *Handbook of child psychology, Vol 3: Cognitive development* (4th ed., pp. 77–166). New York: Wiley.

Brown, A. L., Collins, A., & Duguid, P. (1989). Situated cognition and the culture of learning. *Educational Researcher, 18*, 32–41.

Bruner, J. S. (1966). *Toward a theory of instruction* (Vol. 59). Cambridge, MA: Harvard University Press.

Burke, K. (2010). *Balanced assessment*. Bloomington, IL: Solution Tree.

Camp, G. (1996). Problem-based learning: A paradigm shift or a passing fad? *Medical Education Online, 1*.

Capon, N., & Kuhn, D. (2004). What's so good about problem-based learning? *Cognition and Instruction, 22*(1), 61–79.

Casner-Lotto, J., & Barrington, L. (2006). *Are they really ready to work? Employers' perspectives on the basic knowledge and applied skills of new entrants to the 21st century U.S. workforce.* Washington, DC: The Conference Board, Partnership for 21st Century Skills, Corporate Voices for Working Families, & Society for Human Resource Management. Available: http://www.p21.org/storage/documents/FINAL_REPORT_PDF09-29-06.pdf

Chang, C. (2001). Comparing the impacts of a problem-based computer-assisted instruction and the direct-interactive teaching method on student science achievement. *Journal of Science Education and Technology, 10*(2), 147–153.

Chen, M. (2011). *Education nation.* San Francisco: Jossey-Bass.

Chen, M. (2013). The rise of a*ny time, any place, any path, any place* learning: After-school and summer as the new American frontier for innovative learning. In T. K. Peterson (Ed.), *Expanding minds and opportunities: Leveraging the power of afterschool and summer learning for student success.* Washington, DC: Collaborative Communications Group.

Cognition and Technology Group at Vanderbilt. (1998). Designing environments to reveal, support, and expand our children's potentials. In S. Soraci & W. J. McIlvane (Eds.), *Perspectives on fundamental processes in intellectual functioning: A survey of research approaches* (Vol. 1). Westport, CT: Greenwood.

College Board. (n.d.). Redesigned SAT. Available: https://www.collegeboard.org/delivering-opportunity/sat/redesign

Common Core State Standards Initiative. (n.d.). *Standards for mathematical practice.* Available: http://www.corestandards.org/Math/Practice/

Conley, D. T. (2005). *College knowledge: What it really takes for students to succeed and what we can do to get them ready.* San Francisco: Jossey-Bass.

Csikszentmihalyi, M., & Csikzentmihaly, M. (1991). *Flow: The psychology of optimal experience.* New York: HarperPerennial.

Dean, C. B. (2012). *Classroom instruction that works: Research-based strategies for increasing student achievement.* Alexandria, VA: ASCD.

Dewey, J. (1916). *Democracy and education.* New York: Macmillan.

Dewey, J. (1938). *Education and experience.* New York: Macmillan.

Dewey, J., & Small, A. W. (1897). *My pedagogic creed* (No. 25). New York: E. L. Kellogg & Company.

District Administration. (2014). *Outlook on instruction: Class around the clock.* Available: http://www.districtadministration.com/article/outlook-instruction-class-around-clock

Dochy, F., Segers, M., Van den Bossche, P., & Gijbels, D. (2003). Effects of problem-based learning: A meta-analysis. *Learning and instruction, 13*(5), 533–568.

Drake, K. N., & Long, D. (2009). Rebecca's in the dark: A comparative study of problem-based learning and direct instruction/experiential learning in two fourth-grade classrooms. *Journal of Elementary Science Education, 21*(1), 1–16.

Durlak, J. A., Weissberg, R. P., & Pachan, M. (2010). A meta-analysis of after-school programs that seek to promote personal and social skills in children and adolescents. *American Journal of Community Psychology, 45*, 294–309.

Dweck, C. (2006). *Mindset: The new psychology of success*. New York: Random House.

Ebbinghaus, H. (1913). *Memory. A contribution to experimental psychology*. New York: Teachers College, Columbia University.

Edelson, D. C., Gordon, D. N, & Pea, R. D. (1999). Addressing the challenge of inquiry-based learning. *Journal of the Learning Sciences, 8*, 392–450.

Fennema, E., & Romberg, T. (1999). *Mathematics classrooms that promote understanding*. Mahwah, NJ: Erlbaum.

Finkelstein, N., Hanson, T., Huang, C. W., Hirschman, B., & Huang, M. (2010). *Effects of problem based economics on high school economics instruction* (NCEE 2010-4002). Washington, DC: U.S. Department of Education.

Friedlaender, D., Burns, D., Lewis-Charp, H., Cook-Harvey, C. M., & Darling-Hammond, L. (2014). *Student-centered schools: Closing the opportunity gap*. Stanford, CA: Stanford Center for Opportunity Policy in Education (SCOPE). Available: https://edpolicy.stanford.edu/publications/pubs/1175

Gallagher, S. A., & Stepien, W. J. (1996). Content acquisition in problem-based learning: Depth versus breadth in American studies. *Journal for the Education of the Gifted, 19*(3), 257–275.

Geier, R., Blumenfeld, P. C., Marx, R. W., Krajcik, J. S., Fishman, B. Soloway, E., & Clay-Chambers, J. (2008). Standardized test outcomes for students engaged in inquiry-based science curricula in the context of urban reform. *Journal of Research in Science Teaching, 45*(8), 922–939.

Gordon, P. R., Rogers, A. M., Comfort, M., Gavula, N., & McGee, B. P. (2001). A taste of problem-based learning increases achievement of urban minority middle school students. *Educational Horizons, 79*(4), 171–175.

Guilfoile, L., & Ryan, M. (2013). *Linking service-learning and the Common Core State Standards: Alignment, progress, and obstacles*. Denver, CO: Education Commission of the States.

Guskey, T. R. (2011, Nov.). Five obstacles to grading reform. *Educational Leadership, 69*(3), 16–21.

Guskey, T. R., & Bailey, J. M. (2010). *Developing standards based report cards*. Thousand Oaks, CA: Corwin.

Hackman, J. R., & Oldham, G. R. (1980). *Work redesign* (Vol. 72). Reading, MA: Addison-Wesley.

Halvorsen, A., Duke, N. K., Brugar, K., Block, M., Strachan, S., Berka, M., & Brown, J. (2014). *Narrowing the achievement gap in second-grade social studies and content area literacy: The promise of a project-based approach*. Working Paper #26. East Lansing, MI: Education Policy Center at Michigan State University. Available: http://files.eric.ed.gov/fulltext/ED537157.pdf

Hart Research Associates. (2013). *It takes more than a major: Employer priorities for college learning and student success. An online survey among employers conducted on behalf of: The Association of American Colleges and Universities*. Washington, DC: Author. Available: https://www.aacu.org/leap/documents/2013_EmployerSurvey.pdf

Hattie, J. (2012). *Visible learning for teachers: Maximizing impact on learning*. New York: Routledge.

Hernandez-Ramos, P., & De La Paz, S. (2009). Learning history in middle school by designing multimedia in a project-based learning experience. *Journal of Research on Technology in Education, 42*(2), 151–173.

Hewlett Foundation. (n.d.). *What is deeper learning?* Available: http://www.hewlett. org/programs/education/deeper-learning/what-deeper-learning

Hickey, D. T., Moore, A. L., & Pellegrino, J. W. (2001). The motivational and academic consequences of elementary mathematics environments: Do constructivist innovations and reforms make a difference? *American Educational Research Journal, 38*(3), 611–652.

Hmelo-Silver, C. E., Duncan, R. G., & Chinn, C. A. (2007). Scaffolding and achievement in problem-based and inquiry learning: A response to Kirschner, Sweller, and Clark (2006). *Educational Psychologist, 42*(2), 99–107.

Hung, W., Jonassen, D. H., & Liu, R. (2007). Problem-based learning. In J. M. Spector, J. G. van Merriënboer, M. D. Merrill, & M. Driscoll (Eds.), *Handbook of research on educational communications and technology* (3rd ed., pp. 1503–1581). Mahwah, NJ: Erlbaum.

Kanevsky, L., & Keighley, T. (2003). To produce or not to produce? Understanding boredom and the honor in underachievement. *Roeper Review: A Journal on Gifted Education, 26*(1), 20–28.

Kilpatrick, W. (1918). The project method. *The Teachers College Record, 19*(4), 319–335.

Kirschner, P. A., Sweller, J., & Clark, R. E. (2006). Why minimal guidance during instruction does not work: An analysis of the failure of constructivist, discovery, problem-based, experiential, and inquiry-based teaching. *Educational psychologist, 41*(2), 75–86.

Kim, M. C., Hannafin, M. J., & Bryan, L. A. (2007). Technology-enhanced inquiry tools in science education: An emerging pedagogical framework for classroom practice. *Science Education, 91*(6), 1010–1030.

Knoll, M. (1997). The project method: Its vocational education origin and international development. *Journal of Industrial Teacher Education, 34*(3), 59–80.

Kolodner, J. L., Camp, P. J., Crismond, D., Fasse, B., Gray, J., Holbrook, J., Puntambekar, S., & Ryan, M. (2003). Problem-based learning meets case-based reasoning in the middle-school science classroom: Putting Learning by Design into practice. *Journal of the Learning Sciences, 12*(4), 495–547.

Krajcik, J. S., Blumenfeld, P. C., Marx, R. W., Bass, K. M., Fredricks, J., & Soloway, E. (1998). Inquiry in project-based science classrooms: Initial attempts by middle school students. *Journal of the Learning Sciences, 7*, 313–350.

Lambros, A. (2002). *Problem-based learning in middle and high school classrooms: A teacher's guide to implementation*. Thousand Oaks, CA: Corwin Press.

Laur, D. (2013). *Authentic learning experiences: A real-world approach to project-based learning*. New York: Routledge.

Lave, J., & Wenger, E. (1991). *Situated learning. Legitimate peripheral participation.* Cambridge, UK: Cambridge University Press.

Lee, O., Buxton, C. A., Lewis, S., & LeRoy, K. (2006). Science inquiry and student diversity: Enhanced abilities and continuing difficulties after an instructional intervention. *Journal of Research in Science Teaching, 43*(7), 607–636.

Levy, F., & Murnane, R. J. (2013). *Dancing with robots: Human skills for computerized work* [White paper]. Washington, DC: Third Way.

Liu, M., Hsieh, P., Cho, Y. J., & Schallert, D. L. (2006). Middle school students' self-efficacy, attitudes, and achievement in a problem-based learning environment. *Journal of Interactive Learning Research, 17*(3), 225–242.

Lopez, B., Forgie, G., Dastur, F., & Hoffman, S. (2014). PBL and design thinking in first grade. *Future Forwards, 2*, 82–92.

Lynch, S., Kuipers, J. U., Pyke, C., & Szesze, M. (2005). Examining the effects of a highly rated science curriculum unit on diverse students: Results from a planning grant. *Journal of Research in Science Teaching, 42*, 921–946.

Marconi, P., Cipriani, A., & Valeriani, E., (1974). *I disegni di architecttura dell'Archivo storico dell'Accademia di San Luca.* Rome: De Luca Editore. Cited in Knoll, 1997.

Martenson, D., Eriksson, H., & Ingelman-Sundberg, M. (1985). Medical chemistry: Evaluation of active and problem-oriented teaching methods. *Medical Education, 19*(1), 34–42.

Marx, R. W., Blumenfeld, P. C., Krajcik, J. S., Blunk, M., Crawford, B., Kelly, B., & Meyer, K. M. (1994). Enacting project-based science: Experiences of four middle grade teachers. *Elementary School Journal, 94*(5), 517–538.

Marx, R. W., Blumenfeld, P. C., Krajcik, J. S., & Soloway, E. (1997) Enacting project-based science. *Elementary School Journal, 97*(4), 341–358.

Maxwell, N. L., Bellisimo, Y., & Mergendoller, J. (2001). Problem-based learning: Modifying the medical school model for teaching high school economics. *The Social Studies, 92*(2), 73–78.

Maxwell, N., Mergendoller, J., & Bellisimo, Y. (2005). The high school economics curriculum: Does problem-based learning increase knowledge? *Journal of Economic Education, 36*(4), 315–331.

McCombs, B. L. (1996). Alternative perspectives for motivation. In L. Baker, P. Afflerback, & D. Reinking (Eds.), *Developing engaged readers in school and home communities* (pp. 67–87). Mahwah, NJ: Erlbaum.

Mergendoller, J. R., Markham, T., Ravitz, J., & Larmer, J. (2006). Pervasive management of project based learning: Teachers as guides and facilitators. In C. Evertson, C. M. Weinstein, & C. S. Weinstein (Eds.), *Handbook of classroom management: Research, practice, and contemporary issues* (pp. 583–615). Mahwah, NJ: Erlbaum.

Moll, L. C., Amanti, C., Neff, D., & Gonzalez, N. (1992). Funds of knowledge for teaching: Using a qualitative approach to connect homes and classrooms. *Theory into Practice, 31*(2), 132–141.

Murphy, P. K., Wilkinson, I. A. G., Soter, A. O., Hennessey, M. N., Alexander, J. F. (2009). Examining the effects of classroom discussion on students' comprehension of text: A meta-analysis. *Journal of Educational Psychology, 101*(3), 740–764.

National Center for Education Statistics (NCES). (2012). *NAEP: Looking ahead: Leading assessment into the future*. [Highlights]. Washington, DC: Author. Available: http://nces.ed.gov/nationsreportcard/pdf/naep_highlights_16may2012_view.pdf

New Tech Network. (2014). *Student Outcomes Report 2014*. Napa, CA: Author. Available: http://www.newtechnetwork.org/services/resources/ntn-student-outcomes-report-2014

Next Generation Science Standards. (2013). *Appendix A—Conceptual shifts in the Next Generation Science Standards*. Washington, DC: Achieve, Inc. Available: http://www.nextgenscience.org/sites/ngss/files/Appendix%20A%20-%204.11.13%20Conceptual%20Shifts%20in%20the%20Next%20Generation%20Science%20Standards.pdf

Organization for Economic Development (OECD). (2014). *PISA 2012 results: Creative problem solving: Students' skills in tackling real-life problems* (Vol. V). Paris: Author. Available: http://dx.doi.org/10.1787/9789264208070-en

Palmer, E. (2011). *Well spoken: Teaching speaking to all students*. Portland, ME: Stenhouse.

Parker, W. C., Lo, J., Yeo, A. J., Valencia, S. W., Nguyen, D., Abbot, R. D., Nolen, S. B., Bransford, J. D., & Vye, N. J. (2013). Beyond breadth-speed test: Toward deeper knowing and engagement in an advanced placement course. *American Educational Research Journal, 5*(9), 1424–1459.

Partnership for 21st Century Skills. (2007). *Beyond the three Rs: Voter attitudes toward 21st century skills*. Tucson, AZ: Author. Available: http://www.p21.org/storage/documents/P21_pollreport_singlepg.pdf

Perry, C. (2013). In AP 50, students own their education. Harvard School of Engineering and Applied Sciences. Available: http://www.seas.harvard.edu/news/2013/09/in-ap-50-students-own-their-education

Peterson, T. K. (Ed.) (2013). *Expanding minds and opportunities: Leveraging the power of afterschool and summer learning for student success*. Washington, DC: Collaborative Communications Group.

Piha, S. (n.d.) *Learning in afterschool and summer: Preparing youth for the 21st century*. Position paper of the Learning in Afterschool and Summer Project. www.learninginafterschool.org/position.htm

Pintrich, P. R., & Schunk, D. (1996). *Motivation in education: Theory, research and application*. Columbus, OH: Merrill/Prentice Hall.

Ritchhart, R., & Perkins, D. (2008). Making thinking visible. *Educational Leadership, 65*(5), 57–61.

Rivet, A. E., & Krajcik, J. S. (2004). Achieving standards in urban systemic reform: An example of a sixth grade project-based science curriculum. *Journal of Research in Science Teaching, 41,* 669–692.

Savery, J. R. (2006). Overview of problem-based learning: Definitions and distinctions. *Interdisciplinary Journal of Problem-based Learning, 1*(1), 3, 9–20.

Schmidt, H. G., Boshuizen, H. P. A., & de Vries, M. (1992). Comparing problem-based with conventional education: A review of the University of Limburg medical school experiment. *Annals of Community-Oriented Education, 5,* 193–198.

Schneider, R., Krajcik, J., Marx, R. W., & Soloway, E. (2002). Student learning in project-based science classrooms. *Journal of Research in Science Teaching, 39*(5), 410–422.

Schroeder, C. M., Scott, T. P., Tolson, H., Huang, T., & Lee, Y. (2007). A meta-analysis of national research: Effects of teaching strategies on student achievement in science in the United States. *Journal of Research in Science Teaching, 44*(10), 1436–1460.

Schwalm, J., & Tylek, K. S. (2012, Spring). Systemwide implementation of project-based learning: The Philadelphia approach. *Afterschool Matters, 15,* 1–8.

Scott, C. A. (1994). Project-based science: Reflections of a middle school teacher. *The Elementary School Journal, 95*(1), 75–94.

Sefton-Green, J. (2013). *Learning at not-school.* Cambridge, MA: MIT Press.

Seidel, S. (2011). *Hip hop genius: Remixing high school education.* Lanham, MD: Rowman & Littlefield.

Sizer, T. (1984). *Horace's compromise,* Boston: Houghton Mifflin.

Smarter Balanced Assessment Consortium. (2014) *Sample items and performance tasks.* Olympia, WA: Author. Available: http://www.smarterbalanced.org/sample-items-and-performance-tasks/

Stiggins, R. (2005). From formative assessment to assessment for learning: A path to success in standards-based schools. *Phi Delta Kappan,* 324–328.

Strobel, J., & van Barneveld, A. (2009). When is PBL more effective? A meta-synthesis of meta analyses comparing PBL to conventional classrooms. *Interdisciplinary Journal of Problem based Learning, 3*(1). Available: http://dx.doi.org/10.7771/1541-5015.1046

Strobel, J., Wang, J., Weber, N. R., & Dyehouse, M. (2013). The role of authenticity in design-based learning environments: The case of engineering education. *Computers & Education, 64,* 143–152.

Tans, R. W., Schmidt, H. G., Schade-Hoogeveen, B. E. J., & Gijselaers, W. H. (1986). Sturing van het onderwijsleerproces door middel van problemen: Een veldexperiment [Guiding the learning process by means of problems: A field experiment]. *Tijdschrift voor Onderwijsresearch, 11,* 35–46.

Thomas, J. W. (2000). *A review of research on project-based learning.* San Rafael, CA: Autodesk Foundation.

Tomlinson, C. A. (2011, October). Coaching: The new leadership skill. *Educational Leadership, 69*(2), 92–93.

Torp, L., & Sage, S. (2002). *Problems as possibilities: Problem-based learning for K–12 education.* Alexandria, VA: ASCD.

Vandell, D. L. (2013) Afterschool program quality and student outcomes: Reflections on positive key findings on learning and development from recent research. In

T. K. Peterson (Ed.), *Expanding minds and opportunities: Leveraging the power of afterschool and summer learning for student success*. Washington, DC: Collaborative Communications Group.

Walker, A., & Leary, H. (2009). A problem based learning meta analysis: Differences across problem types, implementation types, disciplines, and assessment levels. *Interdisciplinary Journal of Problem-based Learning, 3*(1).

Wiggins, G. (2014, May). Fixing the high school—Student Survey, Part 1 [blog post]. Available: http://grantwiggins.wordpress.com/2014/05/21/fixing-the-high-school/

Wirkala, C., & Kuhn, D. (2011). Problem-based learning in K–12 education: Is it effective and how does it achieve its effects? *American Educational Research Journal, 48*(5), 1157–1186.

Yazzie-Mintz, E. (2010). *Charting the path from engagement to achievement: A report on the 2009 High School Survey of Student Engagement*. Bloomington, IN: Center for Evaluation and Education Policy. Available: http://ceep.indiana.edu/hssse/images/HSSSE_2010_Report.pdf

# Index

Note: Page locators followed by an italicized *f* indicate information contained in figures.

# About the Authors

**The Buck Institute for Education (BIE)** is a mission-driven not-for-profit 501(c)3 organization based in Novato, California, and is beneficiary of the Leonard and Beryl Buck Trust. Since 1998, BIE has focused its work exclusively on project based learning and is considered the world's leading provider of PBL resources and professional development. Its publications have been translated into nine languages. Across the United States and around the world, BIE provides PBL workshops and coaching to well over 10,000 K–12 teachers per year and provides systemic long-term support to partner schools and districts. BIE also hosts annual *PBL World* conferences and offers online resources at its website (bie.org) and online courses at PBLU.org.

**John Larmer** is editor in chief at the Buck Institute for Education. He authored and/or edited BIE's project based curriculum units for high school government and economics and was a contributing author of the *Project Based Learning Handbook*. He is a writer and editor of BIE's *PBL Toolkit Series*, including the *PBL Starter Kit for Middle and High School Teachers*, *PBL in the Elementary Grades*, and *PBL for 21st Century Success: Teaching Critical Thinking, Collaboration, Communication, and Creativity*. He codevelops professional development workshops and materials for teachers, including 21st century skills rubrics and project exemplars. John presents at conferences and has consulted on PBL curriculum development for the National Academy Foundation, the Oracle Education Foundation, and Pearson Education.

Prior to joining BIE, John was a senior program associate at WestEd in San Francisco. For ten years John taught high school social studies and English. He was a founding teacher at a restructured small high school, and a member of the National School Reform Faculty and school coach for the Coalition of Essential Schools. John received MA degrees in Educational Technology and in Educational Administration from San Francisco State University, and a BA in Political Science from Stanford University.

 **John Mergendoller** joined the Buck Institute for Education in 1989 as its founding research director and was named executive director in 2000. An international advocate for project based learning, he has worked with educators throughout the United States and in China, Taiwan, Brazil, Greece, Romania, the United Kingdom, and many other countries to help them learn about and implement high-quality PBL.

Before joining BIE, he was a senior program director at the Far West Laboratory (now WestEd), a federally funded regional educational laboratory. At Far West, he also established and managed the At-Risk Student Program and the Secondary School Improvement Program. His publications span educational technology, science education, middle grades reform, and project based learning.

John holds an MA and a PhD in Psychology and Education from the University of Michigan, an EdM from the Harvard Graduate School of Education, and a BA in Letters from Wesleyan University in Middletown, CT. He was awarded a Fulbright Fellowship to study cognitive development at the University of Geneva.

 **Suzie Boss** is a member of the Buck Institute for Education's National Faculty. She is a writer and educational consultant who focuses on the power of teaching and learning to improve lives and transform communities. She is the author of several books on education and innovation, including *Bringing Innovation to School: Empowering Students to Thrive in a Changing World* and *Reinventing Project-Based Learning: Your Field Guide to Real-World Projects in the Digital Age*. She is a regular contributor to *Edutopia* and the *Stanford Social Innovation Review*. Her work has appeared in a wide range of publications, including *Educational Leadership, Principal Leadership, the New York Times, Education Week,* and *Huffington Post*. She is a frequent conference presenter and consults internationally with schools interested in shifting from traditional instruction to technology-rich, project based learning.

## Related ASCD Resources: Project-Based Learning

At the time of publication, the following ASCD resources were available (ASCD stock numbers appear in parentheses). For up-to-date information about ASCD resources, go to www.ascd.org.

### DVDs

*High Schools at Work: Creating Student-Centered Learning With Facilitator's Guide* (#606117)

### ASCD EDge Group

Exchange ideas and connect with other educators interested in project-based learning on the social networking site ASCD EDge™ at http://ascdedge.ascd.org/

### Online Courses

*Project-Based Learning: An Answer to The Common Core Challenge* (#PD13OC008M)

### Print Products

*Authentic Learning in the Digital Age: Engaging Students Through Inquiry* by Larissa Pahomov (#115009)

*Personalizing the High School Experience for Each Student* by Joe DiMartino and John H. Clarke (#107054)

*Problems as Possibilities: Problem-Based Learning for K-16 Education, 2nd Edition* by Linda Torp and Sara Sage (#101064)

*Real-World Projects: How do I design relevant and engaging learning experiences?* by Suzie Boss (#SF115043)

WHOLE CHILD The Whole Child Initiative helps schools and communities create learning environments that allow students to be healthy, safe, engaged, supported, and challenged. To learn more about other books and resources that relate to the whole child, visit www.wholechildeducation.org.

For more information: send e-mail to member@ascd.org; call 1-800-933-2723 or 703-578-9600, press 2; send a fax to 703-575-5400; or write to Information Services, ASCD, 1703 N. Beauregard St., Alexandria, VA 22311-1714 USA.

DON'T MISS A SINGLE ISSUE OF ASCD'S AWARD-WINNING MAGAZINE,

# EL EDUCATIONAL LEADERSHIP

If you belong to a Professional Learning Community, you may be looking for a way to get your fellow educators' minds around a complex topic. Why not delve into a relevant theme issue of *Educational Leadership*, the journal written by educators for educators.

Subscribe now, or buy back issues of ASCD's flagship publication at **www.ascd.org/ELbackissues.**

Single issues cost $7 (for issues dated September 2006–May 2013) or $8.95 (for issues dated September 2013 and later). Buy 10 or more of the same issue, and you'll save 10 percent. Buy 50 or more of the same issue, and you'll save 15 percent. For discounts on purchases of 200 or more copies, contact **programteam@ascd.org**; 1-800-933-2723, ext. 5773.

To see more details about these and other popular issues of *Educational Leadership*, visit **www.ascd.org/ELarchive.**

**ASCD®**

LEARN. TEACH. LEAD.

1703 North Beauregard Street
Alexandria, VA 22311-1714 USA

www.ascd.org/el